THREE FACES OF THE DEVIL

DEVIL

Marly Bergerud

A MEMOIR OF COURAGE AND PURPOSE

Books Academy LLC

112 SW HK Dodgen Loop, Temple, Texas 76504
Hotline: (254) 800-1189

Ordering Information: Quantity sales. Special discounts are available on quantity purchases by corporations, associations, and others. For details, contact the publisher at the address above.

Printed in the United States of America.

ISBN: Softcover: 978-1-966567-42-4
eBook: 978-1-966567-43-1

Library of Congress Control Number: 2025903006

TABLE OF CONTENTS

Fame and Failure (1990)   1

Devastating Childhood Trauma (1922)   17

Despicable Man (1929–1952)   27

Tough Times, Tough Women (1865–1965)   35

The Flawed, Wounded Family (1928–1994)   41

My Parents—The Entrepreneurs (1940–1960)   52

Power in the Face of Evil (1954)   64

A Night I Will Never Forget   68

Childhood Joy (1947–1960)   76

Black Man—White Town (1956–1960)   93

Happiness in the Presence of Evil (1954–1960)   101

Broken Promises (1960)   112

Infidelity and Loveless Marriage (1963–1975)   124

The Shattered Dream   134

Achievements along the Way (1942–2021)   139

The Good Ole Girls and the Band of Four (1970–Present)   147

The Worm Infects and Destroys True Love (1973–1985)   155

Single Again, Raising a High
School–Aged Young Man (1985)   168

My Travels Have Shaped Who I Am: China (1989)   172

A Phenomenal Monument—Xi'an   190

The Italian: A Gentleman and a Scholar   192

The Empty Nest and Stark Raging Fear   198

Confronting Addiction, Enabling, and Raging Guilt   201

Two Life-Defining Decisions   211

The Fall of Gorbachev, Communism, and the USSR.   225

Closing a Significant Chapter (1993–1994)   252

A Critical Amend (1993–2003)   262

A Dramatic Change for Me (2000)   268

Wanderlust Is Part of Me: Africa (2005)   285

Facing My Mortality (2005–2014)   298

A Call to Work in High Technology (2007–2013)   302

The Unforgivable (2012)   312

The Devil Calls Again (2013–2014)   319

Italy—On My Mind (2016–2017)   329

Cockeyed Optimism in the Desert (2015–2017)   340

The Great Enabler—No More (2017–2025)   348

A MEMOIR OF COURAGE AND PURPOSE

To my son, Christen, the greatest gift of my life.

For my sisters, **Connie and Sharon**; *their families; and my friends near and far, I thank you for your support and for listening to the saga of my writing journey.*

Along this journey, I have learned so very much from **professional writers' workshops and professional speakers** *at the* **Palm Springs Writers Guild speaker meetings, published and active writing author friends, as well as editors and agents:**
Christopher Vogler,
Charles Robert Masello,
Robert Rutledge,
Rudy Shur,
Judith Briles,
Cynthia Manson.
Developmental editors:
Eduardo Santiago,
Catherine Anne Jones, Ginger Moran, Kathy Weyer
Joyce Bulifant.

FAME AND FAILURE (1990)

*Success is not final; failure is not fatal: It is the
courage to continue that counts.*
— Winston Churchill

I was on top of the world. The event was an all-expense-paid trip to Boston to speak at an international education conference for an audience of more than several hundred teachers of computer technologies from the U.S. and Europe.

It was early in November, and I hoped the weather would not prevent me from exploring the town. Stepping out of the limo at the Fairmont Copley Plaza Hotel, I was greeted by a bone-chilling wind and blowing snow.

I looked forward to the evening's speaker, Buzz Aldrin, the astronaut. As the pilot of Apollo 11, he was one of the first two men on the Moon. I remember watching TV at 3:00 a.m. when he set foot on the Moon on July 21, 1969.

At the gala, I located my table and noticed the place card next to mine, that of Mr. Aldrin.

Marly Dressed for the Gala

He soon approached, introduced himself with a handshake, and courteously pulled out my chair. Smiling with gratitude, I struggled to stay composed. This famous gentleman and former astronaut, appearing to be in his late fifties, facilitated engaging and pleasant conversations throughout the dinner.

I felt pure joy sitting with this distinguished group. I, Marly Bergerud, had reached this level of success.

Buzz inquired, "May I ask your place of origin?"
"North Dakota."

He laughed, "After retiring from NASA, I joined the University of John D. Odegard School of Aerospace Sciences. There, I assisted John in developing its space studies program."
"What a small world. John and his wife, Diane, were close friends from my hometown of Minot."
"The North Dakota winter was difficult for me," Buzz said.
"Yes, the winters can be lengthy and challenging, but we manage to get through them," I replied.

The evening was magical. After dinner, Buzz took my arm and walked to the bar for a drink. Of course, why wouldn't I? We chatted nonstop while I had scotch and another glass of wine. Soon, a group of about six people entered the bar. He recognized his friends and excused himself to join them.

As I sat by myself enjoying my beverage, I suddenly felt a gentle but firm hand on my back. Turning around, I was met with the gaze of an impeccably handsome man with a touch of gray in his hair. He leaned forward slightly and asked in a rich voice, tinged with a subtle Southern accent, "Is this seat occupied?"

I looked into his beautiful blue eyes and immediately forgot about Buzz. I responded, "No, it is yours." Who was this distinguished gentleman?

I extended my hand, "My name is Marly"

"Hello, I am Bill, Bill Clinton." I soon learned he was from Arkansas and the keynote speaker at another hotel conference. We conversed briefly over a drink; specifically, mine was a scotch on the rocks. He inquired whether I was attending one of the conferences at the hotel.

I responded that I was speaking at a business educators' conference. I laughed and mentioned my earlier conversation with Buzz Aldrin when I found out he had worked in North Dakota, my home state. Bill then asked about my experience growing up there, and I shared some family stories and incidents from my life.

"Could you please share your background prior to becoming governor?"

"I was raised in Arkansas, and my father passed away in a car accident shortly before my birth. My mother remarried an individual who struggled with alcoholism and abusive behavior, and I often had to step in during their violent confrontations."

I felt such a bond with this man. His past tugged at my internal, unrelenting pain, which I had mentioned only slightly.
"I am sorry, Marly, but I will be at my meeting tomorrow and won't be able to attend your presentation."
"No problem. I genuinely enjoyed our chat."
As he got up, he leaned over and gave me a quick peck on my cheek as he headed out of the bar. I was amazed at how he listened and talked with me as if I were the most important person on Earth.

The rest of the night was a blur, as if possessed by the devil.

The Morning After

I sat in the nondescript lobby the following day, waiting to meet my friend Maureen, experiencing a splitting headache and having trouble recalling the previous evening. I recalled talking to Buzz Aldrin and later Bill Clinton, but beyond that, my memory was blank.

As I sat there, it felt like I was drifting in and out of consciousness. I vaguely recalled being in a conference room near the banquet hall, off the main ballroom. As if in a haze, I had glimpses of a pool table and my clothes scattered around the room. Panic set in. "What have I done?"

Suddenly, Maureen called out my name, bringing me back to the present moment. She waved from the entrance to the lobby restaurant.

Over breakfast, I asked her, "Can you help fill in the blanks from last night after you left me at the bar?" She glanced up briefly, with embarrassment in her eyes.

"After dinner, you met Bill at the bar with Buzz. Then you joined me." Maureen continued, "We met with some friends, left the hotel, and went bar hopping. She appeared to hesitate, possibly to see if I remembered this.

"I know I had wine, scotch, and then I topped it off with brandy, which I jokingly called 'the nail in the coffin.' I must have thought that was quite funny. It is not that funny this morning." Maureen continued describing the evening. "After several stops, we returned to the hotel bar.

You and I had another drink. I left you in the bar. A little before midnight, I came to the lobby to pick up something at the front desk. As I headed to the elevator, I was surprised to see you still in the lobby. I could not believe it was you." She appeared even more embarrassed as she then told me what she saw. "You were halfway sprawled out on a couch with your blouse partially out of your skirt, and this man's hand was under your skirt," she said. She was now looking at me to see if I remembered anything.

"You were giggling and squealing incoherently. He was laughing. Well, you must have thought you were enjoying yourself."

"None of this makes any sense," I said, bowing my head in shame. Tears streamed down my cheeks as I listened. "I don't remember any of it, Maureen."

At that point in life, I had attained significant success professionally with everything going for me. How could I have allowed this tragic personal failure to happen?

I was oblivious that my first drink would always lead to

another. Then, once I had that third drink, it was all downhill from there. Nobody could persuade me not to have another. It was, in fact, a problem.

I wish I had been capable of seeing it earlier in life. I do not believe I woke up one day and decided I wanted to be an alcoholic. The devil's curse of alcoholism passed from my grandfather to my father, my mother, my sisters, and now me. It did not skip a generation. I felt myself going down that slippery slope, and the devil had a mean grip on me.

My ninety-two-year-old aunt Helen was the sole source of information regarding my ancestors and our family's history, as our father was unwilling to discuss it.

Grandfather (Wilhelm Ernest Balszukat)
Coming to America

Aunt Helen said, "I will recount the story as our mother, Rosa, told me long ago. Just close your eyes and try to imagine what I am telling you.

In 1864, Wilhelm 'Ernest' Balszukat, then ten years old, departed Prussia (now Poland) for America. His parents, Johann and Emelie Berg Balzek, were skilled buggy makers in Gdansk and hesitant to leave their homeland. The family buggy broke down on the way, taking Ernest to the steamer Bremen. His parents told Ernest to run and that he could make it to the ship on time."

The last words of her grandparents to Ernest were, "Run, run. You will be in New York in a couple of weeks. Work hard and find yourself a good woman. You will be fine." As he ran toward the steamer, Ernest called out to the longshoreman as the ship prepared to leave the dock, "Wait. Wait!" Not poetic, but prophetic.

Helen continued, "No one could hear this little ten-year-old boy yelling as he ran toward the very long pier." As Helen spoke, I could almost hear the voice of this young boy.

"The pier's longshoremen had begun pulling up the gangways of the enormous steamer ship Bremen, preparing to embark for New York, USA. An ear-deafening blast of the ship's whistle blew the all-aboard call.

Next, an equally loud, deep-sounding horn; then one loud bell-ringing sound; and finally, an almost toy-like bell sound. The sweaty longshoremen began to untie the thick, rough, heavy golden ropes. The ship's grinding metal engines were loud."

Helen said, "Ernest, the young boy, continued to yell, 'Wait, wait!' No one could hear Ernest over the roar of the engines. His brown hair was wet and hanging over his eyes, and his clothes were damp from running for nearly an hour. The ship's smokestacks blew smoke and steam; loud whistling sounds were deafening, and the longshoremen readied the gangplank to haul it on board. Ernest was now at the base of the gang-plank. One of the longshoremen had been watching Ernest running toward the ship. At the last moment, he grabbed Ernest, and he ran up the plank with Ernest dangling under his strong arm. The Bremen was on its way to America and, ultimately, to the beginning of my family."

I loved hearing Helen tell that story. I have listened to most of our father's family history from Aunt Helen, Father's sister. Our actual family surname of origin was Balszukat, altered to Balsukot during immigration.

Balsukot, my family name, was always quite complex for

teachers and others to pronounce, not in my hometown but everywhere else.

In Helen's story, forty-three years later, Ernest was now fifty-three and still in New York. Continuing, she said, "To make ends meet, he worked various jobs: dishwasher, kitchen helper, horse farrier and groomer, chauffeur, and gardener. But he always wanted more." Then, she continued, our father heard about the government's 1862 homesteading program to encourage people to settle on land west of the Mississippi River. For a small fee, Father could legally own property. It is likely that Ernest felt optimistic regarding his future opportunities.

"Ernest left New York, working odd jobs across the country to reach the Promised Land. He took a train, walked miles, and hitched buggy rides. The nearly 1,500-mile trek took him six years to reach the available land. Our family later felt this journey had hardened Ernest. He became untrusting of those who wronged him and developed a 'me or them' survival mode."

"In 1906, now age fifty-five, hardened by the struggle to make it West, he finally arrived in a barren area of the new West called the Great Plains. There he came upon a town just being developed by the settlers called Plaza, North Dakota.
"That new settlement became one of the lucky breaks for Ernest and, ultimately, what would become my family." Helen continued; Ernest had arrived at just the right time. He could homestead 640 acres of land in Plaza for $16.
"Although our father initially achieved success as a farmer, he always aspired to something greater. He felt something was missing and needed to change his life. Despite his lack of formal education, he possessed considerable practical intelligence."

I thanked Helen for sharing this story. I had never heard this from our father, Winton, nor did he want to talk about his father, Ernest.

My father predominantly recounted narratives concerning immigrants who endured the journey from the East Coast to the modest prairie communities of the Dakotas in the Great Plains. They were primarily of Russian, Prussian, and German descent. He shared some details about Ernest. He said, "Soon after our father arrived in Plaza, he met Rosa Rosenberg, a beautiful young Jewish woman. Many Jewish people, like Rosa's grandparents, had to change their names during that time. Rosenberg was a common name.

Rosa was only seventeen—forty-eight years younger than Ernest when they met. According to family lore, they immediately wanted to get married."

When I heard about this age disparity, the possibility of child abuse often crossed my mind. At a minimum, the age difference made Ernest the dominating force in the family, and Rosa was helpless against him. Ernest's parents, who remained in Prussia, were against this marriage, not only because of their age difference but because he was a Gentile and she a Jew. Without their parents' blessings, Ernest and Rosa fled the town and eloped. I have newspaper clippings telling stories of this illicit elopement.

Father continued his story, "Our mother looked up to Ernest, as he was a good provider, but she feared him. Many people of that era viewed marriage as a means to find companionship and relief from the challenges of daily life.

I thought, "Yes, and a permanent sexual companion."

Father said, "Women, then, were considered little more than property."

I have very few details of Ernest's and Rosa's lives together.

However, it was clear from my father that love, tenderness, and caring were not in Ernest's makeup.

I gleaned from this conversation that Grandfather Ernest was no saint and was demanding and uncaring toward their mother. Nevertheless, Father's demeanor had an undertone of something far worse.

He was not an outwardly emotional man, but I was intrigued by his hesitancy. Then I saw such sadness on his face when he began to describe Ernest.

He said, "Our father was an example of an early 1900s self-made man whose life had not been easy. He was often loud, cruel, and abusive, with a deep, gruff voice that got everyone's attention when he entered a room. His appearance was that of a weathered man. He was a stocky five feet ten inches tall, with mostly grayish-brown hair, and was enormously proud of his short beard and handlebar mustache."

I retrieved from an old scrapbook of family pictures my only picture of Grandfather Ernest and showed it to Father. In this picture, Ernest has thick dark eyebrows that hang low and menacing over his eyes, with a broad, bulbous nose. I asked Father, "Is this a true reflection of Ernest, and who is the other man in the photo?" Father immediately responded, "Yes, that large nose was always red from too much alcohol. It is quite a fair reflection of him. I do not know who the other man is in the photo. In contrast, our mother was petite. She had reddish-brown hair, a light complexion with some freckles on her face, and a slight build, about five feet four inches tall.

Ernest Balsukot (standing) and his friend.

Because of their significant age differences, she wore her hair in a bun pinned on the top of her head to make herself look more mature.

"Fortunately, thanks to mild weather, Ernest's first two years of farming were successful. Our large acreage produced fully harvested crops and a good deal of wealth. Our mother, brother, and sisters were relieved that we had profited well from our demanding work. We all participated in the planting and harvesting. During these times, our affluence in the tiny town of Plaza and the surrounding area was palpable because of our farming success.

Even though our father and his siblings intensely hated Ernest, his blue eyes lit up with evident pride when speaking about Ernest's success. His father had become a successful businessman in Plaza and the surrounding area. Ernest owned 640 acres of open land, the grain elevator, the bank, the general store, and an implement store that carried farming equipment and tools. Father appeared excited and proud when he described Ernest's prosperity. It allowed Ernest to build a sizable three- story home in Plaza for his bride.

Ernest Balsukot family home in Plaza, North Dakota

Father said, "In 1908, our parents began our family of four: me, Harry, and our two sisters, Helen and Rosalie—each was about two years apart." As my father was speaking, I thought Ernest might have some redeeming characteristics. Father said, "Our family, like other farm families, did not have heat, light, or indoor bathrooms like people who lived in town. Ernest considered these frivolities. In those times, as with farmers today, work and play revolved around the farm's growing seasons. Autumn served as a period dedicated to harvesting crops and preparing for the forthcoming cold winter months. After a fall frost, we would pick the corn by hand and store it in a corncrib to dry. Later, we removed the corn kernels from the cob and used them to feed cows, horses, and pigs. We were always working. Weather touched every part of the lives of everyone in the Great Plains, particularly during the late 1920s—the heat of summer and the cold of winter. Life as a farmer was tough.

"No one in the tiny town of Plaza had money. Our family was an exception. Neighbors helped each other through tough times, sicknesses, and accidents. We were all in the same boat. Farm families gathered with neighbors at school programs, church dinners, or dances. Children and adults found ways to have fun for free. Everything was homemade—the food, the games, the music—and there were hand-built portable dance floors. Traditionally organized activities like rodeos and football were popular as well. Neighbors played cards and other games together, and the children loved being together. The church social and school programs allowed people to visit and meet someone new.

"All four of us, my sisters, brother, and me were in school, the girls through the eighth grade and Harry and I through the twelfth. We usually walked to school in rain, snow, or sunshine and spent summers helping in the fields. We produced most of our own food, including eggs, chickens, milk, beef from our cattle, and vegetables from our gardens. Our responsibilities involved milking cows, harnessing horses, feeding farm animals, and maintaining the outhouse. The tasks assigned to our sisters included gathering eggs, washing clothes, cleaning the house, and preparing food for the farmhands.

"Farming was a very physically and mentally demanding way of life. Our entire family's blood, sweat, and tears went into the land. The six of us walked on every bit of our property and planted the seeds into it in the faith that it would grow. Furthermore, from spring to fall, we watched the crop mature and be harvested, used as food, or put back in the ground as seeds to grow again. After the harvest, we prayed we would make some money from it. However, unlike most other farmers, Ernest was unique because he had his businesses in town, which created wealth for our family.

After listening to Helen tell the story of Ernest, I reflected on the complex lives of both of my parents, Winton and Florence, whose parents and siblings were all products of the early 1900s.

I researched that period up to the 1930s and discovered that many men drank to escape their responsibilities.

Plus, I was astounded to learn that during the early 1900s in the U.S., the number of saloons nationwide had grown from one hundred thousand to three hundred thousand. Some small towns had less than five hundred people but as many as thirty-three bars. Like most stories from the early small towns like Plaza, these were gathering places for working-class immigrants and often became the headquarters for political organizations and social centers, better known as brothels.

I asked our father, "How readily available was alcohol in the early 1900s?"

His answer was simple. He said, "Rye, corn, and barley were the three biggest crops grown on our family's land, which we used to make rye or corn whiskey and beer. As a result, alcohol was plentiful for our father and his cronies. Jugs of whiskey and beer sat in barrels on our front porch for our father and his friends. Ernest would spend hours after work at the local men- only saloon, spinning tales of his success, drinking until he could not drink anymore." Father indicated that Ernest once told him that drinking relaxed him and at least temporarily lifted the weight of his responsibilities.

Our father had great excitement in his voice as he told this story about Ernest. "Now, a significant invention had come onto the scene. In 1922, Ernest brought these new machines called tractors into his implement store and, of course, had to be the first to buy one when it arrived. He was ahead of his time and proud to own this shiny red machine with enormous metal wheels.

"Ernest proudly showed the town's farmers how he increased

the acreage of planted crops on his farm and was able to use fewer days and less hired help. Soon, the farmers of the 1920s, specifically in the Great Plains, realized there were new opportunities to increase their crop production using machinery. Through Ernest's bank, he could help his patrons, the local farmers, buy this new machine that was now available, and they could purchase it on credit. Ernest's store excelled in selling new tractors. Using a horse-drawn plow with blades that created a deep furrow in the ground for planting was unbelievably slow work. Now the farmers were excited to see how this new machine could improve their lives."

With tears in his eyes, Father said, "The tractor that Ernest purchased for our farm made working the fields easier. But that tractor would be Ernest's worst investment and my near demise." At this moment, I certainly did not understand his comment.

Now, with a quiver in his voice, Father became quite emotional. He continued, "I assumed that these 640 acres that Ernest had homesteaded would ultimately be mine and that of my siblings, along with his three business establishments in town."

Soon, the Great Depression became a reality that dramatically changed my father, his family life, and the lives of all the people who lived and farmed in Plaza and across America's plains.

DEVASTATING CHILDHOOD TRAUMA (1922)

*I survived because the fire inside me burned
brighter than the fire around me.*
—Joshua Graham

Ernest had become a wealthy and influential man. His treatment of his family was despicable. In the 1920s, he had 640 acres to maintain in America's northern plains, making for a harsh, cold, desperate life. It was a time of poverty and struggle for most other families. Ernest's success or failure on the farm depended on daily labor, the heat, the cold, the dark, the sweat of a man's brow, as weak as the whim of the wind, the rain, and the short growing season.

The day that changed the course of my family's history began like any other day. Ernest's sons, Winton and Harry, had completed the usual milking the cows, harnessing the horses, feeding the animals, and cleaning the outhouse.

The devil arrived on an ordinary August day. No clouds hinted at the sadness, suffering, and evil that this tractor would bring.

Early in the morning, Ernest had noticed that the tractor's fuel line was leaking. He ordered Winton to quit whatever he was doing and get out to the field to look at the tractor's gas line, as it might be just a loose connection. Winton was twelve years old, and Ernest was sixty-one at the time.

From the faded old pictures of Winton, I see a bright, smiling young boy ready to engage with the world. Winton was of average build, a good-looking twelve-year-old. He had slicked-back black hair, blue eyes, and a strong profile. He was thin yet physically strong, having grown up lifting bales of hay, digging deep holes to repair fences, and building a new storage shed.

My father said he liked the feeling that he could help his father and his family. He wanted to please his father, who was unusually demanding, particularly with his wife. That day, Winton grabbed his heavy brown tool bag, put on his tan felt hat, and set out for the cornfield where the broken-down tractor had been sitting in the headland or the turnrow area, leaking gas for two days.

Winton, in his wide-brimmed, light-colored felt hat, North Dakota.

As he was about to pass by his friend Harold's house, he stopped to see if Harold wanted to come along and keep him company. Harold had a heavier build compared to Winton, and he was also a smoker.

The bright sun in the azure blue sky warmed their backs, making this a carefree and enjoyable trip for them. Together, they walked about half a mile through the dry cornfields. The boys eventually found the red tractor. It had stopped in a turnaround spot in the middle of the family's cornfield.

This 1920s gasoline-driven tractor was typical of that era, with tall, wide metal back wheels and small, narrow wheels on the front end. The rear wheels were nearly six feet tall. The large, thin, rectangular red gas tank was only slightly off the ground. The tractor seat, steering column, gearshift, and brake were directly behind the gas tank. When driving the tractor, Winton would have had to crawl up the spokes onto the back wheel to get to the seat. His feet could barely reach the gears. The gas lines were tucked snugly under the tractor between the huge back wheels. Winton removed his felt hat and set it carefully on the ground near a large oak tree. He crawled under the small space beneath the tractor with tools in hand. Quickly, he located the leaking gas line and decided it would be better to remove and replace the line instead of repairing it.

The first step required that he remove the gas line from the tank. In a matter of minutes, the earth and time and everything in Winton's and my life yet to come would change forever. He was only twelve years old, but within a moment, this boy was about to face the devil. His familiar world would dissolve, and the jaws of hell itself would open and take him.

Winton did what he was supposed to do. The gas rushed out of the hose from the tiny leak and the long line stemming from a full gas tank. The pungent, clear stream of gas ran, like a deadly silent snake, out onto the dry corn on the arid ground. Part of the ground had absorbed gas from the leaking line. It also soaked into Winton's trousers and his shoes.

Harold was standing by Winton near the tractor, chatting with Winton, unaware of the deadly new poison staining the ground in front of him. Then it happened.

Harold lit his cigarette and thoughtlessly tossed the match. Within seconds, the gas-stained ground beneath the tractor and the dry weeds strewn around the tractor were engulfed in flames. It only took a moment. Harold knew what he had begun. He ran to safety, escaping the explosion that immediately followed. Winton was not lucky. He was wedged tightly beneath the tractor. Instantly, Winton was on fire. Screaming, he burned. His screams could not douse the fire. Every nerve in his body was lit as he felt the searing pain bite into his flesh, as his trousers caught on fire. The screaming was but a moment's respite from pain.

Winton slapped at the flames to put them out but could not reach them. Now he is a human torch. He beat on the fire with his bare hands. The flames had taken hold and were eating through his gas- soaked trousers. The raging ground fire was spreading to the dry field of harvested cornstalks. Flames were rushing at him from all directions. The day turned into night as the smoke covered the sun and beyond.

My father said he remembered he did not want to die, but he felt it was inevitable. He said he could taste fire; he closed his eyes against the heat and slowly clawed at the ground to pull himself out from beneath the tractor.

His gas-soaked pants were burning from his knees to his shoes. He was on fire. The ground fire would soon surround and trap him. Instinctively, he knew the direction to his house. He had to get through the cornfield to safety, where there was a well; he wanted nothing more than to jump into it. A million thoughts ran through his mind, most of them grim. He ran. He was on fire. The cornstalks cut his face and caught his flames as they began to fuel a more massive field fire. The smoke became even denser. He could barely breathe. Finally, on the open dirt road, he collapsed to the ground.

Bright lights were everywhere. Strange voices seemed to be all around. Winton did not know where he was. Then his mother, Rosa, called his name.

"Winton, it is Mama. You are in the hospital."

He could not move his legs; something was constraining them. He rubbed his eyes with his hands, both wrapped in gauze.

"Why can't I move?"

Rosa tried to hide her tears and red eyes from her son and said softly, "Your legs got burned when you were fixing the gas line." You must stay still and cannot move until they heal."
Little did Winton know what that meant! If only Harold had not dropped the match.

"Harold is outside waiting to see you," Rosa said. "He feels something awful."

"No, never," Winton said with frightening finality.
The entire family considers that moment when Winton's

temperament changed forever. His fun-loving personality and sense of humor were gone. Only the suffering remained for this twelve-year-old boy. Daily he had to endure unrelenting pain, horrific torture of bandage changes, and the frustration of being restrained.

Winton had third-degree burns on both legs, from his knees to his ankles. It had destroyed the entire outer layer of the skin and the layer beneath it. Each day the charred skin had to be cut off. Daily, the open wounds were cleansed and again covered with dressings to absorb the constant drainage from the burned skin. The dressings would adhere to the injuries, and as the bandages had to be changed every few hours, the pain would be horrendous.

Cleaning his wounds was like setting him on fire again. Even though Winton was on intravenous fluids and various pain medications, his screams resounded daily throughout the country hospital. For two years in the hospital, he rarely spoke but mostly screamed from his intense pain.

Rosa, his one constant, sat by Winton's bedside daily for those two years. As his mother sat by his bed and saw his continuous pain, she would be bent over as if choking down her sobs. She prayed for mercy. Nevertheless, seeing none for her helpless child, she despaired. Rosa cried, "How could there be a God who would allow a child such torturous pain?"

Winton continued this horrific story, telling me that Harry, his ten-year-old younger brother, and two younger sisters, Helen and Rosalie, ages six and eight, occasionally found someone to bring them into town to visit him. Their visits were not helpful, as they constantly complained that Mama was always at the hospital.

Winton's siblings had to do his chores and take over Mama's work. They had to cook three meals daily for a farm crew of over twenty-four men who tended to their six hundred forty acres of crops. Even worse, they accused Winton, their dear brother, of being responsible for Ma's asthma attacks. Then, they would leave, saying that his room "stank, and they could not stand it."

Where was Winton's father, Ernest, during this time? Well, that was simple. When Ernest was not drunk, he was maintaining his businesses. Plus, he managed the six-hundred-forty-acre homesteaded farmland he acquired in 1906, making up for the ruined tractor's loss and the burned cornfield. He blamed his stupid son, Winton, for his misery.

Ernest regularly drank his way into oblivion to calm his inner demons, oblivious to the rage the alcohol brought out in him and how it impacted his family.

Winton's constant pain was horrific, but his biggest heartbreak was his father's indifference toward him. He was too busy to visit his son those two years while in the hospital to provide the encouragement he needed for his recovery. Ernest wanted nothing to do with him. He was embarrassed to see him, believing that Winton would now be a useless cripple.

Two years after Winton's horrific encounter with the devil, he left the hospital in a wheelchair. The wounds on both legs were still open and throbbing. While his friends played baseball and football, he endured his painful rehab struggle to walk again. Through this challenging time for Winton, Ernest had no words of comfort.

When Winton, my father, was eighty, I will never forget the tears running down his wrinkled cheeks as he told me this story.

The most attention Winton got from Ernest was a beating when-ever he said or did anything Ernest did not like.

Ernest would hit him with a metal rod or a strap on his back and butt. After the fire, he spared Winton's legs, but the beating continued.

Winton's siblings each got "the rod." When Ernest sent his sis-ter, Helen, to the grocery store to get matches, she was thrilled to be chosen for the errand. However, it happened to be on an amazing day, August 31, 1927, and Charles Lindbergh had just completed the first flight nonstop from New York to Paris. Listening to the men at the store talking about this momentous event, Helen was so captivated that she forgot how long she had been there. When she got home with the matches, Ernest removed his belt and beat her. At age ninety-two, Aunt Helen cried when she told me this story.

In the 1920s, there were no laws protecting children from abuse by parents or siblings as Ernest's children grew into adulthood. Social workers did not visit farms to assess children's home environments. Parents like Ernest had complete authority over disciplining their children. All four of his children feared him significantly. Ernest was physically and emotionally abusive to both the children and Rosa. Such abuse remained undetected by others since his family would not report it. If Winton or any of Ernest's children attended school with bruises, they would provide explanations for them.

DESPICABLE MAN (1929–1952)

That which does not kill us, makes us stronger.
—Friedrich Nietzeche

Father was nineteen when the Depression hit the United States after the stock market crashed on October 29, 1929. This day would come to be known as Black Tuesday. Bread lines, soup kitchens, and the rising homeless became common in America's towns and cities.

In the 1920s, farmers like Ernest struggled with economic challenges due to drought and falling food prices and could not afford to pay a crew to harvest their crops.
Many left their crops rotting in the fields while people elsewhere starved.

In the fall of 1930, the first of four banking panic waves began as large numbers of investors lost confidence. At that time, the United States was the only industrialized country without unemployment insurance or social security. The banking panics forced banks to liquidate loans to supplement their insufficient cash reserves.

By early 1933, thousands of banks had closed their doors. Ernest soon saw that the nation's financial crisis could cost him everything. He was terrified.

At the close of one seemingly typical workday, Ernest routinely locked the bank doors and went home at his usual time. After dinner, he announced that he had to go on a trip, which he often did for a few days. He said goodbye to his family and went to the bank. It was the end of the day, and the bank was closed. There, Ernest emptied the family's bank account and removed and pocketed all his bank patrons' funds. These patrons were his friends who believed their money would be secure in his bank.

That same evening, shortly after Ernest left his home, a fire started and burned all of Ernest's assets to the ground: the bank, the implement store, the general store, and the grain elevator. Ernest never came back. His family was impoverished, left to fend for themselves with no money and with farmland now only a useless dust bowl.

The fire destroyed the successful businesses Ernest had created, which the family could have taken over. Why did he do that to the family and the town he helped create? Speculations abound, but we will never know the truth. That little boy who almost missed the boat from Prussia to America had made the American dream come true, but only for himself.

His shameful escape left the family of five broken and devastated. His cowardly and unforgivable desertion destroyed any of the family's dreams, especially my father's, who had always wanted to attend law school. Now they had nothing to eat; they were destitute.

Nothing would grow in the dry, sun-scorched land. The economic depression, prolonged drought, scorching temperatures, poor agricultural practices, and the resulting wind erosion all contributed to the creation of the renowned Dust Bowl.

At one point, Rosa's sister and brother-in-law, Irene and Mike Mandel, came to Plaza to help. Even with a small amount of help from them, Rosa could not manage the care of the farm. No money came in since the last crops failed in the drought. She could no longer pay or feed the hired farmhands.

Finally, with packed bags, red eyes, and a trembling chin, Rosa took Rosalie and Helen in hand. She said a quick good-bye to Harry and Winton at the train station. How could she leave them? As the three boarded the train, both girls covered their faces with their hands so their brothers could not see their tears or watch them disappear as the train pulled out. The boys watched with stooped shoulders, and their voices were trembling as they said goodbye and waved to their mother and sisters, leaving on a train for Minneapolis to live with Rosa's parents. Rosa did not even ask her sons to come with her. Such were the times.

Ernest abused all four children and Rosa physically, mentally, and emotionally. Of the four, our father, Winton, was the only survivor of his abuse who later in life had children. When Ernest abandoned his family, he left the five of them nothing. It forced the family to split up. The siblings always described how difficult their lives had become and how happy they had been that Ernest had left. The girls lived their young lives through their teens in Minnesota with Rosa's parents and grandparents. Helen used to say that "that was no piece of cake either" because her grandfather was also a " child-beater." The solidifying tone and bond between all four of Rosa's children and Rosa was their hatred for Ernest.

As complex as Harry's and Winton's lives became, they were happy having taken over managing their large farm even though the crops were not doing well. They were away from their drunken demon of a father. Soon, Harry and Winton found it impossible to keep the farm going because of the drought. Together, Winton and Harry left their empty home in Plaza and found small jobs along the way in the little towns of North Dakota.

They worked in Minot at the Waverly Hotel, parking cars and doing bellhop work for $25 a month plus room and board.

Helen, Rosalie,
Rosa, Winton

Winton and Harry

Father's story of growing up with an evil father, nearly being burned to death and years of recovery, his father's desertion, and then that of his mother's—no wonder the devil's rage was emblazoned on his soul. They were the heirs apparent to Ernest's fortune just five years prior. Now, they were barely surviving. The two young men decided they might find something better elsewhere. They quit their jobs at the Waverly and started hitching rides to various little towns looking for work.

One day, they stopped at the edge of a small village where the Barnum & Bailey circus trucks were unloaded and set up a three-ring circus. They moved quickly through the mass of large, sweaty people with dirty, wet shirts and asked if there was work. The men assured the boys that there was plenty of action. Sure enough, Harry found a job with the circus barker selling tickets to the crowd.

Winton found his spot wrestling a grizzly bear for the crowd of circus attendees. This is how the grizzly bear scam worked: First, unknown to the audience, the bear owner would tranquilize the bear. Then, Winton would throw his small frame onto the subdued bear and wrestle the large, friendly bear to the ground. The unsuspecting crowd loved it and thought this was shocking—a wild bear! While Winton was wrestling this huggable, drugged bear, the bear owner was out in the crowd selling many tickets for the next group of guys to wrestle this friendly bear. He worked on the visiting audience of onlookers to collect money for the next show. Men and boys were paying him good money so that they could have a turn wrestling this bear. Each time Winton finished his act, the owner led the friendly bear back to his cage.

Then the scam began. Before the first young man from the crowd was to wrestle the bear, the owner had the bear in his cage and beat the bear to get it angry. Then the owner brought the bear out to wrestle with one of the unsuspecting boys who had paid good money for this opportunity.

The bear was now mean and roared with a ferocious cry. The boys and men had paid their money to wrestle what appeared to be a large but gentle animal. The boys who had become eager to wrestle now wanted nothing to do with this growling, vicious bear. There was a firm no-refund policy.

The bear owner pulled this scam quite successfully three times a day.

After a few months of working in the circus wrestling the bear, Winton felt sad, an unspeakable emptiness that something was missing. He had minimal interactions with other people. Finally, he told his brother, Harry, he wanted to return to Minot, as he felt too restless. Harry said there was more work to be had out West, and he felt that any winter weather had to be better than the 10 to -30F below zero where they lived.

Soon, Harry said goodbye to his brother, hopped on the Great Northern train, and went to California. Winton said he sat for a long time staring at the railroad tracks and remembered feeling very much alone. After Harry's departure, he moved from farm to farm for a short while. For any sum of money, Winton would do farm duties and paint and repair the farmers' buildings at each place. Finally, he returned to Minot.

One warm summer night, Winton felt the need to be more social and have a little fun. He decided to go to a dance at the pavilion near Falls Grove, where Jimmy Dorsey's renowned big band played.

Winton, now twenty years old, was a very handsome young man with deep blue eyes, a broad, bulbous nose, and chestnut-brown/almost-black hair. He had come to the dance that evening with a date, Kathryn Dayton. There, he first saw Florence Martha-Carrie Hall, then age sixteen, who lived close to Minot in a small town called Deering.

Once he laid his eyes on Florence, he could not get her out of his mind. She had a gorgeous face with deep brown hair that waved around her face.

She was very thin and about 5'4" tall. Winton, who stood at 5'8", thought Florence was ideal for him. A few days after the dance, Winton hitched a ride to where Florence lived on her family's farm to ask her for a date.

Florence Martha-Carrie Hall

Two weeks later, Winton borrowed a buggy for their first date. They had a terrific time at a dance and seemed to enjoy each other. He only wished she lived closer.

TOUGH TIMES, TOUGH WOMEN (1865–1965)

The course of true love never did run smooth
— Shakespeare, A Mids ummer Night's Dream

Florence Martha-Carrie Hall, who eventually became my mother, was a quiet woman, the youngest of four children of William (Bill) and Freda Hall. She had three elder brothers who always taught her how to work on their farm.

Mother told me this story about her beginnings: Her grandparents, the Schneiders, had emigrated from Germany and lived in Wisconsin, where her mother, Freda (a.k.a. Fride Schneider, and her twin sister, Martha Carrie, were born in 1873). There, Freda met William (Bill) Hall, one of twelve children. After they married, they relocated to Deering, North Dakota. Like most people in the early 1900s, Bill's and Freda's lives were most often grueling farm life—like that of Ernest's.

Parents BIll, Freda and children
Florence, Leonard, Billie, and Ben Hall

The plains' short growing season was only three to four months because the brutal winters could last six to eight months. Their days consisted of rising at 4:00 a.m., rounding up cattle from the fields, feeding all the animals, milking the cows, preparing food for a farm-threshing crew of twenty-plus men, and tending to the evening chores for the animals.

In 1922, when Florence was eight years old, her father, Bill, abandoned the family, leaving her mother, Freda, to manage the farm and her four children. Bill ran off with Tekla Keating.

Florence Martha-Carrie Hall

Already facing extreme challenges, Freda became even bitterer and struggled to keep the farm going until finally, a drought ruined their crops. No longer could she feed her children.

From 1928 to 1935, drought destroyed most of what the North Dakota farmers had seeded, and Freda's farm was no exception. No crops meant the wind blew across the barren land and created dust storms. Schools were closed. In my lifetime, schools closed because of snowstorms.

Florence, now a quiet fifteen-year-old, climbed up onto one side of the buggy, and she and Freda rode into town and tied up in front of the bank. It was 1929 and the beginning of the Great Depression. Freda walked into the bank with Florence's firm grip on her hand. Her voice, dry and unforgiving like the land, told the banker she wanted to sign over her farm property.

Freda Hall on the combine working the fields.

As desperate as these times were, Freda knew that selling the farm was the only thing left for her to do. She hated her husband, who left her for another woman, and now she was losing the farm. This last act only increased her bitterness, not only toward all men—but toward life.

The banker led them to a big desk and told them to wait, and that a different banker would help them. Florence had never sat in such a big chair; it was smooth leather. Soon, the banker sat at his large brown desk, talked with Freda at length about the farm, and wrote out lots of papers for her to sign. After Freda signed the documents, the angry, desperate woman and the pretty young girl left the bank with enough money to start a new life. Freda used the money to purchase a boarding house in Minot. She paid the farm workers within two weeks and prepared for departure by packing Florence's belongings and her own. With great trepidation about whether anyone could afford to rent rooms in her boarding house, Freda and Florence soon moved off the dry, barren farm into Minot. Florence sobbed as her three brothers, Billie, Leonard, and Bernard, sadly said goodbye to their mother and sister and then went their separate ways.

Florence, my mother, cried as she told me this story. The boarding house was small, with several rooms. Freda took in teachers as boarders to make ends meet. Florence helped Freda with all the chores at the boarding house and found a job at Kresge's five-and-dime store. She had been in school long enough to complete the eighth grade.

Minot became a town like many towns that got their start because the Great Northern Railroad came through that part of North Dakota. Railroad companies needed a place where trains could stop to replenish their water supply. Soon, the townspeople built a railway station. Shortly after, a hotel, a bar, and other amenities emerged to accommodate those travelers' needs, particularly the needs of all railroad workers. Those needs included two incredibly lucrative businesses: saloons and brothels.

The town of Minot emerged between two large hills with a Missouri River tributary that runs through the city: the Souris River, but the locals called it the Mouse River because of its murky brown-gray water. This river, once the source of prosperity, floods Minot nearly every year. The locals clean everything up and hope that it will not happen again. It is a way of life for that part of the country, dealing with disasters and then moving on. That is how Freda survived the devastating challenges that life threw at her. Soon, Florence would learn to cope with hers.

THE FLAWED, WOUNDED FAMILY
(1928–1994)

We are reminded that, in the fleeting time we have on this Earth, what matters is not wealth, status, or fame, but rather how well we have loved and what small part we have played in making the lives of other people better.
- Barack Obama

Father told me how thrilled he was when he heard that Florence had moved to Minot. He still worked nights at the Waverly Hotel, blocks from Kresge's five-and-dime store on Main Street. They would go dancing whenever their work schedules allowed it. He was smitten with Florence. He mentioned that Florence had reservations about him, describing him as controlling and noting his drinking. Father said they would argue and break up often. However, he always brought her around with dubious promises she chose to believe.

In 1931, Winton proposed to Florence, and they were married later that year. Soon, they bought their first tiny house for $6,000.

Winton proposed to Florence.

In 1938, my sister Sharon was born. Soon, that original house was too small for a family of three, and one more on the way—that was me. The expanding family prompted another move to a larger home in a beautiful U-shaped court of about twenty homes called Shirley Court. My baby sister, Connie, came four years after I was born.

Marlyn Kay, Age Two

Marly (6) Sharon (10) Connie (2)

I have various memories from my time living at our home in Shirley Court. When I was four, my sister, Sharon, made me somersault over a footstool. My barrette pierced my head, bleeding on the new rug, which made our father yell at us. He yelled a lot.

Sharon was devious. She would sit on my stomach and hold my hands down above my head. As I could not move, I used the only response available. I bit her in the stomach. This necessary choice of mine did two things: it caused her to go to the hospital and get stitches, and I became the neighborhood "biting" terror. I must give my sister credit for this. Later, I learned that my friends' parents kept an eye on me at my birthday parties to make sure I did not bite their babies. I must have been quite terrible.

The Balsukot Family
Sharon, Connie, Florence, Winton, Marly

When I was six years old, I recall a time when my mother canned peaches on stovetop burners. Something caused the boiling glass canning jars to blow up, and glass began flying. Mother screamed for me to run outside as she grabbed my baby sister, Connie, from her highchair, and we ran out the back door— shards of glass whizzing past us.

One wonderful Christmas, I woke up to a beautiful red bike that Santa Claus had brought. I was so excited that I threw on my storm coat and boots and went outside with my new, shiny bike to ride on the snowy streets. I had never ridden a bike before. Father helped me onto the bike and walked alongside me while I gained momentum. Bravely, I rode down the slushy street of snow and dirt and realized I did not know how to stop, especially in the slippery, slushy snirt (my word for snow and dirt). I crashed into a car toward the end of the street and came running home with dirt, snot, and a little blood now covering my heavy gray storm coat. Both my bike and I survived.

A year later, on a brutally cold Sunday when I was nine, my mother told me to wait outside the church after Sunday school and that Uncle Ben would pick me up and bring me home. I waited for some time. My little legs were cold, even with long stockings covering them. Under a heavy wool coat, my pink dress with flowers and ruffles was blowing in the brisk winter wind. A wool hat covered my curly blonde hair. It had ear covers that stayed on because of that annoying tie under my chin.

I was getting concerned because I was the only one outside the church. Soon, our pastor, Reverend Zerwas, came out of the church and told me he wanted to wait with me. He said he thought I needed company while I waited. It might have been fifteen minutes that we stood in that icy cold spot, our eyes firmly leveled in the distance. To me, it felt like forever.

Finally, Uncle Ben, one of Mom's three brothers, showed up in his battered, squeaking old farm pickup truck. I jumped in and waved goodbye to the pastor. We headed to our house at #13 Shirley Court. Uncle Ben was my favorite uncle because he had a farm a few miles from Minot. When I was eight, I began an annual summer visit to Uncle Ben and his wife Eunice's farm for a few weeks.

I loved experiencing all the adventures of being with them on their farm, like fetching fresh eggs from the henhouse, learning to drive the tractor, helping clean the barn, and learning to milk a cow.

Uncle Ben soon arrived at our house in Shirley Court. Quickly, I jumped out of the truck. Uncle Ben waved goodbye as I skipped up the walk and the front porch stairs. I was happy to be home, planning to stand in front of the fireplace until I could stop shivering. I opened the front door, and with my eyes widening, I gasped. *The house was empty.* All the furniture was gone. The pictures were off the wall, and there was no sign of belongings, mine or theirs. Instead of the roaring fire I expected, the fireplace was dark. It was colder inside the house than outside. No one was there.

Where was my family? Where did they go?

 I sat cross-legged on the bare floor of my bedroom, biting my lip and using my comfort habit of twisting my finger in my curly blonde hair, sobbing. Wiping away the tears with my coat sleeve, I thought I must have been awful. Soon, I became tired, and I was hungry. Finally, I lay down in an empty corner of my bedroom floor and fell asleep. Then I woke to hear the softness of my mother's voice calling, "Marly," and felt her arms lifting me off the cold floor and saying, "We are so sorry that Uncle Ben left you here. We knew what happened when you did not arrive at our new house, and there was no way we could reach Uncle Ben. You must have been so scared that we were gone. I am so sorry that happened."

No one had bothered to tell me.

Mother sounded concerned and sincere and undoubtedly regretful. Nevertheless, that day, I lost something significant. Deep down, I knew she loved me; but somewhere in my little girl's head, I recorded these images and did not know if I could ever trust her again. Or anyone.

I do not remember much about the first ten years of my life. Memories from those early years are mostly what my parents or sisters have told me in bits and pieces. My fondest memories are of my piano and dance lessons.

I do vividly remember my grandmother, Freda Hall, as this hardworking, hardened prairie woman in her sixties. She took a bus to our house during the work week, whether it was minus twenty degrees and snowing, raining, or one hundred degrees. As our mother worked six days a week, Freda came over to help by tidying the house, doing the morning dishes, helping get us kids off to school, and washing clothes. My elder sister, Sharon, by then fourteen, was never around; if she was, she was in her bedroom with a locked door. Freda loved Connie, Connie, my little sister, by then age six. Freda was never happy when I was around. To this day, Connie will admit that often she would purposefully cry and act out that I had done something to her because she loved to see Freda scream at me and call me the "black sheep of the family." Well, let us add a lack of self-esteem to my abandonment issues.

Marly Acting Out

Freda lived alone in a tiny studio apartment a few miles across town from our home. I remember its cold linoleum floor. The living area was so small that it held only one soft chair, a throw rug, and an ancient device, unlike anything I had ever seen. She called it a radio. It was a beautiful rectangular box, like a dark wooden piece of furniture. It stood about three feet high and two and a half feet wide, with a cloth screen in the front where the sound came through and little knobs used to dial in a station.

Grandma Freda Hall

This one room was open to her bedroom, where she had a dou-ble- sized bed, a small dresser with two drawers, a lamp, and a closet full of dresses and two pairs of shoes. She did not have a refrigerator or icebox. She placed her groceries on the win-dowsill in winter. I do not recall how she kept them cool in the hot summers.

I thought her apartment was dreadful. My father was paying for this sad little place. He always yelled at our mother that he "had to take care of all of Freda's expenses," plus our family of five. Also, our father sent a small amount of money to Helen, one of his two sisters, to help pay for the care of my grandmother, Rosa, who was now living near Father's siblings, all in California.

Deep down, it was not the small number of Freda's expenses that bothered Father. He did not like his mother-in-law, Freda, and could not stand being around her and complained about everything related to her. I knew the feelings between them were mutual. I always felt sad that our mother had to get the brunt of his wrath about Freda. Often, I felt terrible that Freda had to live in that place because our house was so big and beautiful. She rarely smiled or seemed even a tiny bit happy. Most memorable was if we ever mentioned anything about "boys" to her, all she could say was, "Men are no good. You should stay away from them and never get married."

A unique memory for me occurs in Freda's later years. One day we were standing outside our house, and Freda looked up and saw an airplane. "Ack-Gott" (her German phrase for "Oh my God"), she said, "I would never get into one of those things. What keeps them up in the air like that?"

That comment made me think about all the "firsts" in her life. These firsts or inventions that would change her life and the lives of most people were telephones, phonographs, the light bulb, the gas-powered car, the radio, zeppelins (balloon planes carrying people), airplanes, TV, and the atomic bomb.

Although the U.S. was advancing technologically by leaps and bounds in the twentieth century, many women were trapped in the Middle Ages. Four women were living in our house with a man who, with alcohol, would come out at night and could quickly drift into becoming a devil, like his evil tyrant father, Ernest.

MY PARENTS—THE ENTREPRENEURS
(1940–1960)

In Minot, our parents worked their entire adult lives six days a week, from 8:00 a.m. to 6:00 p.m. Yet none of my friends' mothers worked. How did that happen? I felt sad for my mother.

Years before I was born, while my father worked at the Elks Club in Minot, he met Andy Anderson. Soon, Andy would become a 50 percent partner in a new venture with our father. With Andy's $2,000 to match our father's $2,000, our father could start his new women's clothing business.
Bear wrestler - becomes an entrepreneur.

Our father, simply because he was a man and the head of the household, got to make decisions that, looking back, were not always the best. He had a high school education.

As I grew up, I realized that our mother was not an intellectual but a strong, hardworking, obedient woman like her mother. Mother did whatever our father told her to do.

Her intellectual growth was from reading Reader's Digest and the Minot Daily News. She also provided the best nurturing environment for my sisters and me that she could.

Florence and Winton Balsukot Grand Opening of The Bon Ton

In partnership with Andy Anderson, our father soon opened his women's ready-to-wear clothing store, The Bon Ton was located on Main Street in Minot. At that time, this was a great business opportunity for our parents. As a result of the clothing store, our mother and father were quite different role models from our friends' parents. Mother had to work six days a week. Father was at the store daily, managing it from opening to closing.

He always ordered the sales help around (several sales clerks, including our mother, and his three daughters, who eventually worked there).

Father would tell the sales staff, "Anyone who walks into this store should walk out with something they have bought here, or you are not doing your job, and your paycheck will show it." Their actions and quiet murmuring showed they were terrified of him when he was not around.

Mother and Father would get home from work by 6:00 p.m., and he expected to eat by six thirty. I do not know how our mother could accomplish all that she did. Mother worked six days a week, raised the three of us, ensured we all went to our piano and dance lessons, maintained our house, and had dinner on the table every night of the week. She was always at our father's "beck and call," meeting his harsh demands. Her significant role as a mother and a working woman was highly unusual then. She was the glue that held the family together in everything she did for us. I remember sitting and talking with her at 3:00 a.m. as she lovingly sewed sequins on dance recital costumes for Connie and me.

In Minot, as in many small towns of that time, social hierarchies existed: the haves (such as the doctors, lawyers, etc.), the have-nots (the very poor), and somewhere in between where our family belonged, the middle class—the merchants.

My appearance and that of my sisters, wearing beautiful clothes from our father's store, set us apart from those at the same economic level or below. As daughters of a women's clothing store, we were subject to our father's insistence that we wear clothes from the store to school to advertise daily.

Often, we would go to school with a new outfit one day, and it would be back in the store the next day. One might think how great that was, but I would not say I liked how it made me feel. Looking back at my life, I realize that many of my friends were poor. I knew some were jealous of my beautiful clothes. Little did they know that I wanted to dress like everyone else and wear jeans like my friends. I did not even own a pair.

Both sisters, Sharon and Connie, and I worked at the store from the age of thirteen. Father expected us to know all the merchandise in his store and be able to sell any of it. I remember one particularly dreadful day working at the store when my customer was our obese high school social studies teacher. Plus, she had a smoker's breath and terrible body odor. I had to fit her properly with a bra. A rule in "fitting" someone into a bra is that the breasts should not spill out of the bra at the sides or in the middle. This fitting was brutal. I added bra expanders to the back hooks but to no avail as her breasts spilled out and made two extra ones.

Our parents traveled to the "clothing market" two or three times a year to buy clothes for the store. Markets for women's retail clothing stores like ours were in Chicago or New York. Going "to market" always seemed glamorous as they got to fly to Chicago and New York. Mother told us they would often spend their evenings seeing Broadway shows such as Bye Bye Birdie, Camelot, Hello, Dolly, and many more, and go to beautiful nightclubs for the best entertainment the cities had to offer.

However, being a clothing buyer for a small store was not a glamorous job. They had only three or four days to accomplish their task—maybe five or six days, including travel.
Once at the clothing market, it became a series of hellacious workdays to visit several hotels to meet various sellers.

It worked like this: In each hotel, sellers of vendors' clothing lines occupied one or more hotel rooms. Their clothing lines were displayed on hotel beds and hanging on metal racks. Our parents had to meet with so many sellers in just a few days that they ran from hotel to hotel to see all the clothing lines they needed to buy from. They would rush from room to room, looking at each piece of merchandise, such as dresses, suits, coats, etc., hanging on racks in these rooms. In a brief period, they would select which clothing lines they sensed would sell best in Minot. Next, they would place an order for the store's upcoming season and dash off to visit the next merchant. Both Mother and Father had a terrific sense of knowing what to buy for the women in Minot. They knew their clientele and often bought clothes with specific people in mind.

Strangely enough, Aunt Helen, Father's sister, was also a buyer for I. Magnin, a chain of high-end clothing stores based in San Francisco.

An example of how different their buying processes were is this: If they liked a specific dress, my parents might buy a quantity of two in each size of 8, 10, 12, and 14 or a total of eight for that one dress. If Helen were to buy that same dress, she might buy ten thousand of that one dress for all her U.S. stores.

Because of Helen's purchasing power and the reputation she carried for her stores across the U.S., she was treated like gold wherever she went. This treatment carried over to Europe, where she spent a third of every year buying in Italy, always staying at the finest hotels.

I loved hearing Helen's stories of when she worked in New York and stayed at The Plaza in Central Park. Her tales of the many months she spent buying in Rome were glamorous. She stayed at the Hotel Hassler Roma, built in 1893, one of the classic grand dames of yesteryear at the famous Spanish Steps base. I thought about how exciting it would be to have that job and spend so much time in Europe. Little did I know how grueling these buying trips were.

Helen spoke quite disparagingly about our father's clothing business. She always put him down for his "little nothing store in godforsaken North Dakota," which gave her joy. The sparks would fly whenever they talked, which was on rare occasions. I remember there was always a screaming match whenever he and any of Father's three siblings got together.

Winton's siblings (Rosalie, Harry, Helen, and Father

Even though Helen had so much in common with our father, it did not make their get-togethers any easier. Separated as a family at ages fourteen and sixteen, they always had an axe to grind about the past. Over the years, I learned that the feud between them was due to our father sending only $25 a month to help support his mother, Rosa. Helen paid for most of her care. He had told his siblings that he had three daughters to raise and send to college and was financially responsible for Freda, Mom's mother. Neither his brother nor his sisters had children. Further, our father had to split the clothing store's profits fifty-fifty with his partner, Andy Anderson.

Of the three of them, Harry had a thriving car business, and Helen and Rosalie, good jobs. The feud between our father and his three siblings was a never-ending battle.

Mother and Father would have a party at our home for all the store staff and salespeople. I remember being up until 1 a.m. with Mother scrubbing the living room rug, polishing the sterling silver, and helping her make hors d'oeuvres. Those store parties continued for years until Father finally said he would stop having them. He never told us why, but I knew deep down that the employees would get tanked and tell Father what a "mean SOB" he was.

During the holidays, the same cleaning process occurred as the preparations when planning for a store party at our home. Mother would make fantastic turkey dinners, and we would set out our best dishes and silverware, even unique glassware. Grandmother Freda would be with us, and sometimes Father's partner, Andy Anderson, and his wife, Pearl. When we were kids, we always looked forward to the Andersons coming over, usually during the holidays— probably because they brought us great gifts.

The Andersons lived outside of Minot in another small town and rarely visited Minot, except on holidays. The Andersons knew nothing about the clothing business and counted on my parents to do everything as the managing partners. Years later, when my father sold the store, I learned the truth behind their partnership, and it broke my heart. If I had known then the raw deal that my father got himself into,with Andy only having a $2,000 buy-in, I would have tried to help him change it.

The only good news was that without Andy's $2,000 investment, Father would most likely not have been able to set up his business, or it would have been delayed. That agreement had been the best and worst agreement of his life. Best—because our father got this business started. Worst—because he agreed to split the profits with Andy fifty-fifty for as long as Father owned the store. Andy never lifted a finger. My parents worked so incredibly hard to make that store a success. It made me sick and very sad for my parents when I learned that they had to give half of their earnings away for all those years.

During my childhood, our father's success in Minot's clothing store allowed him to acquire three additional clothing stores, two in other North Dakota cities and one in Minnesota. The stores were exceptionally successful. Father made a great deal of money in the 1940s and 1950s and provided well for our family. Twenty years into our father's agreement with Andy, he was able to buy Andy out.

Around 1960, I had just started college, and our father decided to get out of the clothing business and sold his four stores. He purchased a hotel from the proceeds, the Clarence Parker Hotel, plus an adjoining hotel, the Parker Hotel.

Conceptually, he planned to turn the combined hotels into a convention center to bring many outsiders to Minot to save the downtown merchants who were no longer competing with the new shopping centers popping up around our small town. Within a few years, our father found that running two hotels was risky. He converted that acquisition into land and apartments in Arizona.

At one point during this last business/work transition, our parents moved to Mesa, Arizona. Mother and Father opened another little clothing store in downtown Mesa called Connie Jean's, named after my little sister. The clothing style or market for women's clothes was quite different in Mesa than the clothing they successfully sold in North Dakota stores. In Mesa, there was a large population of Mormons, or Latter-day Saints. The clientele was required to wear special underwear beneath their clothing, called garments. Additionally, the marketing/buying savvy needed to accurately meet the clothing styles of people living in 100+ Fahrenheit year-round weather was quite different from the clothing worn for -20 to -40F temperatures of snow country. About four years later, our parents decided to retire and sold the last of their clothing stores.

In our father's declining years, he reminisced that he was so sad and disappointed because he had expected one of his three daughters to take over the Minot store. As young girls, all three of us just wanted to get out of his reach and escape the extreme weather of North Dakota.

Secrets in families unfold slowly. I spent a long time enraged at Andy Anderson because he did nothing to earn 50 percent of all income besides his initial $2,000 investment. Soon after, I learned from Connie that she believed Father kept two sets of accounting books for the Minot store and his other stores.

So, Andy Anderson may not have gotten the excellent deal he thought he had. It caused me to wonder if there was some of Ernest's dishonesty in our father.

Fortunately, if there was, our father never abandoned us nor burned down the business, as his father had done. Winton was our father from the beginning to the end.

Another vital family member at holiday or party functions was Aunt Palma Hall. Just like clockwork, Palma took a taxi across town from her tiny upstairs apartment to come to our house every two weeks to bake for us. Her husband, Paul, was a brother of my mother's father, Bill Hall. Bill was the man who deserted Freda and our mother's family when she was eight, and he married another woman and moved to Long Beach, California.

 I was always excited when Aunt Palma was going to be at our house. During those days, when the school bus got to our street, I would jump off the bus and run to our home. As I opened our kitchen door, there would always be the sweet aroma of Palma's fresh-baked caramel rolls and the incredible smell of loaves of freshly baked bread. She made bread, pies, banana bread, unique kinds of cookies at Christmas, and caramel rolls. I would salivate at the thought of eating the gooey caramel and warm bread with a glass of ice-cold milk. It was fun when we thought Palma was not looking, and we would sneak some raw dough with yummy butter and brown sugar on it or eat the fresh cookie dough. Licking the chocolate frosting off the spoon and bowl after she frosted the cupcakes was the best.

Palma did not like any of us in the kitchen with her. She said we were always in the way. Watching her made me want to bake, which I learned to do on my own later in life, and I loved it. Palma and Grandma Freda did not get along very well.

Freda was resentful of Palma for a couple of reasons. Initially, I believe it was because Palma's husband, Bill' brother, deserted Freda for another woman. Whenever Mother and Father went to the market in Chicago or New York, Freda was offended that our parents chose Palma to stay with us instead of her. Mother and Father would never have left us with Freda as they knew I would have run away because I knew she did not like me.

POWER IN THE FACE OF EVIL (1954)

There is always one moment in childhood when
the door opens and lets the future in.
—Graham Greene

Winton was our father, and he became the fire that once ravaged his body. He incinerated our family with words and fists. Our mother got the worst of his abuse. I incurred his rage as I stood up to his anger and refused to cry. I remember hating the sound of his gruff voice when yelling at her and me. It was bone-chilling. She was afraid of him. Living with my father, my mother and I experienced emotional and physical abuse.

My sisters and I observed a lack of genuine affection or physical care between our parents, which provided us with poor examples of how adults should interact respectfully. Since our parents came from broken homes, they had no role models of love to transfer to us. Our father never told me he loved me or was proud of me. If I did ten wonderful things and one not so great, he would only dwell on the "not so great."

I was an incredibly accomplished tap dancer and performer who played concert piano and received all A's throughout high school. He would complain about the A-grade. Never did I hear, "That was great, Marly Kay." Nor did he attend my recitals—just as his father never played ball with him. Mother would tell us she loved us, but I was not buying into her kind of love because she did not protect me from our father.

Growing up, I learned that neither of our parents could manage alcohol. In retrospect, our father's genetic predisposition to alcoholism and his beatings as a child seemed to bring out the devil—his inner rage. Mom went along with the crowd and was a happy, sloppy drunk. My sisters and I were always waiting for the other shoe to drop whenever they would enjoy their nights "out on the town" at the Elks Club or the Riverside. These were regular weekend occurrences.

Father was a Shrine Potentate, better known Potentate was a position like a chairman or leader of an organization. They had multiple events for their members. These evening balls were often formal events with many of their friends. Mostly, these were nights of drinking. Mother would always get excited when one of these special events was on their social calendar. She could leave work at the store early to get her hair done. I loved watching her put on her sparkly rhinestone and pearl jewelry and enjoyed seeing her smile and how happy she was in a beautiful new gown.

Winton Ernest Balsukot, Potentate of the Shrine

Our father was the big grand pooh- bah of the Shriner society's highest order, known as the Potentate.

Winton and his Shrine Friends ready for a parade

A NIGHT I WILL NEVER FORGET

One freezing, dry winter night when I was twelve, our parents had gone to a Shriners event at the Riverside, a local club. That night, our sister Sharon had to babysit our little sister, Connie, and me. Sharon had been asleep in her bedroom next to ours for a few hours. I could not sleep. So, in my red plaid flannel pajamas, I got out of bed to look out the bedroom window. I knew it was the time of the year when the northern lights, also the Aurora Borealis, were often seen in North Dakota. Sure enough, I was so excited when I looked out the window. That night displayed the beautiful northern lights in their most brilliant greens throughout a vast stretch of the night sky.

The varied shades of green were vivid and flashing in the night as the new-fallen snow swirled across the frozen ground.

It was magical. I felt lucky and excited to see such a sight. I stood quietly, looking out at the barren trees with no leaves and the brilliantly lit midnight sky. I was delighted to see the beautiful six-sided snowflakes that clung to the windows in their lacy patterns. Each seemed different from the others.

Suddenly, I saw the bright headlights of our car entering the driveway. Quickly, I closed the curtain, shut and locked my bedroom door, and jumped into my little twin bed next to my sister Connie's bed. She was sound asleep. Mother and Father were returning from an event they loved to attend with their friends. I could hear the crunching sound of snow as the car slowly drove down the frozen ruts of our very long driveway. Even though I had warm, flannel pajamas, I was shivering. I pulled up the thick red wool blanket and bedspread covers and waited. With dread, I feared what would happen next. I heard them as they came into the house. Still, I was shivering.

Like clockwork, I could predict what would follow next. Our parents would enter the house and soon go to their bedroom (it was down the hallway from Connie's and my bedroom, separated by Sharon's room). Their bedroom door would close. Then it would begin.

I could hear hushed tones of them talking, and finally, Father yelled, "Florence, you are a big, fat, sloppy drunk, and you made a fool of yourself again tonight! "

Our mom responded, slurring her words with something like, "Now, Winton, it was not all that bad," and he began yelling.

"Do not argue with me; you are a lousy drunk!" I could hear Mother crying.

The verbal abuse went back and forth, and Mother cried with a pitiful sound, "Stop it, Winton! Stop it!" I knew he was hitting her. Her cries were that of a helplessly abused woman and became louder as he continued to hurt her.

It was a common occurrence, but that night felt different. I threw the bed covers off my little twin bed, leaped out of bed, ran around Connie's bed, unlocked the door, ran down the hall, and threw open their bedroom door. What a hideous sight.

I saw it all happening so fast—yet, in some ways, in slow motion. Father swung his fist on Mother's body as I entered the room. I watched as she fell backward, like a rag doll, into a heap on the floor in her beautiful gown. Simultaneously, he dropped to the floor, jammed his knee into her stomach, and wrapped his tie around her neck, choking her. Her face was red from being slapped. She gasped for breath, and her eyes were wide with fear.

She struggled to get him off her but could not speak. I could only hear the gurgling sounds of her choking. I now had come fully into the room. I stood there, frozen in fear. Yet I yelled at him, "Stop it! Stop it!"

He turned toward me with fury in his eyes. In that moment he had become the devil. I stood there terrified at what was happening and again screamed at him, "Stop it!"

I did not move. I could hardly breathe. I screamed louder, "Stop it!"

At that moment, after my third attempt to get him to stop, he let go of my mother and, like a lion ready to assault his next prey, sprang up and lunged toward me. I knew I was going to get it.

He grabbed me by my left shoulder and used his other hand to repeatedly hit me across my face and the side of my head. Then he struck me so hard that it knocked me over, and I fell onto my mother's makeup stool several feet away.

My right ear rang like a church bell—my rib cage throbbed in searing pain. I got up. He grabbed me again, viciously hitting and punching me everywhere, yelling, "So you wanted to see how it felt?"

Mother was shouting at my father, "Stop hitting her! Leave her alone! Marly, run back to your room!"
I refused to cry. I will never know where I got strength as a petite physically strong twelve-year-old. I just could not let Father think he got to me.

"You little bitch!" he yelled. "Who do you think you are?" The more he hit me, the more I became determined not to let him get to me. Each time I would get up off the floor and just glare at him in defiance, bracing for the next blow. I refused to cry. This decision to be defiant and not cry was a life-defining moment that has affected my entire life. Finally, he stopped his vicious attack, then yelled, "Go to bed!"

I ignored him and carefully stepped through the broken shards of glass and makeup, now spread all over their bedroom rug. I helped our pitiful, injured mother get into her nightie and watched her agonizingly climb into bed. I picked up her soiled, ripped, beautiful gown and placed it on a chair. I did not look at him but left their door open and limped slowly down the short hallway to my room. Then I closed and locked our door. I crawled into my twin bed; our little sister was still sound asleep. I pulled the covers over my head while my body throbbed. I wiped my tears away as I whimpered until sleep came.

The following morning, I woke up feeling tired. My chest, arms, and head instantly reminded me of the battle of the night before. I hated my father for the devil he became in the dark of the night and what he did to Mother and me. I often wondered, If there is a god, why would God let bad things happen to children? And yet a better question haunted me: What have I done to deserve this kind of treatment from a parent? I felt sad. There must be something wrong with me for our father to want to physically hit me, and verbally, and psychologically threaten me.

He created a type of hidden abuse for Mother and me that caused us to have underlying emotional fear as our constant companions. My sisters did whatever our father wanted and never responded defiantly, which saved them from his abuse. At times, I felt such hatred for him that I wished terrible things would happen to him. One time, I can remember wanting him dead.

I could not understand why he was so quick to devil-like rage and seemed to have a wave of underlying anger. Most days, growing up, I felt like I was holding my breath, waiting for the next shoe to drop.

Underlying the emotional and physical pain of living with a raging nighttime alcoholic, I desperately wanted my life to be different. I wanted to leave home and be far away from him, but I did not dare to leave home for fear of what he would do to me.

The next day, our father was busy reading the newspaper at the breakfast table, drinking his coffee, and our mother was getting breakfast for all of us. They both functioned as if nothing had happened—just a typical day. I cannot believe he could not feel bad for what he did to our mother and me. As I had to go to school, I hid my bruises with my sweater and wrapped heavy tape around my rib cage to help it heal.

There were no apologies from him—nothing—ever. It was like those incidents never happened. I felt sad for my mother and our family. He broke her wrist in one of their battles, but the excuse was that she fell at a party.

I asked my mother, "Why don't you get a divorce?"

Her response? There was none. She just glared at me.

She did not say anything. I did not understand how she could continue to endure such constant abuse or protect me from it. In those days, divorce was out of the question. I remember when one of my mother's friends got a divorce, she left town. She could not remain in that small town of Minot because of the rejection and judgment that would rain down on her.

Like many abused women, what would Mother have done with three children, no education past eighth grade, and without Father and the store, no job?

I knew other terrific, fun, loving, kind, and supportive parents existed. My best example of what I consider good role models was my good friend Karen's mother and father. They treated me like one of their own. They were sweet and fun and always wanted to talk with me about everything I did. I would often take refuge at her house and stay until I received the call to come home.

My closest friends felt like a real family.

My guy friends felt like brothers I never had. The guys I would date in my teens were never serious boyfriends. I dated guy friends who loved to dance at the YMCA.

My sisters were savvy and figured out ways to avoid our father's abuse. They never got hit—just Mother and me.

Neither of them did anything to protect or help us. If our parents were fighting and something got difficult, Sharon would sneak out of the house and run to her girlfriend's house and stay overnight or close and lock her bedroom door and turn up her radio. My younger sister, Connie, was six to ten years old when my parents' alcoholic battles occurred. I did not expect she could do anything to help me, but she remembers those nights, the screaming, what I did, and the abuse. Later, Connie told me, "I was going to do whatever I needed to do not to ever get in trouble. You, somehow, had the inner strength to stand up for your beliefs, which defied and angered him.

Drunken fights late at night were commonplace, our screams stifled. The violence stayed within the family. I assumed that if we were quiet, no one in the town would know that inside our house, the 1922 cornfield fire erupted again with devastating frequency; no one in the city would see that we were all being burned alive.

All those years, I thought no one outside my family had a clue. Later, I learned everyone in the town knew our father beat Mother and me.

As a twelve-year-old, I stepped in to save my mother from what could have become a deadly fight during one of my father's alcoholic nights. I swore I would never drink and be abusive like our father or passive like our mother and take such horrific abuse from a man. I would marry someone I genuinely loved and not drink and get drunk like my parents.

I could hardly wait to escape from the daily psychological and emotional trauma our father created and my never knowing when the next shoe would drop. Soon, I knew I would no longer be there to protect our mother from his brutality and abuse.

CHILDHOOD JOY (1947–1960)

Find a place inside where there is joy,
and the joy will burn out the pain.
—Joseph Campbell

To me, much of my childhood was a sad and miserable affair. I loved my parents but did not trust them to love me the was I thought my parents were supposed to. As a result, I was lonely and felt unloved and isolated in many situations at school and home. Even so, some brilliant, bright, and shiny childhood memories made me smile with deep and satisfying joy. When I reflect on these times, our parents showed us tremendous love through as many material things as one could ever want, some things they never had as children. Specifically, two gifts for Connie and Sharon, and most precious to me, were our piano and dancing lessons. Intense practice of these lessons was my salvation when life at home was intolerable.

Our parents showed their love through gifts and must have spent a fortune on our many years of training and dozens of costumes. Without fail, we each began piano and dance lessons at age five.

Mitzi, Marly, and Brownie perform
The Darktown Strutters' Ball

When Sharon was ten, our dance and piano teachers told our parents they were wasting their money on her. Those calls ended Sharon's days of piano and dance, but then she chose the violin. Her practicing the violin nearly killed us all. Sharon would close her bedroom door when she practiced. However, the screeching of wrong notes and the repetition of her trying to get it right resounded through the house like the brakes of a train coming to a quick stop.

Usually, I sought refuge in the basement from the irritating sounds emanating from her upstairs bedroom. Even being in the basement gave me little relief.

Shortly into Sharon's musical studies with the violin, somehow, magically, she ended up with a brand-new clarinet, and we all were much happier. She loved the clarinet because she knew she would now be in the high school's marching band, as were her friends and many boys. During special parades in Minot, I enjoyed watching her march down Main Street with the Minot High School band, dressed in a maroon uniform with gold tassel trim. Then, during Sharon's senior year, the band was so excellent that they traveled to an invitation-only competition in Colorado Springs. This trip was one of Sharon's first days away from home without our parents. Little did we know that her boyfriend, Gary, was on that same excursion and four-day glorious bus trip away from home.

Connie took dance and drama lessons up through her senior year. She liked her dance lessons but loved and excelled in drama. As an adult, she told me she was delighted when I left for college so she could be out from under my shadow and do her own thing. I had been a straight-A student and excelled at piano and dance. After I graduated and went on to college, I learned that my teachers would say to her, "Well, you are certainly not like your sister Marly." That made me feel terrible for her. No wonder she was happy to see me leave home.

I didn't cherish my piano lessons, but I loved playing the piano and all types of music. For thirteen years, I diligently studied and practiced piano. I found that perfecting the sound and tempo was indeed a challenge. I remember working on my "piano touch" versus striking a piano key. I learned how the key's touch provides the specific sound I was trying to create. Practice, practice, practice on our upright blond spinet piano while our little yellow canary, Dickie-bird, warbled away. The louder I played, the louder he sang.

I vividly remember one piano competition I entered as if it were yesterday. It took place in a large auditorium with a magnificent, raised stage. Beautiful maroon velvet curtains framed the proscenium arch.

A gorgeous, glistening eight-foot Steinway grand piano sat in the middle of the stage. I learned that the wood used to create this fantastic instrument's soundboard helps make the resonant sound as I rocked each key. It was thrilling to perform using this magnificent piano as I played Mozart's Concerto in C Minor. I recall that I won a Superior ribbon for this competition.

As much as I loved playing the piano, tap dancing was my true love. I practiced my routines, dancing in the basement of our house, down the sidewalk near our home, and rehearsing my steps quietly under my school desk. I rehearsed rigorously at home and worked hard during many weekly dance lessons. I could hardly wait for the next dance lesson to master each new routine.

Dancing was a fantastic way to forget about the pain within. From age five to eighteen, being a terrific dancer was all I could think about during most of my waking hours.

Marly – Dances to "Mr. Sandman"

I wanted to be good enough to go to New York and become a Rockette or move to California and live my life dancing. Little did I know that the minimum height even to be considered for a Rockette tryout was 5'9". I was only a mere 5'5" standing on my tiptoes. Both of my sisters are taller than I am. Maybe I will still grow?

Father promised me that if I got good grades throughout high school and did not smoke, drink, or screw (I think he referred to that as doing nasty things with boys), he would send me to any college in the nation. Hurray! Well, that was it. I got perfect grades and did not smoke, did not drink, or did not do nasty things with boys; in fact, I did not have any boyfriends with whom I was serious.

In retrospect, I wish I had done all the above Nevertheless, I used nearly all my time and energy outside of school taking piano and dancing lessons, practicing, practicing, practicing, practicing, practicing, practicing, and practicing. I loved tap and jazz dance routines. No matter how much time passed or how old I became, my goal was to become a great dancer and hit the stages of New York. I performed in the usual recitals, the county fair in Minot, and other venues in small towns. Besides solo tap performances, I had one duo I performed with a boy who took lessons. Also, I was part of a dance team of fifteen girls. This group learned and performed several dance routines at the Elks Club and other settings. One night at the Elks, the group did a lively cancan on a raised platform walkway down the middle of a banquet room. I vividly remember concentrating on not stepping onto someone's mashed potatoes on the tables butted up to the runway. Even today, that does seem weird to me, young girls at the Elks in front of grizzled, usually intoxicated, old local men of North Dakota.

I enjoyed playing various dancing parts in school plays, like Fiddler on the Roof. However, I loved my solo performances. My friends said, "What a great dancer you are! Your tap dancing is like listening to the rapid-fire sounds of horses on the run." Somehow being thought of as a wild horse on the run makes those memories feel light, pretty, and free.

Marly performing tap routine to "Cheek to Cheek"

My closest girlfriends—Karen, Judy, and Diane—and I would gather at the YMCA after most school days. Our Minot High School was two blocks from our parents' clothing store in downtown Main Street in Minot. We might do homework together at the "Y" and talk while having a Cherry Coke with marshmallow syrup.

On Friday nights, around twenty of my friends and I would meet at the Y, as the Y usually sponsored a dance in the newly refurbished basement room, the Canteen.

This large room contained a jukebox, and we all brought our quarters to keep the music flowing. One dear friend, Karen, had a brother, Mike, who was also in our class. He was a great friend, and I loved doing the swing and jitterbug with him at parties. He would grab my waist, flip me onto his hips, and swing me over his back. It was wild and fun! We would dance nearly every dance until they closed for the evening.

The pinnacle of what I considered my serious dancing career was when my dance coach, Virginia Maupin, told me I should perfect this one routine for a TV audition. She would set up an audition for the Ted Mack Amateur Hour, a TV talent show produced in New York. Ms. Maupin knew my parents would soon be traveling to New York on a buying trip for their clothing store. She told me that if she could get an appointment for me to audition, now would be an excellent time to try out my polished routine on a chance at the "big time."

I almost stopped breathing; I was so excited when she told me. I left the room and began crying. In my mind, I was on my way. This audition could lead to a career in television or possibly on stage. It was a chance that could catapult me toward success that had always been the focal point of my dreams. I was fifteen. How lucky could a fifteen-year-old be to go to New York and have this opportunity? In my hometown, people who saw me perform always complimented me and said I was a great dancer. Now this! It was about to happen just like I had dreamed it would—finally, recognition for my talent and years of hard work and dedication. I was going to be a star.

My parents allowed me to take a friend, Judy Anderson, to New York. Judy joining us in New York made the trip even more special because I could share it with my buddy, two giggling teenage girls from Minot, North Dakota, with stars in our eyes.

We arrived in New York and stayed across Central Park at the Hotel St. Moritz on the Park, a hotel celebrated as an icon of New York hotels.

Marly overlooking Central Park, New York

I remember going up to the Sky Room Lounge and feeling the presence of the rich and famous who stood there. It was a moment I shall never forget, looking out over Central Park's massive green area.

Its 750 acres have existed since 1853 as America's first significant landscaped public park, created to improve public health and provide a recreational area for the city. Shortly after our visit, the hotel closed, and its contents were auctioned off. Today it is the Ritz-Carlton New York, Central Park, with only the building's name intact.

My audition was on the second day of our trip to New York. My mother, Judy, and I wore our best dresses and took a cab to the CBS Broadcast Studio at 527 West Fifty-Seventh Street.

Father did not come with us as we would be away most of the day, and his buying days were limited. He could not afford the time, as he had to finish buying clothes for our store in Minot at the renowned New York clothing market in the Garment District between Thirty-Fourth and Forty-First Streets, west of Sixth Avenue.

On our way to the CBS studio in my first taxi ride in New York City, Judy and I were in awe of the width of the streets, the constant din of taxis honking, and the unending number of massive skyscrapers looming above us. The tallest buildings in Minot were possibly the two hospitals, which were six stories high. We marveled as these buildings were so tall that we could not see their tops until we stopped and got out of the taxi. It was thrilling to be in New York.

Soon, we arrived at CBS. Mother quickly paid the taxi driver as he pointed us toward the CBS studio. This nearly block-long facility was in the Hell's Kitchen section of Manhattan.

It served as the CBS News headquarters, the CBSN live-streaming news channel, and was the primary broadcast facility for CBS News. It was nearly a block from the curb to the building. Stunning fountains and massive containers overflowed with vivid, colorful flowers along the way. We remarked on how everyone seemed to be moving at a fast pace, almost at a run. As we entered through one of the building's three massive rotating steel doors, we saw six banks of elevators. People were hurrying as if they were all late to work. It was as if they were all in Alice in Wonderland, whispering, "No time to say hello." Goodbye. I'm late. I'm late. I'm late!"

An information desk loomed large in the center of the lobby. A welcoming young woman behind this circular desk gave us directions about the elevator that would take us to the studio. Immediately, the elevator bell rang as its door opened, and we dashed in. We were surprised to see an elevator attendant. He wore a very formal uniform, including white gloves, and politely asked us, "What floor do you wish?"

We told him, "The sixteenth floor, please," and giggled in delight, getting our first escort in an elevator. We entered a vast lobby leading to CBS Studios' multiple areas as the elevator door opened. We were greeted by a gorgeous young woman with red hair and bright, red-painted fingernails sitting behind a large walnut desk. Seemingly annoyed, she asked us why we were there and then instructed us to be seated.

She did not appear to be a pleasant person. It almost felt as if we had intruded into her space. We chose to sit on three magnificent, plush gold velvet chairs. Finally, after some time of silence, I asked her, "Where may I change into my costume?" With a seemingly disgusted look, she got up from her desk and paused at the door on the far side of the room. Opening it, she pointed to a door down the hallway and said, "Use the second door on the right to change your costume."

I thanked her and then skipped down the hall. I was so excited and nervous. There were only two doors on the right in this hallway. I opened the second door as instructed and gasped. It was a tiny, dingy, sad closet that appeared to house a janitor's pail and mops, not the star-studded dressing room I had always imagined. I looked down the hallway to ensure I had not miscounted the doors. As I stepped inside the tiny closet and closed the door, I reached up and pulled the worn string to turn on the light bulb that hung precariously from the ceiling and now swung back and forth. Carefully, I removed my red-flowered dress and shiny black patent leather street shoes and placed them into the duffel bag carrying my gorgeous costume.

I removed my mid-calf-length, royal-blue chiffon dress from the duffel bag with its flowing multilayered rhinestone-studded skirt. Then I stepped into it and quickly zipped it, carefully keeping the multiple ruffles from falling into the janitor's water pail.

The deep blue of the dress contrasted with my lily-white skin and golden blonde hair. I removed my black patent leather street shoes, put on my sparkly silver tap shoes, and returned to the office where the others waited. As soon as I reentered the office, the same woman in her gruff voice said, "You are next to audition. Go down this other door to room 29 and wait." "They will call your name when they are ready for you."

Excited and anxious, I picked up my sheet music, said goodbye to my mother and Judy, and quickly walked down the hallway. My silver sparkly tap shoes echoed clickety-clack, clickety-clack on the granite floor. I found room 29 and stood patiently waiting outside the audition room. My stomach gave me a signal of my stress level, which always happened before I performed.

I was alone. Soon, a short bald man stuck his head out of room 29 and brutalized my name as he called, "Marly Ballzekutt?" As I was the only person in the hallway. I nodded and quickly followed him. Immediately upon entering the room, I was startled, as it was a small room, maybe 12 ft. x 14 ft. An upright console piano was at one side of the room. The bald man sat on the piano bench hunched over the keys.

Another older man sat next to him. The bald pianist, with a cigar hanging from his mouth, grumbled, "Where is your sheet music?" I handed it to him. Then he mumbled, "Give me the tempo and tell me when you are ready."

 I responded, "I am ready. 1—2—3—4." The bald old man with the cigar began to play.

My audition routine consisted of rapid-fire tapping with a combination of turns and expansive smooth jazz moves. Unfortunately, this routine needed a large room or a stage.

I struggled to redirect my movements to fit the space. I did my best.

When I finished this well-polished routine, the stone-faced bald pianist looked at me, handed my sheet music back to me, and with a gruff voice said, "Thank you." I do not know what I expected. He gave me no hint of approval.

As I walked out of the audition, tears were beginning to surface. Given that my routine truly needed a large area to show off, I thought I had done a great job.

Back at home, I hovered over the mailbox for a few weeks, looking for news of my audition. Finally, the envelope arrived from CBS Studios. I was shaking so hard I could hardly open it. It said, "Thank you for auditioning, but we do not need more tappers." It felt like someone had stepped on my heart. I whimpered but told myself that this little setback would not stop me. Mother passed the rejection off lightly. This negative response was devastating for what could have been a beginning to achieve my dream as a dancer.

I returned to my dance lessons and reflected on my technique. People who watched me dance said, "How do you remember all those intricate steps?" I never thought about the next steps once I learned a routine.

In dance, as well as in learning to play the piano, rigorous practice is the key. Repetition made the dance steps happen, and the fingers performed using the correct piano keys. For me, it created a mental process that some might call muscle memory—as in any sport. For my dance and piano training, I would often use markings. These elements in the choreography or the music became signals for me to do a specific dance piece or change a piano piece's tempo. One of my best-loved, four-and-a-half-minute dance routines performed at age sixteen was a jazz/tap interpretation of three great dancers: Fred Astaire, Donald O'Connor, and Gene Kelly. This multi- layered three-part costume and dance routine was unique butforthat era. It consisted of a black tuxedo jacket over a long-sleeved white shirt, black pants with cuffs, a black top hat, and a shimmering cane.

As the music began, I would glide effortlessly with a few spot turns that moved me across the wooden stage to the song "Top Hat, White Tie, and Tails." This beginning displayed Astaire's style of fluid, arms wide,free-flowing movements, slides, and rat-a-tat- rapid- fire yet soft tapping.

The music soon became a lighthearted, bouncy tune, "Make 'Em Laugh." I then ripped off the velcroid-on tuxedo jacket and white shirt, revealing a scruffy-looking blue shirt. Quickly, I grabbed a different, scrunched-up hat with a turned-up brim off the hat prop rack. Simultaneously, I jumped onto a platform stage prop with three steps as Donald O'Connor would do and performed fast "buck wings" on the platform. Next, the tricky steps –a carefully rehearsed tap, tap, tap, while sliding backwards down the edge of the three stairs to whirling-dervish movements (like Michael Jackson's moon walk but on stairs).

Finally, I ripped off one more layer of clothing to reveal a sailor's suit beneath. Quickly, I grabbed a sailor's hat and began my Gene Kelly dance interpretation of "Singing in the Rain."

This routine was great fun, and it displayed various dancing skills. The audiences attending these performances loved it, as was apparent in their applause while demanding, "More!"

I love to dance. Performing on stage was pure joy. It was all I ever wanted to do or be - a dancer.

As I have fulfilled my promises to my father, now, what I needed to do was to get to California.

BLACK MAN—WHITE TOWN (1956–1960)

A Man Who Crossed Barriers and Built Bridges
—Robert Polk

Growing up in Minot, I only saw one young Black person in our schools, never on the buses or homes on our streets. Nevertheless, while in high school and working at our parents' clothing store, I realized some other Black people lived in town. One day, while working at the store after school, three pretty, tall Black women came in and asked for Winton. Well, blow me down. My father knew them and greeted them by their first names and with a hug. He greeted many customers that way, but this seemed far more friendly. I thought, how could that be? I heard the only Black people in town were some "ladies of the night" up on High Third Street. Not only did Father know them, but he knew their dress sizes and had Mother order special, fancy, and expensive cocktail-style clothes for them. Oleg Cassini and Ceil Chapman, these dresses were $300–$600 each back then. Even our mother only had one of these dresses for special events, and she got it at the wholesale price.

I brushed off this new awareness of our father's apparent "knowing" these women. I realized that our parents knew most women's sizes in this town as they ordered clothes for them.

I told my older sister, Sharon, what I had observed when the three Black ladies were in our store. Soon, she and her buddy Sandra decided to check out High Third Street, which was Minot's tenderloin or red-light district in the early twentieth century. It was often known as the neighborhood of a "haven of brothels and bootlegging." In ill repute at this point, there were still a few functioning houses of ill repute.

They would sit in Sandra's car at night because our father, if visiting these houses of ill repute, would not recognize that car if he spotted it there. They put their hair up in men's hats, waited until about dusk, and drove up to Third Street to "stake it out" and see who showed up there. They would eat sunflower seeds while waiting. Sure enough, the mayor, the dentist, and our father were guests at these ladies' " houses." Poor Mother. She must have known. How sad for her. We would not have dared to confront Father about it at home.

One day after school, upon entering the Y, my friends and I were greeted one day after school by Reverend Robert Polk, the new youth program secretary for the YMCA. He was well-received and appreciated as the new assistant pastor at the First Congregational Church.

Several of my friends belonged to this church and told their congregation was 100 percent Caucasian and thrilled to have Reverend Polk join them.

Bringing Reverend Robert Polk, a black man, to the 99 percent white town of Minot was for two reasons:

(1) to help prepare this all-white community to become a more diverse, multicultural town. A new Air Force base had just opened on the city's north end, and an older radar base was on Minot's south end, composed of people from multiple ethnicities.

(2). to work with the Y's youth. The Y helped with character building for all its members, emphasizing Christian values, morals, and a proper lifestyle.

All my friends and I were to call Reverend Polk, Mr. Polk, or Bob. As we all got to know Mr. Polk, we learned that he was easy to talk to, friendly, helpful, and interested in what we wanted for activities at the Y. We all liked him. He was interested in every one of us and had great ideas for improving our activities at the Y.

I learned that there was one other Black professional in Minot. He worked for the Minot Daily News.

Bob Polk wrote a memoir of his time in Minot called Crossing Barriers and Building Bridges. In it, he wrote, "I seemed to be the right person at the right time to help ease the way when the troops of color came to the Minot Air Force Base, which was just under construction, as well as the Radar Squadron. Bob's new book, Fly in the Buttermilk: One Black Man's Odyssey Out on the Prairie, is now fifty years since his two-year sojourn to Minot, where he recalls the words "the first Negro" which were usually attached to his name and his wonder of how this young Black cosmopolite from the South Side of Chicago survived this journey.

When deciding to visit Minot, Reverend Polk knew he was coming to what many described as "the coldest spot in the nation."

It has a record low of -41F. He knew that Minot had a predominantly Nordic population with a religious diversity that ranged from the Church of Norway to Evangelical Lutheran and a tiny group of Asians, Native Americans, Jews, Greeks, and other nationalities. It held all the typical Midwestern town elements, beginning as a central hub along the Great Northern RR.

One morning during our family's daily breakfast routine, we all squeezed into our kitchen's "L-shaped nook." Father took the chair outside of the nook. I slid in and always felt trapped in the back corner. One morning at the breakfast table, I told the family about this great new man, a Black minister, hired as the new youth director of the Y, Reverend Bob Polk. As kids might say about others they enjoyed being around, I said, "I just love that man."

Father practically flew up from his chair with that familiar look of the devil in his eyes, reached across the table, slapped me across the face with the back of his hand, and said, "Do not let me ever hear you say such a thing again about a Black. You are forbidden to ever go to the Y again."

What? All my friends would goto theY daily with their brown bags for lunch and after school. Terrific— another ultimatum.

I ran to the bathroom and put cold washcloths on my face to calm down the red hand mark. I did not cry. I was just angry. How could a father be so mean to me and be such a bigot?

I did not see color, poor, rich, intelligent, or dumb in people. On the inside, I wondered where my father's embedded anger and bigotry originated.

As I often did, I paid no attention to my father about many things, or I would have lived in a glass bubble. I never did anything illegal or wrong; therefore, not going to the YMCA was not an option. The YMCA was one block from the high school. The day after my father yelled at me that I could not go to the Y after school, I walked directly to the Y, as I always did. When I saw Reverend Polk, I asked him if I could speak privately. We went into his office. He closed the door. I told him what had happened at home with my father. Mr. Polk said he appreciated knowing that and would be sure never to do anything that would cause me any problems. I cried because I felt terrible saying something like that to anyone, especially this courageous human being who dared to come to this pristine little all-white town.

Bob would later write in his book Crossing Barriers and Bridges, "Prostitution had interesting implications and consequences as far as race relations were concerned; my work in the YMCA and with the families of Minot." When those students had come to my office and informed me that their parent objected to my appointment as Youth Secretary and demanded that they withdraw their membership from the Y, a typical follow-up statement was that their fathers or some male member of their family regularly frequented Third Street.

It was okay for the men of Minot to be sexually intimate with Black prostitutes but not okay to speak with respect and affection about a Black pastor. This was the hardest thing for me to understand and decode. I did not understand the phenomenon or how it played itself out, but its antecedents were a constant puzzle. I was one of a handful of Black men in Minot, yet most of the prostitutes were colored. Black men owned or operated the places of ill repute, often fronted as cafes, Bar-B-Q, or rib joints.

He further wrote, "I was often confronted by a comment about Third Street. The community would say to Bob, "If it did not exist, we as a community would probably be more open to the idea of the colored troops coming into our community."

Bob said, "What they failed to understand was that Third Street would not exist without the white male population in Minot, its surroundings, and white visitors from across the state."

Father and I walked down Main Street together to the drugstore soda fountain the next week, and I spotted Mr. Polk walking toward us. When Mr. Polk saw us, he crossed the street to avoid running into Father and me. What a considerate, caring man.

One of the many YMCA youth activities was raising money for some of our Junior Hi-Y Clubs to take them to New York City for a holiday and learning experience.

Four members went on this trip with Bob and returned without incident, or what one might say without a critical incident. However, for Bob Polk, it was a turning point in his life. While in New York, he visited a friend of his, Andrew Young, who had become a congressman, ambassador to the UN, and mayor of Atlanta. Also, Bob took the four Y youth he was supervising to visit the spectacular Riverside Church with its Gothic cathedral. They stepped inside to feel the soul of the Christian faith. The inside was a sight to behold with its vaulted ceilings, sculptures, and stunningly colored stained-glass windows with their religious stories. Little did Bob know until later that his students had stolen the cathedral's silver communion cups.

Several weeks after this trip to New York, Bob received a letter from the Riverside Church. He was afraid to open it for fear of repercussions regarding the stolen communion cups, which he had just learned occurred while he was away. Rather than open it and possibly ruin his weekend fishing trip with some Y youth, Bob waited a few days until returning from that trip. Then he opened it.

A pleasant surprise awaited him. The letter was an invitation to apply for the position of youth minister at the Riverside Church. His answer was an immediate yes. After a long process, he would begin his work in the prestigious Riverside Church. Andrew Young had sent his name forward and that of four others. Bob Polk was the chosen one to be a leader in this distinguished church. His departure would leave a hole in the hearts of countless people he influenced in many ways.

HAPPINESS IN THE PRESENCE OF EVIL
(1954-1960)

Around us is the presence of evil. The devil is at work.
But in a loud voice, I say God is stronger.
—Pope Francis

One weekend, Father said we were all going for a drive. The five of us were excited, as this was not a regular occurrence. We hopped into the car and drove for about ninety minutes. Finally, we got off the main highway onto a newly cut dirt road and stopped at the top of a hill. He said, "I just bought the cabin at the bottom of this hill." Well, I could not have been more excited. Our family would have a summer cabin on the edge of a beautiful lake. What a fantastic gift for the family! Only later would I realize how much more work this did create for our mother.

My sisters and I quickly ran down the hill to the lake. We were at Lake Metigoshe, located in the Turtle Mountains, fourteen miles northeast of Bottineau, seventy-six miles north of Minot, and along the US-Canadian border. The Chippewa called the lake Metigoshe Washegum, or "clear water lake surrounded by oaks."

When my father purchased the lake cabin, my sisters and I were fourteen, ten, and six. Sharon hated going to the lake because she was entering high school and was into boys. I, on the other hand, thought the lake was perfect. Connie loved the lake and had a good new friend who lived next door. Our cabin had three bedrooms, one bathroom, a living room with three 8' x 8' windows across the living room, a kitchen, and an entry mudroom for dropping boots and fishing rods. Later, our father had a wide porch built around the front half of the cabin with a large BBQ on one side.

Our wonderful home at Lake Metigoshe State Park
This is our lake home in Bottineau County, North Dakota, and the Rural Municipality of Winchester, Manitoba, on the Canadian border.

The new porch added considerable space to finish our beautiful lake home. Beneath the porch, Father had built a boathouse where we would put the ski boat and outboard motor when we closed the cabin for each winter. I would help pull the dock out of the water and prepare the house for the brutal winter.

When the boathouse was empty during the summer, I would use it as a favorite place to create my movie-star scrapbooks. I could often invite a girlfriend over, and we would sleep in the boathouse if the mosquitoes were not too bad. It was as close to having a tent as we could get.

Initially, we had to dig a massive hole for the septic tank to get the cabin in working order. Because I had good physical strength from all my dancing and acrobatics, I had the privilege of assisting our father in this project. Plus, I must have loved doing these things because he gave me attention and made me feel good. You might refer to my behavior as somewhat of a tomboy. I learned to prime the oil pump to help light the oil stove/heater and wore rubber waders to help put in and take out the dock before and after each season. I remember how cold the water was some months in May, as there were still deep ice blocks in the middle of the lake. During the summer months, our mother did not have to work at the store for a month for the first time since I could remember. Nevertheless, work was in their blood—Mother and I painted the outside of the cabin, and I helped Father tar the roof.

Next door to our cabin lived Norm and Vesper Shirley and their two children, Skippy (William) and Mary. Skippy was a year older than me, and Mary was Connie's age. It was perfect having them as neighbors.

Skip and I could take out their boat or ours and roam around the lake. He was my best buddy—the brother I never had.

Marly with William (Skip) Shirley

I truly loved him for his caring, sweet friendship, and wonderful laugh. One summer, we decided to raise money to buy a tent to sleep in outside. The project involved selling frogs to all who loved fishing in this lake.

Frogs change locations where they hang out each summer, and this summer, they decided to hang out on our shore. To contain them, Skip and I built little wooden boxes to keep them in with mesh screens so they could stay in the water. We put up signs around the lake that said we sold frogs for $0.25/dozen. We made $47.00. If you do the math, that is 2,256 frogs.

We were happy with our business venture because now we could buy a tent. We went to our parents and told them we needed a ride to Bottineau to buy the tent. They said, "No." What? We could not imagine why both of our parents said emphatically, "No."

Well, in hindsight, as I got older, Skip and I figured out that they thought we might want to play house, doctor, or something like that. I honestly was so innocent that that thought was the last thing on my mind.

I love to fish. Skippy and I would get in our fourteen-foot row-boat with its one-and-one-fourth horsepower Evinrude motor. We would use it for fishing from 5:00 a.m. to 7:00 a.m. and troll our lines behind the boat using frogs for live bait or lures. Our catch was always walleye pike and northern pike. Also, surprisingly, we could catch perch right off the end of our docks.

I quickly learned to clean and fillet the fish, making Mother happy because she did not have to touch them. I did not particularly appreciate eating fish—probably because I caught and cleaned them.

What did Skip and I do with our $47? I believe we put the money toward a yellow surfboard. This yellow board is not the kind of surfboard you see people use in the ocean to catch big waves. This surfboard was rectangular with a rounded top edge and a large hole for a long rope tied to the boat. When you stood on the board, there was a handle with two lines connecting the handle to the front edge. You would start by hanging on to this handle, leaning back while sitting in the water, and yelling, "Hit it!"

Then the motorboat's power and speed would pull us up to the top of the water behind the boat— Skip's and my initial " surfing " experience on the lake.

Next came water skis. We started waterskiing using a pair of long, rectangular fiberglass skis while being towed behind a boat. I laughed and said this was our version of "walking on water." Waterskiing was exhilarating, gliding across the lake's surface at about 18–25 mph. The motor's speed must pull people up and on top of the water. So, the heavier the skier, the more power the motor needed. Our fourteen-foot boat and Skip's family boat each had a 100 hp (horsepower) Evinrude motor.

Later, as we got better at skiing on two skis and learned to drop one ski, we were ready to step it up and bought a slalom ski specially designed for skiing on one ski. There were always two people in the boat, one driving and another watching the skier, looking out for other powerboats in our path, and calling out when the skier fell. I loved waterskiing. It is a great sport.

The lake covered approximately 1,544 acres and had a shoreline of nearly 28 miles. This site may not sound significant, but some of my friends lived at least forty- five minutes away by boat and about the same by car. So sometimes, if I were caught out on the lake in a sudden wind or rainstorm too far from home, I would have to stay at someone else's cabin until the storm blew over. Plus, those days were not the days of cellphones, so everyone would worry if you did not come home at a designated time.

One friend from Minot, Phyllis Thorson, lived on the other side of the lake. She went to Model High School, and I went to Minot High School. Next door to Phyllis and her family lived the Dahles, Thomas, Philip, and their parents. Phil was a great-looking guy, about five years older than I. He was tall with jet-black hair, piercing brown eyes, and a smile that could melt a girl's heart. When I turned sixteen, he and I became an "item."

Soon, I met other neighbors of Phyllis's: Les Turner (a gorgeous tall hunk Phyllis liked very much), Marlo Brackelsberg, another well- built tall young man from Mohall, North Dakota, and Leo Jostad, the last of the gorgeous guys with whom Phyllis and I would spend our summers while at the lake. My parents liked my involvement with the "guys" as we were learning great skiing techniques from them. They became a little reticent when I began dating Phil because he was older.

When we were at the lake, my date with Phil would consist of picking me up in his white convertible and driving the forty-five minutes it took to get around the lake to his parents' cabin or Phyllis's. Since the guys were mainly of drinking age, there was plenty of alcohol around, and I soon attempted to imbibe. I only tried drinking beer, but that was a disaster as, after some hefty tossing at my first and only beer-drinking evening with the gang, I tossed my cookies in Phil's brand- new white Ford Fairlane convertible. Not good. However, that did not deter Phil, as we dated mainly over the summer months for a few years. When not at the lake, he drove sixty miles from his hometown to visit Minot.

He had other things on his mind than light kissing and would get carried away trying to get into my knickers, but it never happened.

Little Goody Two-shoes probably drove him crazy, but he remained a gentleman. Soon, that relationship fizzled out as I was very busy with high school, piano, and dancing lessons.

The subsequent events at the lake happened quickly: Les, Marlo, and Leo were awe-inspiring water-skiers. Phil drove the ski boat for all of us when we skied. These three tall, muscled farmer boys proceeded to show us how to ski. Soon, we were all doing good to excellent slalom skiing, using trick skis, and having good fun. Then we began teaching kids in the neighborhood to ski. In 1958, we created the Club de Skinautiques or, informally, the Skinautiques.

This group added skiers like Terri Larson, an unbelievably talented barefoot skier, and others who performed death-defying tricks on their skis, including skiing through lit fire hoops.

The Skinautiques decided to put on a ski show on the north side of the lake. There was a long stretch of straight open water and plenty of room to pull many skiers at varying speeds. Holding us back was that the entire shoreline area of the lake was full of reeds. Before using it for skiing, we realized the entire shoreline water area needed dredging, as reeds caused much havoc with outboard motors. We soon learned that the Lake Metigoshe Improvement Association existed and consisted of many of our parents. At some point, they assisted us by clearing that shoreline out so we could put on our water show without damaging all the props on the motors of our ski boats.

The first ski show was in 1958, and we made several hundred dollars, which revved us up for the following summer's show. In the second show, we built a sixty-eight-person pyramid (I was on the second level); another act featured a line of six girls carrying flags, in which my sister Connie participated. The exciting acts included our barefoot skier, speed skiing, tricksters spinning 360 degrees, and a clown jumping through fire hoops.

The skiing pyramid was something we practiced on land. We used a long wooden pole, possibly twelve to fifteen feet, about two and a half inches round, for practice. Then the guys hooked the massive wooden pole to chains and wrapped the chains around the base of a huge tree. First, the four guys would be the sturdy, manly bottom of the pyramid.

Then the second level of three women would climb up and stand on the shoulders of the bottom row of four guys. Next, very light, small people, one guy and one small girl, would climb up two levels to form the third level. The success of these shows required much practice, and a few suffered injuries along the way. The club pyramid performance recently had fifteen skiers in this exciting act.

Another act I loved was being part of a set of three tandem or double skiers. Each pair of two skiers consisted of a man with a woman on his shoulders, and each pair had the ski ropes set at different lengths. All six persons (three men for the bottom and usually three lighter women for the shoulders) would be pulled out of the water simultaneously. Then the women skiers would drop their right ski, lift, and cross that leg for their partners to grab our foot. As soon as they each had a good hold on our foot, we would slip out of the left ski, and simultaneously, the men would hoist us upward while we swung our left leg around their necks. Once the three women were up on the shoulders of these powerful men, the men would slalom and dip us in and under the other ropes leaning at about a forty-five-degree angle as we crossed by each other in the teams of two.

I always prayed my neck would not get caught in the lines as we crossed under the lines of each other. This event was a great crowd-pleaser. In the last ski show I participated in, we made over $10,000. Then, the Skinautiques bought better skis, other new equipment, and a new motor that could easily pull up to ten people.

As the group had grown over the years, the club bought a beautiful ski boat with a powerful outboard motor. As a result, this group grew dramatically in size, ability, and reputation. In the last two summers, I was part of the group that taught about 250 children to ski, and today, they continue to do so. The Club de Skinautiques performs today at the lake and other venues.

Soon, I began college, rarely going up to the lake, the setting of some of my fondest growing-up memories.

In my later teenage years, there were many proclamations my father gave me of "do not" and "cannot." At a very early age, I learned that due to my father's aggressively suspicious nature, if I wanted to do certain things, I would tell a little white lie and convince my dates to do so. My high school dates were afraid to come into my house, as they had heard so much about my father and howawful he would be to me if I came home even a minute late. A few left me at the curb and would not walk me to the door.

Sadly, my relationship with my father was about to take a horrid turn, foreshadowing that he would renege on the deal we had previously made about my going to college.

BROKEN PROMISES (1960)

We must be willing to let go of the life we planned
so as to have the life that is waiting for us.
— *Joseph Campbell*

Remember, I could go to any college if I did not smoke, drink, or do bad things with boys. Well, this little virgin was ready to attend the college of my choice, USC, the University of Southern California. I had pre-enrolled and could hardly wait to get involved in their Gloriya Keufman school of dance. I had been accepted by many of the top ten universities in the US because-my grades were excellent. Besides, as USC is in Los Angeles, a comfort to my parents would be tha twe had five relatives in California upon whom I could rely on if needed. My father's mother, Grandmother Rosa, and his two sisters, Aunts Helen and Rosalie, lived in Los Angeles. My father's brother, Harry, also lived in California but in Northern California in Sacramento. My bags were packed. In a few weeks, I will leave and begin my new life. I could hardly sleep. I was so excited, anticipating this next step toward my dream— attending a university that would expand my dance abilities.

Then everything crashed. My father called me into the living room one summer evening and said, "Marly Kay, I know you have your heart set on going West, but I have decided you will not go to California. Dance is a career that will get you work that is no better than if you were a whore. Therefore, next week you will drive to the University of North Dakota, as your sister did, where I can watch you. If you want me to pay for it, you will get a degree in business, enabling you to take care of yourself. "

He might have shot me through my heart right then and there. I was devastated. I could not believe what I was hearing. If only I had saved enough money, I would have gotten on the train that day, said, "Screw you," and left for California. But I did not have enough money saved to pay for a train ride, much less to pay for college. If I had known he would do this, I would have applied for scholarships or worked until I could save enough money to go. Looking back, I wish I had just run away and never looked back.

I was always doing things to get approval from my father. If I was not getting perfect grades, I would excel with my piano and dance talents, yet it was never enough. I had fulfilled my promise to him. Once again, he had broken his promise to me. I felt crushed.

I was devastated.

Two weeks later, colleges were ready to begin their fall semesters at the end of August.

My California dreams dashed, I packed my beat-up little 1951 Ford and sadly drove to Grand Forks to attend the University of North Dakota.

UND is an excellent university for many fields of study, but not for dance. They did not even have a curriculum for people becoming better dancers.

I pulled up to Fulton Hall's dormitory, found my room, met my two roommates, unpacked, and settled into my new life. I did not want to be there. I did not even care if I failed.

A few days later, I did the rah-rah thing and went through sorority rush week. The school year begins with a week of recruiting new students to join a Greek- letter organization. A sorority is a Greek-letter organization for women, and men's organizations are called fraternities. I became a Gamma Phi Beta pledge.

Gamma Phi Beta sorority, Grand Forks, North Dakota
1960 (I am second row, third from the right)

The members of this Gamma Phi sorority were excited for me to join their "house." They viewed me as this talented, straight-A student from Minot. All sororities on campus compete for new students called pledges who would bring more prestige to their organizations and raise their members' overall grade point average. Little did they know that as much as I liked my new friends, I did not want to be at UND, home, or anywhere in North Dakota. UND is a terrific university. My new friends were fantastic, but my heart was set on being elsewhere—California.

At the end of the first term or semester, when it came time for the pledges to stand up in our Monday night meetings and read off our grades, my grades were the worst I have ever received. Even though I knew what I was doing when my grades slipped, I felt sad that I had let my sorority sisters down. They were shocked. They were pretty upset with me and assigned me a sorority sister who was a senior to monitor me. I was embarrassed. She had to go with me to study every night to get my grades back up. I had made a big mistake—trying to prove to my father that I did not want to be there by failing French, and my other grades were not so hot either. Finally, by completing my bachelor's degree, I had pulled my grade point average up to a B, but it was murderous. I thought I would have to sleep with my calculus teacher to get a decent grade—but I did not.

I longed to be in a supportive, loving, and monogamous romantic relationship. I did begin to meet and date a few different guys in various fraternities through my sorority and fraternity mixers. This part of being at UND was working for me. I was particularly interested in Larry Bergerud, the president of Sigma Chi.

He was a good-looking Norwegian from Minnesota, loved by his fraternity brothers. He was a good dancer, a talented musician, and an artist. We started dating on weekends. However, since he and his friends jammed in a small jazz quartet on weekends, I would show up toward the end of their "gig." Afterward, we would spend time together. I loved listening to them and watching while he artfully made his alto saxophone sing.
He was talented in many ways, both musically and as a painter and sculptor.

Gamma Phi Beta sorority, Grand Forks, North Dakota
1960 (I am second row, third from the right)

One night, Larry and I were at the downtown bar called the Riviera, having a drink, alcoholic or not, and having great conversations with our friends. The "Riv" was a restaurant/bar that had always been a fun hangout for UND college kids. In walked the Devil, my father. As he stormed into the bar, he was screaming my name. When he spotted me and got to our table, he grabbed my shoulder and lifted me out of my chair. Then he took hold of a chunk of my hair and dragged me out of the bar, yelling at me. As we left, he hollered at Larry, my date, " You, meet me at my hotel tomorrow morning!"

I was horrified! The devil himself was dragging me out of the bar in front of my friends. I wished I was a man or a boy, like David with a slingshot, as I would have taken this version of Goliath down or beaten him. My long-felt internal rage for him was now boiling. I felt pure hate. Father dropped me off at the sorority house and said, "I have someone watching you, so do not think you can get away with anything."

The following day, with great trepidation, Larry met my

father at the designated time. Larry told me after they began their meeting, he calmly said to my father, "I do not think that Merly's behavior deserved your being physical." That made my father furious.

He yelled at Larry, saying, "How dare you tell me what a father can and cannot do?

You were both under the drinking age, so I had asked my good friend in town to check on Marly to see if she was going out drinking!"
He asked Larry, "Just what are you trying to prove? "

Very respectfully, Larry responded, "After sorority and fraternity Monday-night meetings, many of my friends and Marly go to the Riviera to socialize. Not everyone drinks while there."

Father responded, "Well, she had better not be there."

After this horrific and humiliating episode in front of my friends, my internal rage and defiance caused me to be more determined than ever to continue doing whatever I felt like doing. Now, my father was right to be worried. I was one of those Goody Two-shoes in high school. I did not drink or sleep with the high school basketball star, but when let loose and away from home at college, I became one of those over-the-top drinkers because I could!

This last episode with my father only replenished my hidden, private reservoir of rage.

Looking back at those days, after an evening at the Riv and returning to my dorm, I vaguely remember that once I had to crawl along the hallway, not even realizing I was blind drunk, counting the doors until I got to mine. At least once, I crawled into the wrong room. At that time, I did not even consider that I was drinking too much.

I was having fun—like all my friends. I did not get sick. I did not wake up with a hangover. I did not miss any classes. So, what was the problem?

Despite my father's horrible first interaction with Larry, we dated for a year. We became pinned, like a pre-engagement ceremony. Larry was two years older than I, and when he graduated, he took his first job in California.

Several years before our wedding, after my sister Sharon had been home for Thanksgiving, she returned to UND. She then wrote a note to our parents telling them she was getting married in less than a month. That little note did not go over well. The following day, our parents drove the four hours to the university to stop this. They returned the next day, and we were planning a quick, colossal wedding.

It was a gorgeous Christmas wedding and reception. I was only fourteen, but I vividly recall sitting in the living room and sobbing when they drove off after their reception. Even though Sharon did nothing to protect me during our father's tirades, she understood how evil our father could be. She was always there to listen to me.

When our father was on a devil's rampage, Sharon removed herself by immediately going to her friends' homes, or she would lock herself in her room and turn on loud music. After her wedding and now having left on their honeymoon, I remember thinking that my sister, Sharon, age eighteen, would be free from the clutches of our father.

In the fall term of my junior year at UND, Larry graduated and left for a job in Merced, California. I only returned to UND because of my commitment to the sorority as their fall rush chairman. Then I said goodbye to my sorority friends when UND's fall semester finished. After enjoying the Christmas holiday with family at our home in Minot, I said goodbye to them and my Minot friends and got on a train to Sacramento.

I was a junior in college and transferred for the spring semester to California State University, Fresno, California. I would live in Merced with Larry—in sin, as our father would soon call it. Being with Larry was not what being in love was supposed to be.

Our lovemaking was not what I thought it should be. It was like a slam, bang, thank you, ma'am, and often hurt because foreplay was not in his repertoire. Both of us were clueless about tender lovemaking. We became engaged during our first Christmas holiday together in California. Mother was excited to help plan a summer wedding on my twenty-first birthday.

Larry and I drove back to Minnesota in June to see his family and later to Minot. My mother and I planned a huge church wedding for the end of July. It was an exciting time, believing we were in love and ready for marriage. Plus, getting caught up in planning a grand, beautiful wedding and ignoring all the warning signs was easy. Ahhhhh, so many women dream of "what it might become" rather than what it is.

Some girls dream of their perfect wedding day: what dress they will wear, the shoes, the food, the music, whom to invite, and where to go on a honeymoon. I was not one of those little girls. I never really dreamed of my perfect wedding. Nevertheless, we had a perfect wedding.

My parents went all out by providing us with a magnificent church wedding. We chose five attendants, including my sisters, Connie and Sharon, and girlfriends: Brenda Oland, Diane Rosedale, and Lana Elliott, who wore beautiful royal-blue dresses. My wedding gown and veil were simple yet gorgeous, and my talented girlfriend Lana's soprano voice echoed through the sanctuary.

Marly and Larry Bergerud's Wedding – July 1963

Father's hotel held our incredible reception for five hundred friends and family members. We all celebrated and danced to a twelve- piece band. Giddy in our honeymoon outfits, we returned to the party, said our goodbyes to our friends and family, and took off for Bismarck, a little town one hour away. Whoopee, this is our honeymoon. Our car barely limped into the motel parking lot as we heard our tire blow.

Larry ordered a pizza. We ate and talked about the beautiful wedding and the fun of seeing all our friends again, and he immediately fell asleep. That scenario pretty much describes what was going to be my emotional and physical life with Larry.

Two weeks after our wedding in Minot, Larry and I packed up our car and drove to Merced. There, Larry needed to use our only vehicle to get to work. Once I found a job, I needed a car to get to work and finish college. We needed that second car, but we did not have any money. Within a few days of arriving in Merced, I took a bus to Sacramento, where my uncle Harry, Dad's brother, owned a used-car lot. Harry was always a kind, gentle, and wonderful man, the opposite of his brother, our father. I used to confide in him about my issues with my father. Harry gave me a 1949 Plymouth that he had on the lot. Harry said, "When you no longer need the car, just bring it back!"

He was the best uncle ever! This car was quite a sight.

I was thrilled to be in California, even though we were in a town where we knew no one. Knowing that my sister Sharon, her husband Gary, and soon their little princess Wendy were living in Granada Hills, California, only four hours from us, gave me a sense that I was not on a lonely planet with just Larry. We were able to visit them occasionally. Also, we made a few trips to the Los Angeles area. We got better acquainted with my father's mother, Rosa, and his two sisters, Helen and Rosalie.

Although I was happy to be in California near my family, Larry and I should not have married. At that time, I believed that if we were intimate, marriage had to follow. Reflecting back, neither of us was ready emotionally or physically for marriage. What do young people know about it at such an age? We had taken the typical steps one did in those days. We became pinned (a fraternity/ sorority ritual where the man gave the woman "his fraternity pin" in a big ceremony). Soon after, we made love, and you had better get engaged and married.

Our marriage was a coexistence of two kind and fun people who truly cared about each other. Neither was mature enough to be in a relationship or a passionless marriage.

Larry came from a family of Norwegians, sincerely kind, sweet people. He grew up feeling cared for, but no demonstrative models of physical or emotional interactions existed. Indeed, neither my father nor mother was a role model for an emotionally and physically healthy marriage.

Was I emotionally available? At that time, I did not know what being emotionally available meant. Can this marriage be saved?

INFIDELITY AND LOVELESS MARRIAGE
(1963–1975)

Cheating is a choice, not a mistake.
*— **Kushandwizdom.tumblr***

When I completed the remaining year and a half at California State University, Fresno, to receive my bachelor's degree, Larry was ready to move to Southern California. He intended to get a Master of Fine Arts with an emphasis on sculpture through the Roski School of Art and Design at the University of Southern California. The thought of him at USC pained me deeply as I relived my dashed dreams of attending USC and having a career as a dancer. I could not help but wonder how different my life would have been had I gone there for my college degree.

As it turns out, he was enrolled correctly through USC's general admissions. However, he never received clearance from the School of Art and Design. His second college choice was the Master of Fine Arts program at Claremont Graduate University in Claremont, California. This decision was logistically appropriate as we resided in Upland, California. Larry taught high school during the day and attended college in Claremont in the evenings.

I deferred pursuing my master's degree until Larry completed his Master of Fine Arts.

Larry earned an annual teaching salary of only $6,500. That is the correct yearly salary. We needed additional income to live on. Besides, Larry needed about $500 per month to buy bronze for creating his incredible sculpture projects. His salary was barely enough to pay for our rent and to eat. As a result, before he started his MFA program, I applied for jobs in Los Angeles.

I was offered a job at S and W Law Firm and IBM in downtown Los Angeles. I chose the law office because they would allow me to start three weeks later. I wanted to go to North Dakota to see my family before I began any job, as I knew I would not get a vacation for a year. I often wondered how my life would have been different had I chosen IBM.

During my college years, I frequently considered pursuing a Juris Doctor (JD) degree to become an attorney. However, my immediate priority was to obtain my business degree. In retrospect, our choices remain unchanged, regardless of their outcomes or what one initially intended.

In the interview with the office manager before hiring me, she walked me to a desk nearby and asked, "Can you use this machine? No one else in the office can or will use it."

I looked at it and saw no mechanical keys that popped up like standard typewriter keys designed to lift and strike the paper. This machine was quite different. It had this peculiar ball with letters on it. I was clueless about how it worked, but I said, "Sure, I can use this." It was an original IBM Selectric typewriter. The other secretaries, all women thirty to fifty years older than me, looked at me with glee as the office manager placed me at this desk with the strange new typewriter. They had refused to use it and figured the "new girl" would get stuck with it. It worked well, but not when I needed to type interrogatories with eight carbon copies.

Soon, I met PJW, my new boss, Pete. He was a new hire as an associate at this firm and focused primarily on corporate law, which I found quite stimulating. He had just finished a year as a law clerk to Chief Justice Earl Warren. As I got to know him, I realized he was brilliant and exciting to talk with but a hard-driving taskmaster.

I loved working at the law firm, the people, the excitement, and the pressure. At that time, the firm had only sixteen male attorneys, and this location in downtown Los Angeles was their first office. Today they had over 3, 500 lawyers with offices in 14 countries.

PJW had never had his own secretary when he was a law clerk, as he did all his work for the Chief Justice. That meant he was clueless about how much work he could pass on to me or any secretary.

Immediately, PJW was pouring on the work. I typed very fast, and this Selectric typewriter worked fine except when using multiple carbon copies. Then, when striking any key on it, the little round ball did not have enough physical weight to imprint the eight carbons needed on interrogatories. However, I managed, but slowing down my typing helped. I soon learned with PJW that I could not make one mistake on any work page. He would hold the paper up to the window to see if I had erased anything.

I worked from eight to five, but most days, I had so much work piled up on my desk that I would stay until seven-thirty. They paid me in cash for working overtime. Plus, I would miss some of the downtown Los Angeles rush hour traffic driving the thirty-eight miles home in my 1964 red MGB. Often, I would stop and pick up dinner or take Larry out for dinner using my evening's overtime pay.

Larry and Marly's red 1964 MGB

PJW was handsome, sexy, and thirty-two, ten years older than me. After a short while on the job, PJW began making sexual advances talking about my looks and shoulder-length platinum-blonde hair. Of course, those were the days of miniskirts, along with three-inch spike heels. I certainly was not getting this attention at home.

When I accepted this position, it was in the second year of my marriage, which was not going particularly well. My boss and I often went to lunch together, especially if we had to do an interrogatory at a client's office. He would ask me questions about my background, where I grew up, and how I met my husband, ultimately leading to whether my marriage was happy.

As I became comfortable talking with him, I would tell him what was and was not happening at home. Reflecting on my marriage, I remember thinking that something must be wrong with me for it to be so bland. After a few months on the job with PJW offering me all the accolades of verbal attention missing in my marriage, my relationship with PJW proceeded from lunch to dinner, to multiple martinis, and soon, to a motel. This infidelity was between two people who unwittingly formed a deep, passionate connection before they realized they had crossed the line from a business relationship into romantic love.

My initial experience of having a physical relationship with PJW was magical, learning what real passion, sex, and love-making were supposed to be. While with him, that is how I thought I felt with a few martinis under my belt. In truth, emotionally, I felt horrible. He, of course, just wanted to get me into bed. I just craved and absorbed all the attention that came my way.

I knew I should not be with him, but after a few drinks, my capacity for any judgment did not exist and, in its place, was an "I did not care what I did" attitude.

On my forty to sixty-plus-minute drive home from Los Angeles after being with PJW, my emotions ran from ecstasy to pain. I wondered how I could have let that happen. It never occurred to me that I had a drinking problem. Or was I so starved for love and affection that I did not care? This roller coaster of an affair lasted for a year. Larry must have known something was wrong with all my late-night work. He knew he could not complain because nothing was happening at home. Mentally and emotionally, I felt damaged.

Finally, one day, I made up my mind. I told PJW I was quitting. He could not believe it. I told him I wanted to save my marriage or give it my best. I could not continue drinking and having sex with him. He was married and had three children. Even if I had deep feelings for PJW and wanted to be with him, I was not a homewrecker. Besides, there was no way he would ever leave his wife and kids and jeopardize his new position in the firm. He begged me not to go. Besides the sex, I truly enjoyed his intellect and stimulating conversations about law, life, and love. This decision to leave was difficult for me. It made my heart hurt. I gave him two weeks' notice and quit.

When Larry asked why I quit, I told him I had had it with the drive and late hours. Immediately, I got another job closer to where we lived. I did not want this new job because I wanted to return to school for my master's degree.
\
Within a year, Larry finished his MFA. I quit my new position of just one year and enrolled in USC's education master's program. I realized that if Larry and I were both in teaching positions, we could have the same holidays and time off. As much as I admired the teaching profession, a teaching career was far from what my heart desired.

At last, USC! Nearly every time I drove on the USC campus, I would think about how my life would be different if I had attended USC and studied dance. Also, I often asked myself these questions: When did I lose my intense desire to dance—the one thing I had always dreamed of pursuing for the rest of my life? Or did I? What kept me from following my dream when we lived near Los Angeles? Did I let our financial constraints and existence in the complacency of a typical American life, each of us working forty-plus hours a week and me driving seventy miles a day for work, keep me from following my dream?

Did I not have the guts to do what it took to pursue my dream? The summer after I quit working at the law firm, I began USC's master's program in education in the evenings after work. Being in Los Angeles nearly daily and close to the law firm was emotionally challenging.

My supervisor at USC immediately placed me in a student-teaching position at a high school nearby where Larry and I lived in Upland. Simultaneously, I interviewed for a high school teaching position at Brea-Olinda High School in Brea, California.

Even before I finished my student teaching, the superintendent hired me on the spot. At that time, I only needed a bachelor's degree to teach.

Two months after completing my student teaching, I started my new career teaching business classes at a high school. I was twenty- four years old. My students were six years younger than I. The senior boys did their best to challenge me with their flirtations but quickly learned they could not get away with much. Nevertheless, it took me a while to figure out who was throwing gross spitballs while facing the blackboard. One young man who did not deserve more than a D for his semester's work in our accounting class told me he would bring in his father to straighten me out. He did not want to lose his place on the basketball team because of low grades. They came in for the parent-teacher-student conference. Much to the young man's surprise, his father agreed with me, and the challenge ended. I did not win any popularity contests with his basketball team.

I must admit I did enjoy the students, my teacher friends, and participating in their school activities. I was on the Faculty Donkey Basketball team.

They needed a step stool to get me seated on top of this animal, which was much taller than I had imagined it would be. His back height was about 4 feet from the floor. With no saddle or stirrups, I clung to this feisty donkey with my knees and thighs, clutching the basketball. I immediately realized I might die if I fell and landed on my head while using both hands to toss the ball. I was scared. All of this for the love of my students.

Brea-Olinda Faculty Meet Police for Donkey Basketball Game

Completing my master's degree while working full-time was no easy feat. I would leave my teaching position in Brea at 3:00 p.m. on Tuesdays and Thursdays and drive thirty-three miles to Los Angeles to attend USC. I took one class each day scheduled from 5:30 to 7:00 p.m. (one Tuesday, one Thursday) and two other classes from 7:00 to 10:00 p.m. those same evenings. In the dark night, I ran from class to my car in some semi-empty parking lot on the outskirts of the USC campus in downtown Los Angeles. I would pray that I could get to my car without any problems. Only once did a car full of young guys try to block me from getting to my car, but I asked a young couple if they would walk with me the rest of the way, and they did.

My drive home from USC to Upland was from forty to sixty minutes. I had this hectic schedule for two semesters and two summers, including one online course.

Teaching at Cypress College, 1970

THE SHATTERED DREAM

Those who have walked the path filled with broken promises
and shattered dreams are the ones who arise with the strongest wings.
—Dane Thomas

Christen, Age Two

From the beginning, I loved Christen and cherished every moment spent with that beautiful baby boy. After six weeks of maternity leave, I hated leaving him, but I had to return to work.

Unfortunately, nothing changed between Larry and me. You always hear about people breaking up and then "buying a house, having a child, that will fix everything." That is what we did. Wrong. Things do not fix the problems. I think Larry thought that now Christen was in our lives, that would take all the pressure off him for my emotional and physical needs. I would beg Larry for any intimate or physical interaction with me. The more I cried, the more he withdrew. I felt like I was dying inside. As a woman, I felt this rejection must be my fault.

I went to a therapist near work in Los Angeles, and he said, "You are reaching into the cookie jar, and there are no cookies."

I did not want to be a spectator in my life any longer. We both seemed to need and want a different life than the one we had together.

Larry was a gentle, kind person, so what was my problem? I felt there was something wrong with me as a woman. I must be unattractive, not sexual! I was clueless. Internally, I felt empty in my marriage—alone. I deeply loved Christen and wanted so very much for my life with his father to be different, but that was asking him to be something he was not. I cried a lot and tried to explain to him how I felt. The more I said to him, it seemed to pressure him, and he would withdraw even more.

When we met in college, our young love and his being the first person I went to bed with made getting married seem all right.

What do most people know about love, marriage, and life at ages twenty-one and twenty-three? For many women and me, it is that elusive dream of what it may become. I needed joy in my life. I wanted to go out and have fun, entertain friends more than we did, travel, dance, learn to sail, and snow ski. I mastered waterskiing in the summers at the lake and imagined snow skiing would be just as thrilling.

I knew that divorce was a big deal, that it would dramatically change everything, especially with a small child. I felt alone and unhappy with the way things were in our marriage.

I did not feel like I could go on like this anymore. Being honest with my feelings was the biggest favor that I did for myself. I was honest with my feelings and finally accepted that Larry was emotionally and physically unavailable. I wanted to end our ten-year marriage. I knew there was nothing I could do to change my husband's behavior. I could only change myself. I was willing to be open and vulnerable to share how I felt with Larry and ask him for what I wanted or needed emotionally and physically. The more I asked, the further he withdrew.

Beyond the emotional and financial aspects of divorce, it is a legal process. I completed all the divorce paperwork. It was simple. The feelings surrounding divorce took their toll emotionally on all of us. Having a one-and-a-half-year-old baby caused me the most significant emotional pain.

For many years, I was concerned about the potential long-term effects this decision might have on our son's life. That pain and fear of its underlying mental and emotional impact on Christen, that he would feel an underlying fear of abandonment, stayed with him and me even today.

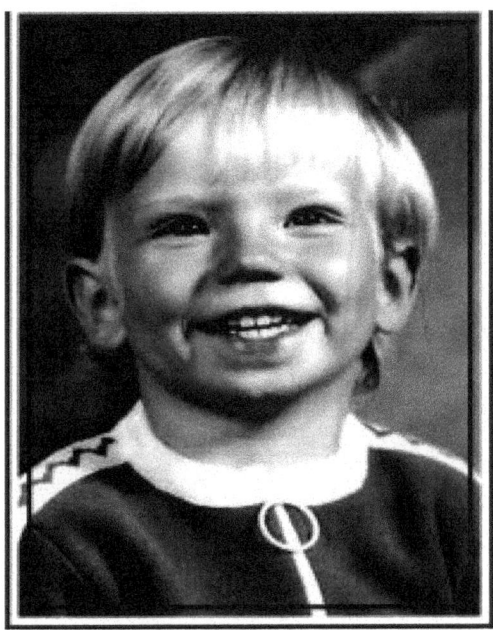

Christen – Age Two

In 1972, after nine years of trying to make things work with Larry, I packed up Christen, this adorable blond-haired, blue-eyed baby boy. We moved to an upstairs apartment near the college where I was teaching. Larry helped us move with little discussion. Honestly, I cried nearly daily for three years about our breakup. Larry was an every other weekend father most of the time.

Some mornings at 3:00 a.m., the stark realization hit hard on some nights when I had to do hospital runs with a sick baby or stay home from work because Christen was ill. I was now alone and the primary caretaker of this beautiful child. Quickly, reality struck, realizing what life had become—a divorced parent with an infant child.

ACHIEVEMENTS ALONG THE WAY
(1942–2021)

A woman with a voice is, by definition, a strong woman.
But the search to find that voice can be remarkably difficult.
—Melinda Gates, philanthropist

Honestly, I do not know where I derived my strength as a child, a woman, a mother, or a businesswoman. Despite childhood challenges, my strength, courage, and resilience took me beyond unbearable pain and propelled me forward to persevere. Being in the right place at the right time was a part of it. I thought for some time about the answer to this question. The reality is it was many things: emotional intelligence, my ability to multitask, passion, assertiveness, perseverance, the intensity of who I am, communication skills, faith, humility, risk-taking, compassion, gratitude, and, very high on this list, were opportunities.

What had caused opportunities to be available to other women and me in the twenty-first century? The plight of women in the U.S. during the nineteenth and twentieth centuries was fraught with immense issues that women fought through and suffered to pave the way for women today.

I worked as a legal secretary in downtown Los Angeles while my husband, Larry, finished his M.F.A. Then, I began a career in education teaching high school in Brea, California. Simultaneously, I attended USC, taking four classes a week after teaching all day. While working at the high school in Brea for over two semesters and three summers, I received my master's degree in education by attending USC. Then, I began teaching business classes at Cypress College, one of the one hundred sixteen California community colleges

.

Discrimination in hiring and salaries in the workforce has still been among women's significant battles since our country's beginning. In the 1960s, before working in the field of education, being a woman had impacted me in getting a home loan. The loan officer told me, "We can only use one-half of your income toward qualifying for a loan because you are a woman and would most likely get pregnant and not be able to work." Another instance, I lost a job at a private business college to a man applying for the same position for which I was a finalist. The agency said, "You are more than qualified, but they wanted a man, as he would garner more respect from our clients." Once I entered the teaching profession, salaries were pretty cut and dried. In most states, salaries are determined based on a person's higher education levels (bachelor, master's, and doctorate degrees) and years of teaching or education management.

Some educational institutions give salary credit for years of work outside the education industry if that work directly relates to the position.

In education, discrimination occurs in more discreet ways than salary placement. While working at one college, I overheard my immediate male supervisor talking about me to a male peer in very derogatory terms.

My female colleagues told me, "Watch out. He does not like strong women." At that time, I, like women still today, did not feel I could do anything about what I heard. Fear of being discriminated against occurs in education in other ways, such as being transferred to another location or given an unreasonable work schedule (part day, part evening, five days per week rather than three days per week in the morning). I was never concerned about losing my position, but some authority figures, including board members and faculty, sometimes made things difficult for me because I spoke the truth.

While teaching at a community college, I started co-authoring textbooks with my friend Jean Gonzalez, a teacher and friend of mine at Cypress College. The original textbook was called Word Processing: Concepts and Careers.

At that time, textbooks on office technologies did not cover the computer technologies that were beginning to affect businesses. For faculty, the process of implementing new courses into the curriculum often requires that textbooks be selected simultaneously when creating a new course.

We both searched to determine what texts the publishers had available. When I spoke to several publishers, they believed that word processing referred to a book concerning words. We laughed a lot about that. Jean and I decided we needed to create the book (see Word Processing: Concepts and Careers).

One publisher, John Wiley & Sons, believed in our plan for a book. They flew us to New York to sign a book contract. Our publisher would now be the prestigious John Wiley & Sons. Before agreeing to their contract, I negotiated a separate agreement with the publisher. It was for them to arrange speaking engagements for me with educators at colleges and universities across all major cities in North America. I felt this type of marketing was essential to assist the teachers in learning about new technologies.

Writing that book was a fantastic team effort between Jean and me, especially with our full-time teaching schedules and my son, Christen, now a six- year-old.

Once the books were in print, I traveled and spoke to educators every two weeks for almost six years. For most trips, I would leave Christen, my son, and my second husband, Donald, on a Friday night, speak to educators all day on Saturday, and fly home on Sunday.

My husband Donald's support made this possible. Christen and Donald occasionally joined me on speaking trips to places like Hawaii, Atlanta, Mexico City, and Washington, D.C.

Marriage to Donald Hucker 1981

Early one fall day, I heard from some colleagues that I should apply for a management position that had just opened at Saddleback College in Mission Viejo. Immediately, I sent in my application for the job. A few months later, I began this new career as the Dean of the business science division at Saddleback College in Mission Viejo, California. I was excited to start this role, which I held for seventeen years, enjoying my work with the faculty on laying out their new 88,000 sq. project. ft. facility. Over time, I enjoyed helping them launch Orange County's newest technology classes and computer systems.

Dean of Business Science, Saddleback College

At one point in my position as dean, I was responsible for working with and scheduling twenty-one full- time faculty and two hundred ninety-seven associate faculty or adjunct faculty who were available on the books of the Business Science division. Being dean had broad responsibilities, and aspects of it were complicated. As relevant to my new management responsibilities, one of my initial primary tasks was working with the construction contractors to complete, furnish, and equip a new 88,000 sq. ft. ft. ft. facility. About eight months later, the Business Division full-time faculty, staff, and I would move into this new building. I was eager to help the faculty plan a new computer lab with a capacity for 150 workstations. The IBM personal computer had just entered the marketplace. The Business Division's dead mainframe computer was no longer relevant.

Today, Saddleback College has just under twenty-six thousand students!

I enjoyed working with Saddleback College administration, faculty, and support staff. Our president, Constance Carroll, was a brilliant leader and instrumental in supporting me, my vision, and my achievements. Assisting the faculty was highly rewarding and fulfilling. I supported the college in enhancing its reputation as a technology leader by addressing the training needs of the business community. I thoroughly enjoyed being in this new position. It felt like I had come home.

My last position working in education was as a vice president of workforce and economic development for De Anza College, another California community college.

As I reflect on my life, I realize I have a personal desire for relentless improvement no matter what I do, from my life of dancing and playing the piano to unlocking the highest levels of performance from myself, my teams of faculty, and various organizations, making work a more exciting place to be for me and those around me. I remember going to conferences to learn from high-performance leaders and those at the cutting edge of technology and business.

I brought nine colleges and universities together to create a central facility for them to bring their students to learn about all the latest computer technologies. After retiring from my positions in education, I was asked to become a contractor for a virtual reality company to assist colleges and universities across North America in implementing a new technology: virtual reality. This technology marked the start of using rear-projected "caves" and virtual objects to transform learning methods. I never thought, "no" but rather, "how can we do it?"

Leading at the edge involved moving beyond my comfort zone and making calculated decisions to achieve significant outcomes. I consistently sought out the most compelling strategic opportunities.

After my tenure as Dean of Business at Saddleback College, I received an award from my faculty for fifteen years of visionary and innovative leadership. I enjoyed guiding them to incorporate the new technologies and to succeed.

THE GOOD OLE GIRLS AND THE BAND OF FOUR (1970–PRESENT)

Many people will walk in and out of your life, but only true friends will leave footprints in your heart.
— Eleanor Roosevelt

Over the next twenty years, I experienced various changes and events alongside my two-year-old son, Christen, while handling a full-time college teaching schedule and subsequently taking on the role of Dean of Business. My sisters, Sharon and Connie, along with several close friends, have consistently served as foundational influences in my life.

Marly, Sharon, and Connie.

Their families typically reside within a few hours' drive or a brief flight from my location, facilitating regular visits.

My close friends live primarily in various cities of Orange County, California, where I lived most of my adult life, as did Christen until he left for college. Maureen Smith, Don Busché, and Angela Satterlee are three exceptional friends comprising the Band of Four. Since the late 1970s, we have traveled much of the world together and experienced many of life's joys and tragedies. In 1983, all four of us worked together at Saddleback College when I was the dean of business. Angela and Maureen taught classes in the Business Division. Don served as dean before me. We have also co-authored numerous computer text-books and traveled internationally together. Angela, Don, and I chat regularly and still see each other as often as possible.

Maureen Smith, Don Busche, Angela Satterlee, and I.
The Band of Four

The other group of longtime close friends consisted of six re-markable women. We call ourselves the Good Ole Girls.

The Good Ole Girls (GOG's)

In 1976, each of the Good Ole Girls was teaching at one of six different community colleges, all located in Orange County. Initially, we met at meetings of a new organization called International Word Processing.

The organization started with approximately twenty-six founding members and expanded to more than two hundred fifty members over several years. It was composed chiefly of new high-tech computer industry salespeople, plus about twenty-two educators. The Good Ole Girls (GOGs) began gathering to assist with the organization's growth. The GOGs had great fun and much in common and decided to start meeting regularly. Our get-togethers began while working on mailings for the organization. Soon, we started meeting for each other's birthdays, second marriages, divorces, funerals, illnesses, and all that goes into friendships of over forty-nine years. Even today, when one person has an issue (a fall, sickness), the call goes out, "Good Ole Girl is down," and we all rally.

Christen was raised around these individuals from the 1970s and is aware of the role they played in my life then, as well as the part they continue to have today.

As dean of business at Saddleback College, I was honored to receive the Courageous Leader Award from California's 116 community colleges. It was for the vision and leadership I had provided by facilitating a collaborative environment that empowered faculty to embrace the vital changes necessary for implementing the new technologies of the time. Some close friends, including my sister, Connie, Saddleback's President, Constance Carroll, and the Good Ole Girls, flew to Sacramento to celebrate this special award ceremony.

When I resigned from Saddleback College and moved to Northern California for a new college management position, the Good Ole Girls still found ways to meet. However, it was always easier for me to travel than for all five of them.

This gaggle of women spent a few glorious days together in Albuquerque for the hot air balloon festival and then on to Santa Fe. Four of us took an Adriatic cruise.

All attended Ohio for a wedding of the daughter of one of them. We rallied with great joy for five marriages to second husbands within this group of six women. However, the Good Ole Girls and the Band of Four did not escape unbelievable heartbreak. The Good Ole Girls lost one young daughter to cancer, and a tragic car accident took one young man. Two daughters succumbed to cancer within the Band of Four.

I will be forever indebted to all the women and men who helped make my journey possible. I feel blessed to have had incredible opportunities available and grateful for the strength and courage to move on to them.

Marly and Don Busché

As life would have it, Don Busché, my colleague, co-author, and fun traveling buddy, and I began another co-author writing stint. Don is an author, a forever great friend, and an excellent educator and presenter.

We published textbooks on each of the new IBM operating systems. Continuously, we were doing book revisions because of ever-changing technology. We knew we had to begin writing the next release when we sent in the last edits to the book on one version of the latest operating system. An updated operating system was constantly in the works.

That writing period for us ended with our completion of twenty-five published textbooks. Some publications were only new editions of prior versions. However, each text went through the same grueling research and writing process. While working on writing about a new operating system version, the new software would often display "Under Construction."

When that statement appeared on our computer screen, it halted that piece of our writing. It meant IBM had not yet finished developing that part of the operating system, making our writing complex.

Simultaneously, I loved being on the speaking circuit at colleges and universities across North America. I felt as alive at the podium, talking with educators, as in front of any classroom. Working with people across the U.S., Canada, Mexico, and China was enjoyable.

Additionally, Don and I often presented together, and those presentations were often hilarious. We had great fun as our personalities played off each other during our presentations.

One of our days on the road went like this: We had ended an eight-hour day of presentations, had dinner, and then returned to the hotel conference room to prepare for the next day's sessions. It was after midnight, and we had finished preparing for the next day. We were ready to call it a day and realized the conference room doors were locked and chained shut. Don said, "The last thing I want is to be locked in a room with you all night." He does have a great sense of humor.

We were lucky that our next day's presentation was all about telecommunications. We could use our barely functional, old-fashioned, relic-type 1980s telecommunications device on our computer to call the hotel operator—no cell phones in those days. We called the hotel operator and asked her, "Would you please help us get out of our conference room? The doors are chained shut." She thought we were kidding, said, "Yeah, right!" and hung up. We called her back and quickly said, "Please do not hang up. We were so busy working that we did not realize chains had been wrapped around the door handles, locking all the conference room doors. We are locked in."

Then she asked us, "What conference room are you in?" "We do not know. "

Finally, at about 1:00 a.m., the hotel manager sent an employee around, shaking all the conference room doors until they finally found us.

Another unusual time was when Don and I discovered that Joy-cee, one of the Good Ole Girls, was conducting a presentation simultaneously at the same hotel in Washington, DC. After our separate seminars, we met and drank with the editors from our respective publishing companies.

The three of us had a few too many drinks, including after-dinner drinks. Mine was brandy, which I always laughed at and called "the nail in the coffin." After dinner, the three of us left our editors. We decided to visit the Washington Monument and go to the top to view the city. The guards at the monument would not let us in and indicated it was because we were inebriated. We giggled and then found it quite freeing to do cartwheels and somersaults down the lawn of the Washington Monument. Then, we danced down the empty streets of DC. Don was never one to drink too much, but that evening he undid his tie. I always felt great, happy, and successful spending time with Don. Plus, having multiple drinks may have helped loosen our otherwise hidden inhibitions.

I look back on these times with immense gratitude for the opportunities to travel and the speaking tours provided by the publishers of our co-authored two dozen-plus published books. As a result, this travel allowed us to visit most U.S. and Mexico states. On these speaking trips, our time was limited, so we did not tour much in these cities, but we enjoyed traveling and meeting new people from all over the country. Still, I looked forward to the day that I would travel to other continents.

Think where man's glory, most beginnings, and ends, and say mine was I had such friends.

(William Butler Yeats)

THE WORM INFECTS AND DESTROYS
TRUE LOVE (1973–1985)

*It's like a switch, clickin' off in my head. Turns the hot light off
and the cool one on, and all of a sudden there's peace.*
Tennessee Williams, Cat on a Hot Tin Roof.

As a mother, I tried relentlessly to create a childhood for Christen different from mine—without suffering the pain of alcoholism and physical abuse. However, Christen comes from a broken home. I have had issues with alcohol. My family has had a generational genetic predisposition to alcoholism. So, was his childhood genuinely different?

Christen was only one and a half years old when we left his father and moved into an apartment. It was not easy to find babysitters who would come to the apartment. Within a few days of moving and visiting more than a dozen daycare facilities, I found a daycare facility nearby. However, the trek each day to get him there was not easy.

Each day I was dressed for work in a suit and high heels, carrying Christen and the day's baby paraphernalia.

I feared falling down the apartment's steep stairs. By age two, Christen displayed typical two-year-old temper tantrums when frustrated.

Also, he became upset when his friends came to play and would leave all his toys out, which seemed to overwhelm him. He seemed to have high standards even then.

At this point, Christen was an adorable little boy with platinum- blond hair, bright-blue eyes, and a smile that melted everyone's heart. He was by then walking and running. Initially, Christen uttered baby garble a mile a minute. He soon spoke multiple-word sentences that made sense. I did not want him to be in just any daycare facility but in a caring learning environment.

Before he was born, I had devoured reading everything I could about brain development. From the research, I learned that his formative years, primarily ages three to four, could have the most critical impact on shaping language and cognition. After researching eighteen preschool environments, I felt a nearby Montessori school was an excellent, academically oriented, calming educational beginning. He began at age two and a half.

I drove him to his school on the way to the college where I worked. He was always the first child at Montessori in the morning at seven- thirty, and the last one picked up after my work. It was heartbreaking to see him standing at the fence, crying when I would leave him and drive away to work. He quickly adapted to school and soon looked forward to seeing his friends daily. Even Christen potty-trained himself by watching the others at school. He was not supposed to be at this school until he was three years old and potty-trained. However, I felt they took mercy on me because I was an educator, as were all the people at this Montessori.

In 1973, Christen was two and a half years old. I borrowed $2,000 from a teacher friend at the college. That, along with my remaining savings, allowed me to make a down payment on a $36,000, three-and-a-half-bedroom, 1,263 sq. ft. ft. condominium into which Christen and I soon moved. It was a terrific small home for us. I felt it was a safe place where he could ride his tricycle in our tiny backyard and have friends in the neighborhood, and it was close to my work.

I completed our divorce paperwork two years after moving out of my life with Larry. I walked into the courtroom with little three-and-a- half-year-old Christen in hand. The divorce was final in 1975.

I began teaching in the Business Division at Cypress College a couple of years before moving to the apartment with Christen. I enjoyed the classes I taught, the many new colleagues, and the students. Their friendship as faculty was precious during the tumultuous time of leaving Larry. One great guy, Donald Hucker, was among six faculty members with whom I became good friends. We all shared office space with partial five-foot partition walls, so nothing too personal got shared at work. Donald and I began going to lunch together.

He listened to my reasons for leaving Larry, especially making that choice with a small child. We learned a lot about each other, and after several months of lunch outings, we began dating. Going with him to live theater, sailboat racing on his thirty-foot sloop moored in Long Beach, romantic dinners out, dancing, movies, and snow skiing was exciting. We fell in love.

Donald's zest for life was beautiful. Spending time with him helped me climb out of the trauma of divorce and see a new beginning. He is a kind, gentle soul, very bright, an excellent writer, well-read, and has a good sense of humor. He has great guy friends and a caring family. Donald was twelve years older than me, a good-looking, tall guy with a great smile and an infectious laugh.

Donald moved in with us a few months after Christen and I moved into the new tiny condominium in Westminster.

Christen, Marly, and Donald

After being together for eight years, we finally decided to get married. I loved learning to sail with Don and his crew and took piloting and navigation lessons so I could race with them. Donald and I attended a ski and sail symposium in Vail, Colorado. While Donald enjoyed the sailing sessions sponsored by North Sails, I began learning to snow ski using the Graduated Length Method (GLM) approach.

The GLM method started me on skis not much longer than a

shoebox. Gradually, the instructor moved me into longer and longer skis. I did like skiing, but like most sports, one must do it more than a few times a year to be good at it. Donald and I enjoyed several skiing vacations with Christen, my sister Connie, and her husband, John. Donald is a beautiful skier. Larry, Christen's father, taught him to ski when he was five, and he became an excellent skier.

Weekends came and went. I hated packing up Christen and driving him to his father's every other weekend. Because I worked full-time, weekends were the best uninterrupted quality time I had with Christen when he was not at his father's home for the weekend. Nevertheless, emotionally, I was torn on those weekends when Christen was at home with Larry. Donald wanted me to crew in races with him and his other four crew members. A sailboat race was not a place for a small child.

To race his Santana 30, a monohull keelboat, Donald needed a five-person crew. Crewing in races during our many warm-weather weekends was incredibly exhilarating. Our longest offshore race was to sail from Long Beach to Avalon Harbor on Catalina Island. The crew continually wished for the westerly to come in during our "twenty-six miles across the sea." Alternatively, the race may have been from Long Beach around the end of the island to Two Harbors, a seaside village located at the isthmus on the island's backside. Donald and other sailors sometimes had harrowing stories of sailing in a race from Long Beach to the island and storming down the backside on an all-night return to Long Beach.

Life with Donald was continually active. We enjoyed sailboat racing, snow skiing in the winter, exciting outdoor theater at the Shakespeare Festival in Ashland, Oregon, in the summer, and other theater performances at various Orange and Los Angeles

County, California, venues. We loved the theater. I felt fully engaged in life; I enjoyed working as the dean, loved my energetic darling son, and had an active life with Donald. It was exciting. I rented a piano to renew and reconnect with my long-lost, well-honed skill.

Donald's Santana 30

Marly relaxing on the boat.

Donald was an outstanding male role model and influence during Christen's growing-up years, from age two to his late teens. Initially, Donald was afraid to get too close to Christen but soon began to love and enjoy him.

One day, Christen, then age three, came home and told us that he had worked on a trinomial cube at school. I did not know what that was but soon learned it was a box with three wooden cubes: red, blue, yellow, and eighteen square-based prisms. The building of the trinomial cube was considered a preparation for mathematics. He was in the right place at the right time for his preschool development. He devoured learning both then and always.

When Chris was only four, Donald coached him in the nuances of playing chess. Nightly, he used to read books with him. When the three of us were in Hawaii, Donald taught Christen the names of many beautiful flowers and how to identify birds by their sounds and colors. We eventually bought a lovely house together.

Life with Donald and Christen may sound terrific, and much of it was, but there was an issue that soon would become a problem. Donald was a sailor, and most of the crew would chug down beers on a sailboat race and a quantity of scotches at the yacht club afterward. His drinking did not seem like it impacted him in any way. When I could not crew with him, I would meet him at the club and join him by imbibing a new drink for me, scotch on the rocks. Previously, I had been a martini drinker and then moved to just wine. Now, our alcoholic drink repertoire includes, before dinner, a couple of scotch drinks and a couple of glasses or more of wine during dinner. Soon, it seemed to follow that after these evenings of drinking, we would have arguments that led to lots of anger and yelling—mostly me.

One morning after a great evening at the yacht club, we woke up in our new house and stepped into eight- plus inches of water, mud, and silt. Our home had flooded during the previous night from what was called the "one-hundred-year rain." The mile-long flood control channel behind our backyard block wall fence could not empty the planned drainage areas as debris and water had plugged them.

Consequently, the force of this mass of water in the channel, the size of a football field and six feet deep, broke through the weak spot in our next-door neighbor's cement block wall.

During the night, the water in the neighbor's house broke through the wall and into our yard. It moved into our backyard and down the side-walled patio at the back of the garage, which it could not penetrate. Then, at some point during the night, it backed out, leaving about twelve to fifteen inches of muddy floodwater in the backyards and the insides of eight homes, including ours.

The water and mud had come into our house underneath the two closed sliding glass doors when it could not get past the garage wall. While we were sleeping, the water quietly entered the house and rose to about fifteen inches. Then, quietly, it flowed back out when the channel behind the house emptied, leaving several inches of murky black water, mud, and silt about twelve inches up all the walls, fireplace, and new furniture, soaking the rug.

Within moments that morning of our getting up and stepping into this mess of water and mud, the neighbors, unaffected by the rain, helped us move all the newly purchased, mud-soaked furniture to the garage. Then nothing remained in the house but our clothes hanging in the closets and sopping wet, wrapped Christmas presents floating on the closet floors. Luckily, Christen was at his father's that weekend.

That night, after a painful day of feverishly trying to dry out the house, we got dressed up. We needed to attend Donald's much- anticipated sailboat racing trophy dinner in Long Beach. During the event, we drank wine and scotch. Donald won a trophy for being first in his class in our round-trip race from Long Beach to Catalina. He had a reputation for being a great skipper with a lean, fast crew and boat to watch in many of our races.

We began arguing after returning to the damp, musty-smelling, filthy house. We got into our usual rant that seemed to occur when we drank. This evening had the added feeling of being emotionally distraught because of what had happened to our new home. Most likely, I had stoked an internal fire with too many drinks at the trophy dinner. Our arguing might have begun with something like, "I felt bad that you spent so much time talking with some other woman!" Then, standing in murky silt on the soaked, smelly carpet with Christen's toys floating down the hallway, I cried uncontrollably. After shouting at each other, Donald grabbed some clothes and ran out of the house.

I remember throwing the wind-up alarm clock at him and screaming, "You had better take this with you or you will miss work!" Then, as he drove off, I ran barefoot down the street after his car, yelling at him, "Please do not do this! Please do not leave!" I was an emotional, pathetic mess who drank too much, but did I know that? Donald did the right thing by leaving, spending time on his boat, and returning in a few days.

A few years later, we moved from the little house in Westminster to another in Huntington Beach.

Christen, Age 6 and Marly

At this time, some notable traits of Christen as a young boy surfaced. They were perseverance, tenacity, and an attitude that he could do anything he wanted. Two examples were a school reading contest and a McDonald's contest. In the fourth grade, one of his classes had a four-week reading contest to raise money for the school library. Christen solicited all our family members and the neighbors to pledge a certain amount of money per book they wished he would read from a teacher's prepared reading list. His teacher would verify that he had read the books. Our parents and other relatives quickly pledged $1.00 per book, and the neighbors pledged more like $0.25 or $0.50 per book. He e read twenty-two the ooks rom ooks from the list. Afterward, his teacher tested him to validate that he had read them. The relatives and neighbors had to cough up the funds. I believe he raised close to $120 for the school.

The other contest he entered was sponsored by McDonald's. The prize was a shiny brand-new red Schwinn bicycle, awarded to the person who clocked in as having ridden the most miles using their existing bikes between the start time of 9:00 a.m. and 6:00 p.m. The route consisted of one repetitive mile loop from beginning to end. To prepare, Christen cleaned up his heavy all-terrain bike with its wide tires and his little red BMX bike in case he needed it.

The day of the race came. The whistle blew, and the race began. At first, I sat at the McDonald's starting point for the contest and waited until he had completed the first few laps. Then I had lunch and drove around the bike race path afterward, as Christen had not shown up at the McDonald's check-in point for a while. I rounded the last corner, and he was walking his bike with a flat tire. I told him to keep walking, and I would get his little BMX and bring it to him. I did that and took his big bike to get repaired. When the bike shop repaired the tire, I found

Christen, exchanged the bikes, and put the BMX back into the trunk. Sure enough, he was the last to finish the race at 6:00 p.m. He won the competition with the miles clocked and took home that shiny new red bike. I was so proud, wondering what that perseverance and tenacity would do for him later in life.

Then, there is a story of Christen's Garbage Business. He went through the neighborhood and invited the neighbors to partici-pate in his garbage haul-out/return business. He charged $0.25 for one garbage can, $0.50 for two, and $1.00 for three or more. Twenty-five neighbors signed up for this business. There was only one problem with this business model. What happened when he was away every other weekend at his father's? You guessed it. Donald said, "Do not look at me!" Picture this—the smiling mother hauling out the neighbors' garbage cans. The garbage haul-out business did not last too long.

During this period, while moving to Huntington Beach, I had changed jobs from teaching business courses at nearby Cypress College to becoming the dean of business at Saddleback Col-lege. Soon, the drive taking Christen to his school in Newport Beach and my drive to work in Mission Viejo was taxing on us. Yes, then another move—to Dana Point. Donald hated moving. This move was for me to be closer to my workplace at Sad-dleback College, and I wanted to get home earlier. Donald's teaching hours were more flexible than mine. Christen was now entering high school.

Christen and Marly – Dana Point

While teaching and then as the dean, I co-authored many textbooks during this period. Plus, I traveled to speak at education conferences for the publisher for about six years. Every few weeks, I would take a flight out on Friday after work, present to faculty all day Saturday, and return on Sunday. I will always be grateful to Donald for being with us and caring for Christen as he did. It made me feel comfortable doing all the traveling needed for the publisher's speaking engagements. Unfortunately, in 1985, shortly after moving to Dana Point into this beautiful and unique home for the three of us, Donald ran out the door during an alcoholic screaming fit of mine. He never returned.

Why did Donald leave? Our twelve years together were mainly terrific. I shoved him away when I needed a man to show love and affection.

The devil, alcoholism, had returned to do harm again. Christen and Donald have remained in touch by phone and through occasional visits and are still very close to this day. Donald remarried, and we continue to be good friends and stay in touch.

After Donald left and during the next five years, my alcohol consumption escalated. When I drank, I was clueless about the amount of alcohol I had consumed. After that second drink, friends said it was "Katy, bar the door." I never drank during the day, but I drank at night with Donald or out on Saturday with friends.

Had the devil's curse taken hold? Am I now a high-performing, forceful, and successful person during the day, yet on nights out with friends when I drank, a raging drunk like my father?

SINGLE AGAIN, RAISING A HIGH SCHOOL–AGED YOUNG MAN (1985)

Having not grown up in Dana Point, Christen and a few others new to the area became a "gang of several" as the new guys on the block. Quickly, he assimilated and was getting excellent grades. While attending a parents' night, I remember talking with his literature/ writing instructor, who commented on Christen's superb writing ability. I asked the teacher if he could suggest anything outside the classroom to push that writing ability. He indicated he would think about it. A few weeks later, Christen returned and said that his writing instructor had recommended him as a local San Clemente News sports reporter. That was terrific.

Christen attended Friday night high school football games in his new job and then went to the newspaper office to write about them. He might call home to say he would be there very late. The articles had to be accepted and ready for the next day's paper. Sometimes Christen would be there until 1:00 a.m.

The newspaper owner trusted and thought so highly of Christen that he was given keys to the office to lock up when he finished late. While in high school, the Los Angeles Times brought him in to do local sports writing, articles about exchange students, and another one of his works with Amnesty International. Most notably, I saw his leadership skills surface when he became editor of his high school newspaper. His team renamed it, The Paper.

As I was returning home from work one evening at about seven, I gasped when I saw cars had filled our driveway and both sides of our street. The front door to our house was wide open. Would Christen have a large party and not have said anything to me about this? Christen's friends were sitting on our second story outside on the balcony. I could not imagine what was happening. As I entered the house, I quickly realized that our home's three levels were overflowing with his high school friends. Were they partying? No. These young people were sprawled out all over the floors, writing something. Immediately, I learned that they were here writing letters on behalf of an organization Christen had begun as an offshoot of Amnesty International.

He had tried to hold these Amnesty International meetings on campus; however, he was not allowed to have these meetings on the high school grounds. The administrators indicated this was an international organization, and its meetings could only occur off campus. He and his friends appeared before the high school's board of trustees. They asked the trustees to consider changing this ruling by the school. The Los Angeles Times covered that board meeting, but the school's board policy prevailed.

Christen and his friends continued to meet at our home on behalf of Amnesty International. When they met, each person wrote letters to various countries taking issue with grave violations of human rights, freedom of expression, and freedom from discrimination. Amnesty's mission had expanded to include supporting reproductive freedom, holding corporations responsible for human rights violations, and preserving human rights in national security policies. I was incredibly proud of Christen and these fine young adults.

Letting Go

During one summer of Christen's high school years, he applied for a six-week summer program in France to travel abroad and improve his language skills. He had studied French for many years and had hoped he could live with a family in France to work on his language proficiency. As that student placement did not work out for him, he accepted the program in Switzerland. He flew to Zurich and Basel, where he lived with a kind, loving family for several weeks. They spoke French, German, and English. He loved his Swiss family, Peter, Anita, Grandma, and their two teenage children. Peter was an architect, and Anita was a very caring mother. Their children, a son and a daughter, became fast friends with Christen. I fondly referred to Anita as his "Swiss mama." He had a terrific time with his "Swiss family." He traveled across Europe with them during their vacations.

This six-week trip was as much for me as it was for my son, Christen. I needed to get ready for the "empty nest" and learn to let go. My only child would be leaving soon for college and life without me. Naturally, young people at that age are eager to gain independence.

Christen Graduates High School 1989

MY TRAVELS HAVE SHAPED WHO I AM:
CHINA (1989)

To move, to breathe, to fly, to float,
To gain all while you give,
To roam the roads of lands remote,
To travel is to live.
—Hans Christian Andersen, The Fairytale of My Life:
An Autobiography

President Constance Carroll, Ken Yang, Marly, and other faculty.

During Christen's time in Europe in 1989, Don, my colleague, coauthor, and great friend, and I had an excellent opportunity to travel to China. It would be my first trip out of North America. Don and I have often traveled together. Constance Carroll, President of Saddleback College, supported the time Don and I, both deans at the college, needed to be away from college responsibilities to go on this important trip.

I am still drinking a lot. Why? I guess for fun or habit because it was the thing to do with friends, colleagues, and family. We were all drinkers. It did not seem to enter my mind in those days that alcohol, drinking, and drunkenness were a vein of sickness and disease in my family. I am not my father or his father or my mother, for that matter.

I was a successful woman invited to China as a recognized professor, a strong leader, a published author, and a speaker on new technologies. I stood before both men and women and told them how to succeed, sent by an American university to bring light to darkness.

Ken (Yang Guang-Hau), our good friend and exchange teacher at Saddleback College, requested President Constance Carroll's permission to allow Don and me to travel to Kunming, China. The purpose was to set up a sister-college agreement at his college, the Yunnan Institute of Finance and Trade. In addition, he asked us to provide several presentations to their three-hundred-plus non- English-speaking instructors on "the new technologies." Ken would be our native Chinese host and interpreter during our trip to China. His English was impeccable because he learned it from Americans building a road in the neighboring province of Burma, now known as Myanmar.

Dinner at Marly, Christen, and Donald's Home in Dana Point (Christen, Marly, Julia Yang, Donald Hucker, Ken Yang, and Don Busché).

In June 1989, Don and I left on our adventure to China. We flew to Hong Kong and transferred to a tiny China Airlines plane. This second flight we will never forget. One passenger brought tires on board with him that occupied the seat next to mine. Another brought a crate of chickens aboard. A giant hog in a flimsy wooden crate smelled bad, bellowed loudly, and grunted the entire cross-country trip. I was afraid it might break loose and devour one of its chosen. There were hordes of fleas in the carpet surrounding my feet, and they found their meal, my ankles, causing me significant discomfort. Finally, we arrived in Kunming and landed. As our plane landed and taxied to the gate, about a dozen Chinese armored tanks surrounded the plane at the gate. Getting through customs was unlike anything I had ever seen. Chinese soldiers surrounded us, took our passports, and handed them to a soldier perched on a platform about eight feet above us.

We did not get them returned to us until we left the country. The government always knew precisely where we were while inside China.

Finally, after spending an hour getting through Kunming customs, our friends Ken and Julia were waiting for us with a driver to take us to the Institute of Finance and Trade.

Yan and Julia Yang met us at the Kunming Airport.

Welcoming dinner for Don Busché and Marly,
Ken Yang and the president and faculty of the Yunnan
Institute of Finance and Trade

We stayed in a large multistory, whitewashed building, and our rooms were on the fifth floor. I struggled to haul my heavy bags up the five flights—a lesson learned. This dormitory was not a first-class hotel with a doorman and bellhops. They locked us in at night.

While staying at the Institute, Don and I heard about student protests in Beijing. Privately, I asked Ken to tell us about them. We knew they were in Tiananmen Square, where we would travel next. We were anxious about how the student protests might affect us and our ability to attend the Beijing China Pacific Economic Development Conference the following week.

For good reasons, Ken was fearful and preferred not to talk about it. He did not want his family to be involved in these conversations. If the family did not know what was happening in Beijing, they would have nothing to tell if the government interrogated them. Ken and his family had been severely impacted during the Cultural Revolution thirty-plus years before. He did not want to take any chances of speaking out in a way that could affect his family again.

Ken privately told Don and me the following story about how the Cultural Revolution affected him and his family. It began in August 1966 and was known as the Great Proletarian Cultural Revolution. Mao Zedong ordered a massive assault on the institutions built by eighteen years of Communist rule—and the educated population and social remnants of the past. He shut down the nation's schools, calling for a massive mobilization to take current party leaders to task for embracing bourgeois values and a lack of revolutionary spirit. The government caused over one and a half million deaths during he Cultural Revolution, and millions of others suffered imprisonment, seizure of property, torture, or general humiliation.

Ken, or Guanghua Yang, told us that he and other professors had been taken from their homes by soldiers of the Chinese military. They were driven far out of Kunming to a very remote and barren part of the countryside. Finally, their truck stopped. The drivers, bearing rifles, tossed their human cargo out onto the dirt. Ken had only the clothes on his back and a book in his jacket. The soldiers left the professors to die. A potato and a couple of carrots had been smuggled in unnoticed by one of the prisoners. A potato has several "eyes." Those are the spots where a potato's roots have yet to form. Almost immediately, these intellectual prisoners secretly planted potatoes and carrots. Within weeks to a couple of months, the professor cultivated vegetables. They lived on wild berries, grass, and water from a nearby brook. Ken was on this makeshift farm for three years.

Meanwhile, Ken's wife, Julia, was a doctor still living in Kunming with their two children. As a doctor's livelihood was essential, the government put her to work seven days a week. Finally, Ken was allowed to return to Kunming three years after being taken and held prisoner during this tragic time. He believed his return was only to give his wife more hours to work by taking care of their two children. Others were held captive for ten years.

The long-term effects of the Cultural Revolution would impact China's intellectual growth and progress for decades to come. It ended in 1976. Deng Xiaoping came to power in the late 1970s and remained as such until he died in 1997. He had abandoned many orthodox communist doctrines and attempted to incorporate elements of the free-enterprise system into the Chinese economy.

The actions of the People's Liberation Army (PLA) in Tiananmen made news across the world. The PLA is the principal military force of the People's Republic of China and the armed wing of the Chinese Communist Party (CDP).

I knew Christen would be worried about me. One evening, we were allowed to place a call to my home in California while at the residence hall in Kunming. We came down from our rooms on the fifth floor to make the call. Soldiers surrounded us with their rifles in hand to ensure we did not say anything they felt was against their government. They requested our friend Ken to interpret what we were saying.

Don and I visited Ken Yang's family in Kunming.

In 1989, we flew to Beijing after Don and I visited our friend Ken and his family in Kunming. After this visit, we were off to Beijing, where Don and I had each personally paid $4,000 to attend the first economic development conference between the U.S. and China. Don and I felt it would be a unique opportunity to see the formation of new relationships between China and the U.S., with many informed U.S. diplomats in attendance, such as James Lilley, U.S. ambassador to China under President George H. W. Bush.

All conference attendees were kept together on buses when visiting many of the famous ancient sites in Beijing. No one could go out independently to see any part of the city or surrounding villages.

At that time in history, 1989, Beijing was still a magnificent display of ancient China. It was a spectacle to see millions of people riding bicycles and oxen-driven carts carrying goods from one place to another.

The main mode of transportation in Beijing, China, in 1989

There was little evidence of modernization. There were very few cars or modern buildings. Beijing was still ancient China. Bathrooms in some hotels still only had holes in the cement within open stalls for one to use. I never got used to people watching while I used their bathrooms. However, I realized the citizens were curious and not used to seeing Caucasians.

On June 4, 1989, we joined other conference attendees on a bus ride to tour Beijing. Our bus driver drove slowly along the edge of the vast Tiananmen Square.

Soon, the protesters surrounded our bus. The size of the crowds of people (young and old) in the square was enormous.

Marly's photo of Tiananmen Square taken during our group bus trip.

The people of China completely covered the wide-open square, which occupies 109 acres. All of us on our bus were feeling intense emotions being among the thousands of young and old Chinese people who were now surrounding our bus. Carefully, our driver ushered us away from the square. The vast sea of assembled Chinese people appeared to be very peaceful. They had gathered seemingly without a good plan. I felt this massive gathering of hundreds of thousands in the square would not end well. The storm must come. The government response will come. There was no choice for their government, no way to avoid it.

Before pulling away from across the square, a sight, barely discernible but a tall white creation, brought tears to my eyes. In the distance, this white figure was the students' creation of a replica of our Statute of Liberty, called their Goddess of Democracy. Whether these are their exact demands or not, our guide told us that the students' needs were (1) to live where they wanted to live, (2) to go to a school of their choice, (3) to marry a person of their choosing, and (4) to allow China to have more significant economic expansion with the rest of the world. The government never agreed with these statements.

Soon, the Times Magazine published a picture of a man in China in front of a tank. He was a little man; everyone knows it. He was small in comparison to the tank. All these years later, the picture is iconic, and no one can forget it. Everyone has seen the photo of the small man. I mean, everyone knows him from the picture. You know the image of him, a little man, no, the little man in front of the tank. I read that he lived. I believe he and I are in some way the same. Of course, not in bravery, but he was a courageous man, and as far as I know, he was saved by his friends, as the story goes. However, I feel a little like I know him and what he might have thought in the face of the tank that day. He knew he was helpless in front of the enormous army tank. He could only give his life to death. He held no real physical power, of course. Why did he stand there? I do not know, or maybe I do. I am not sure. Perhaps we both saw the same thing: no way out or forward, just stuck. People around him, maybe friends or family, were being killed. What could he do? What could I do? For a moment, the little man in front of the tank and I both looked into the face of darkness and the uncertainties of life.

When I was twelve, our father was strangling our mother. Not to death, although that is not the most critical issue. Our burned and drunken father was a serial abuser, and I looked at him and stood before him, a twelve-year-old girl—a little girl in my "jammies"— against his attack on my mother. I was unable to take any action against him. Like the little man in front of the tank, there was no question— who would win the fight?

So, littleness and the outcome of the battles are not the issues. My two sisters did not join me; I stood alone, helpless to fight Father, my father alone. At least, that is the way I remember it. A night for a strong, resilient young girl, I remembered with terror and evil. Where were my sisters that night? One was older and, at night, closed and locked her door. The other was much younger than me. I failed because, of course, the abuse continued. And I lived with our father and mother.

As the soldiers began coming out of the tank after the small man standing in front of the tank, he was rushed away by friends, so he lost. The tanks and the soldiers won, or did they?

In some ways, I feel that I lost to my father. I succumbed to him in that I did not run away. I served him by being obedient. Even though there was more abuse over the next ten years, I bowed to him and was respectful and kind. I loved the father he became on occasion and hated the evil devil that came out in the night. I was a good girl, always seeking his approval and wanting to be like him. I regret not leaving home and following my heart's desire to dance. If I had realized that he would deny me the promise he made, I would have worked hard to save money so I could have more easily left home.

Like most little girls, I desperately sought my father's love and approval, even though I knew him and his horrible ways. Though I knew his weakness, I still yearned for his love and support, as does every child for their parents. Yes, the little man and I were brother and sister in some ways. On this visit to China, I saw the strength and rebellion in the small man in front of the tank. Where he stood in bravery, I felt not courage but shame. I bowed to my father. I served him for ten more years and then left home.

The Chinese government said this is what occurred on June 4, 1989: Following the death of pro-reform Communist leader Hu Yaobang in April 1989, thousands of Chinese students, public servants, and intellectuals gathered in Beijing's Tiananmen Square and in over four hundred cities in China to march in his memory. Within days, a gathering of up to a million people had transformed into a mass demonstration against government corruption with calls for democratic reform.

As our bus drove by the tens of thousands of protestors, I felt the yearning of these young people. Growing up with an autocratic, tyrannical father, I felt brotherhood for their hunger for honor and simple freedoms. As I watched them in the square, my heart was pounding.

This account did not jive with most of the comments in the reports from the Chinese government. After June 4, I read about and talked with some of the people in China. I believe this is the truth of what happened in Tiananmen Square. On June 2, 1989, nine of China's top leaders of the Politburo Standing Committee met to decide what to do about the weeks-long protests. This meeting was two days before the military crushed Tiananmen Square's young people, the purge that would change Chinese history. Deng declared that the people in the square were manipulated by outside influences, specifically the U.S., to replace socialism with capitalism. He knew he had to clamp down on the protests—violently, if necessary. Of course, thousands of other students who participated in the protests did have grievances against the government. That meeting of the nine men, particularly the words of leader Deng Xiaoping, helped set China on the course of that week and the thirty-two years that followed.

Deng argued that only by using the force of violence to clear Tiananmen Square would end the unrest. He felt that ending the uprising would only work if the committee agreed to allow the economic reform the students were asking for to prevent it from happening again. He knew that force was the only way he could get an agreement for economic liberalization for China. The loud voices within the Communist Party did not want economic liberalization, blaming it for the unrest. Instead, they wanted a return to state-dominated socialism.

Deng closed the meeting by asking President Yang Shankun to order the military to declare martial law that night and "finish it within two days." Within forty- eight hours, the storm clouds grew and closed in on the square early on June 4. The military included ten thousand soldiers and fifty People's Liberation Army (PLA) tanks. The tanks were to take control of Beijing and clear Tiananmen Square on June 4. The sound of the tanks rumbled into the streets. Some heard them coming during the night.

The force of the PLA in Tiananmen and what followed shaped China's politically authoritarian stance. Plus, the one student demand the PLA agreed to was their wish for economic liberalization (outreach to other countries, a more open-door policy). This one concession the government gave the students was the beginning of what made China the economic giant we know today.

The Chinese students' demands were things I have always been able to take for granted living in the United States. The United States still has some severe issues yet to be resolved and new protests. Nevertheless, I am even more grateful for living in a country with democracy and great freedoms. Recent uprisings of societal factions within the United States have shown our country that democracy can be fragile.

During the week of the Chinese student demonstrations in 1989, Don and I spent hours trying to change our flight to leave earlier than June 6 because Beijing's tension was palpable. Finally, we got confirmation to be at the airport by 6:00 a.m. on

June 5. We arrived at the airport and did not know what had happened in the square the night before. A friend on tour with us was staying in the China Great Hall Hotel next to Tiananmen Square. We met her again at the airport. She reported that she and others barely missed gunshots fired into their hotel lobby. She told me she paid a soldier to transport her out of the hotel to safety.

Before entering the airport, a well-dressed, blonde Caucasian woman approached us and said she was an American from CNN. She asked us if we were going to Hong Kong, which we were. Then she asked, "Would you carry this videotape to a CNN person on the other end? I must get it to her."

I had many other videotapes in my luggage from the Yunnan Institute. I thought one more would not be a problem. I told her, "I will. "How will I know who this CNN person is?"

She replied, "You will."

Don said quietly, under his breath, "You are going to get us killed or hauled off to jail yet!"

As we checked in for our flight, our passports (which the government had held during our entire visit) were returned. I felt like I could breathe again. After a short flight, we landed in Hong Kong, retrieved our bags, and placed them on a luggage cart to move them to our next flight home. The departure from the baggage claim inside the airport funneled to a narrow point where people were waiting to greet and pick up passengers. As we came down this inverted V-shaped ramp with our luggage, I noticed only one Caucasian among the mostly Asian crowd waiting for passengers. She looked at me and nodded. I nodded in return. Don and I moved our baggage carts through the terminal. We exited the terminal and were now outside the airport. We moved our loaded luggage cart out and over to an open sidewalk area where we would soon get a taxi. Then I dragged one of my suitcases off the luggage cart and opened it. I began pulling out several videotapes, placing them on the pavement as if repacking my bag. I placed the one tape I was transporting for CNN onto a cement post next to me. Within a couple of minutes, the blonde, Caucasian woman walked by us, took the videotape, smiled, thanked me, and walked away.

Today, I would never take anything from a stranger and transport it on an airplane. I shudder to think what might have happened if someone had searched my luggage at the Beijing Airport while carrying this serious CNN tape. At that time, there were only FAX machines—no internet and very few cell phones. What was on that tape? CNN's reporting to the world of actual footage of what occurred the previous night in Beijing's Tiananmen Square, which Don and I were now viewing from our hotel in Hong Kong.

In Hong Kong, we could only sleep for a few hours. We had spent most of the early morning hours (3:00a. m., 4:30 a.m., and finally, 6:00 a.m.) attempting to take a limo to the Hong Kong airport three times. Three times we got dressed and, with our luggage, left our room and waited outside on a transport bus. Each time, shortly after boarding the bus, the hotel manager would enter the bus to tell us our flight was once more delayed.

In 2007, on a return trip to China for a Three Gorges Dam tour, we attempted to discuss historical events with officials or educators. We mostly received blank stares and no comments. The bedrock of the Communist Party's approach to the demonstrations and massacre is to remove it from history.

Accurate accounts of this incident cannot appear in published books, school textbooks, media, or the internet. While in China in 2007, every time I spoke with someone about 1989, I received no acknowledgment that any historical events occurred. Eighteen years after this horrific event in Tiananmen, it had been whitewashed. Enforcement of memory is an age-old policy of the Communist Party's rule. Facts of their history are off-limits: the Cultural Revolution, the Great Famine, the Great Leap Forward, and the anti-rightist campaign, the genocides of landlords and Tibetans—you name it, all are off-limits.

One exception was our guide. When I spoke with the guide about the 1989 event, he answered most of my questions in near-silent words with either a yes or no. However, as we left the tour, he pulled me aside and whispered, "Most Chinese citizens have no idea what happened on that dreadful day, eighteen years ago. If they do, they know better than to talk about it."

A PHENOMENAL MONUMENT —XIAN CHINA (1989)

Travel makes one modest. You see what a tiny place you occupy in the world.
—Gustave Flauber

After leaving Beijing, one of our stops was Xian, where we had the experience of a lifetime viewing the massive partially uncovered graveyard of thousands of terracotta warriors discovered in 1974. It depicts the armies of Qin Shi Huang, the first emperor of China in 246 BC, who ordered this mausoleum to protect him in his afterlife. It took seven hundred twenty thousand builders thirty years to build the Terracotta Warriors. Each warrior's face is sculpted to be different from the next one. In September 1987, French President Jacques Chirac praised the Terracotta Army as the Eighth Wonder of the World. I felt honored to witness such an amazing creation and historical site.

Terracotta Army Soldiers and Horse Tomb-figurines

Our last city before leaving for home was Lhasa, Tibet. Even today, the People's Republic of China (PRC) still claims Tibet is an integral part of China. The Tibetan government in exile maintains that Tibet is an independent state under unlawful occupation. Lhasa is famous for the Himalayan Mountains and its Potala Palace. The palace is a dzong fortress and was the winter home of the Dalai Lama and one hundred thousand others, who are still refugees and have lived in exile since 1959. Our visit to Lhasa was breathtaking, seeing its people and the beauty of its surroundings.

Potala Palace, the 7th Century of the Dali Lama

A few years after we visited Tibet, I attended the Tibetan cultural studies endowment announcement at the University of California, Santa Barbara. At this event, I felt fortunate to have had the privilege of talking with and being blessed by the Dalai Lama. After the Dalai Lama shook my hand, he placed a long white scarf around my neck that he blessed and squeezed my earlobes with both hands as he talked with me.

THE ITALIAN: A GENTLEMAN AND A SCHOLAR

George Peele's
Merrie Conceited Jests of 1607

One evening, at a professional meeting, I was about to step up to the podium to speak. Addilyn, one of my closest friends, grabbed my hand. Quietly, she leaned in close to me and said, "You are such a pretty, sophisticated, smart woman, dressed to the nines, but with a scotch in one hand and that cigarette hanging out of your mouth, you look hard." Only a very close friend would tell me the truth.

I was addicted to smoking and hated that I was, and I figured if I did not buy cigarettes, that would be a good start. Initially, I smoked a pack to half a pack of cigarettes daily. Then I stopped buying them and bummed off everyone else, which did not earn me any points. I quit smoking a few months later, and this plan worked for me. I had been smoking for the past ten years and decided I wanted to quit. Some of my more sophisticated friends used to tell me how unladylike and hard I looked when smoking.

These were the days when I was out on the speaking circuit for the textbooks, still working endless hours like a crazy person at the college, raising a young son, and writing books halfway through the night. One night at home, I was looking for a cigarette and could not find one. I was sure I had some at home somewhere. I tore the house apart and scoured every purse in the closet and the pockets of my jackets and coats. Finally, in desperation, I went to the curb and looked for partially finished butts.

Was this a problem or what? Then, of course, I got into my car, went downtown to the local liquor store, and bought a couple of bottles of Chardonnay and a carton of Marlboro cigarettes. When I got home, I took a chair up to the third-floor flat roof deck of my home in Dana Point, went back inside, put on a coat, grabbed a down comforter, and wrapped it around me outside. Then I said, "I will sit here and smoke as many cigarettes as possible until I cannot stand smoking another one." I refer to it as my rendition of the Bergerud Schick Center approach to stopping smoking. And I did. I sat out on the roof deck for hours, smoking and drinking my Chardonnay until I had a disgustingly large pile of cigarette butts and could not smoke one more. Plus, I now have the dry heaves. That is a beautiful image!

I said, "Let's see how my quitting smoking worked because next week, I will be on a speaking trip driving from Minnesota to Wisconsin with two of my publishers' editors, one of whom was a chain smoker." Yup, inhaling his secondhand smoke on this trip in the back seat of Dave's car, at first, I thought I would never make it. Soon, I got used to it. That drive may have helped ease me out of smoking.

At that point in life, I did not acknowledge that I might have another addiction: alcohol. I honestly did not recognize or dare to admit that I did. What I did do, though, was to ask my medical doctor various things about the signs of alcoholism. I knew I came from a family with a genetic predisposition to alcoholism. However, I swore I would never let that be me.

I began having disturbing drinking experiences and asked my doctor about them. He explained various signs that are indicative of alcoholic blackouts.

What I learned from my doctor about blackouts was alarming. I had told him about several incidents where, according to witnesses, I continued to function. However, I did not remember most of what happened after my second drink—or very little. He told me these incidents might be alcoholic blackouts. However, my drinking did not erase the memories I formed before becoming intoxicated. Finally, I began to accept that, besides being a binge drinker, I might also be a blackout alcoholic. This devil has maintained a presence in my life for some time.

Here is a pathetic example of an evening out for dinner with my darling niece, who temporarily lived with me. We went to Dana Point Harbor for dinner at a terrific little restaurant, then to the bar to listen to music and have drinks. Pretty soon, I began to read everyone's palms! Did I know how to read palms?

Hell no! Nevertheless, there was a line around the bar of people waiting for me to read their palms.

The next day, my sweet fifteen-year-old niece told me she tried to save me from taking one of those cute guys home with me, but to no avail. What a horrible role model I was. I felt awful about exposing her to my weak addiction and its resultant behavior.

I vaguely remembered the palm reading but not taking someone home.

During this same period, my publisher, John Wiley & Son Inc., assigned Joe, one of their New York editors, to work with Don Busché and me on our new textbook on computer operating systems. This editor was also to go out on the speaking circuit with us to help market the books. His name was Joe T. When the publisher gave Joe this assignment to work with us, the story goes that one condition was that Joe had to be able to dance, as my publisher knew I loved to dance.

Joe seemed great, highly intelligent, good- looking, and continually told stories. He was very attentive. Later, while I was presenting to educators, Joe always provided critiques and great accolades regarding my content and delivery style while presenting to educators about the new technologies. He made my being on these road trips fun. John Wiley's created the education conference program to market our books. Joe accompanied or met us in many cities across the country. We developed a great friendship. Boy, did we dance! I loved working on the initial textbook with the publisher and Joe T. and being wined and dined at some of New York's finest restaurants. Joe was always with the publisher, Sara O. We had many laughs and drinks at these events. The books were selling exceptionally well; the publishers were happy with how lucrative this venture had become.

I was thrilled. We were constantly working on revisions because it seemed a more recent operating system was released as soon as our manuscript was published.

When working on some aspects of the book's development in New York, Joe and I often attended incredible Broadway shows. I loved the excitement of being in the hustle and bustle of New York. Usually, I stayed at the publisher's apartment reserved for visiting authors. If that apartment was unavailable, I often stayed with Denise, a good friend of Joe's, at her loft in SoHo, a neighborhood in Lower Manhattan.

Soon, my friendship with Joe drifted toward something much more profound.

Joe and Marly Celebrate Her 50th Birthday

I fell deeply in love with this sweet, brilliant man. However, soon, I discovered that he, too, had his demons.

When Joe and I arrived at the hotel where the conference was to take place, we checked in, went to our rooms, and then met at the bar. Sometimes after dinner, we would find a club with live music, cut loose on the dance floor, and do crazy dancing. The more I drank, the more inventive my dancing became. Before leaving the bar in whatever hotel we were staying in, we carried two glasses of double scotch on the rocks to one of our rooms, drank, and had fantastic sex.

With Joe's gentle nurturing, I began to accept my sexuality more fully for the first time. I thought the best I could ever hope for was to get better at it to please him more. I needed the comprehensive "how- to" manual because my relationship with my son's father was nearly void of loving sexual interactions.

The publisher booked me on the speaking circuit during this same period in most major US, Mexico, and Canadian cities. Joe attended each of these events for the publisher. We spent more time together in towns across the U.S. on my weekend speaking trips. I finally came to my senses and realized that sex could be terrific with a caring, loving partner. One day after Joe and I had a night of drinking and fun dancing, we felt great, with no hangovers from too much alcohol. It never occurred to us that we might have issues with our drinking.

THE EMPTY NEST AND STARK RAGING FEAR

Give the ones you love wings to fly, roots to come back,
and reasons to stay.
—The Dalai Lama

Most of the time, while I was working and traveling on the speaking tour for the publisher, Christen was attending a university in Northern California, where he lived with friends. He loved every minute of this newfound freedom, as most kids do. I missed him terribly.

Since his departure, the "empty-nest syndrome" was like a punch to the stomach. I missed Christen, his banter, his friends, and watching him become such an intelligent, energetic, good-looking young man. During a school holiday, on one of his trips home, I was outside on our back patio when he returned. He came through our house to the patio and greeted me with a big hug and kiss. I tried not to gasp as he had shaved his head. For him, that was quite a statement. I said nothing about it as if I had not noticed.

On one of his summer breaks between semesters, I agreed to help fund a trip for Christen to trek through Europe, meeting friends from college along the way. Soon, he left the US. He decided to check in weekly by calling either me or Anita, his previous host during an earlier visit to Europe. As a result, I felt no pressing need to be at home in California. I arranged with Joe to arrive in New York in three weeks to spend a few months with him.

All went well during the first few weeks of Christen's trip. I had not yet left California. Then, I had not heard from him for ten days, nor had Anita. Another week went by, and we still had not heard. I panicked. After three weeks had passed, and neither Anita nor I had heard from him, I was terrified that something had happened to him. He had been sending postcards. The last one was from Berlin. My mind was racing about him lying somewhere in East Berlin. I was trying to be optimistic but was terrified of what might happen to him. Thoughts tore through my mind that I would never see him again or know what happened to him. I was about to engage Interpol, a European agency that acts as a liaison between the United States and European law enforcement agencies. Anita and I decided to give it another two days.

Two days after my last call with Anita, Christen called Anita. He had run out of money traveling through Austria and was in the small country of Slovakia. A kind gentleman in a store in that little village told Christen he could stay in a cabin he owned on the mountain nearby, but it did not have any heat. Christen would have to chop wood for heat. This cabin was a few miles out of town. The only phone in this village was in the post office. The post office was closed every time Christen trekked into town to use the phone.

At last, he connected with Anita on one of his treks to this little village. She wired him some money so he could take the train back to Basel. My heart resumed beating normally. I was immensely relieved.

Looking back on how I felt during my internal trauma of Christen's temporary disappearance from Anita's and my radar, I realized that I looked to Scotch to calm my nerves.

Despite acknowledging that I may have a drinking problem, my drinking escalated. The possibility of something horrible happening to Christen caused me indescribable emotional pain. Was my increased drinking out of worry and concern for him, or just habit and an excuse on my path to alcoholism?

Interestingly, Christen doesn't remember this happening as I described it, which is most likely because I was just "a typical worried mother" and he was "just having a great time."

CONFRONTING ADDICTION, ENABLING, AND RAGING GUILT

Once the enabling stops, the recovery is given the opportunity to start.
—Healthyplace.com

Extremely relieved knowing Christen had returned to Basel, I soon would leave for New York to spend time with Joe. He lived in New York, and I was still in California. We spoke nightly, sometimes for hours, while I sipped scotch. Since we were on the phone, it did not feel like I was drinking alone. If I ran out of scotch, I would switch to whatever else was in the liquor cabinet. It never occurred to me what impact my newly formed drinking patterns had on me.

Joe drank as much as I did. We often talked about our drinking habits, mostly when I lived those three months in New York with him before my speaking engagement in Boston. I asked Joe and my friends to be truthful with me about how and what they observed regarding my drinking behavior. Initially, I was a binge drinker, meaning I might only drink when out with friends on a Saturday night. I did not know what had happened to my brain after that second drink. Then, while drinking, unfortunately, I learned that a part of my brain would shut down—thus, as happened in Boston, I had become a blackout drunk.

While visiting Joe in New York, we walked along some streets in Midtown after our previous evening out to dinner and the theater. I stopped walking, turned to him, and said, "I have to ask you something."

"Of course. What is it?"

"What did I do last night after dinner and the play? Did we fight?"

Then, with downcast eyes, he said, "Yes." He went on to tell me what I said and did.

All I could do was cry. Was it possible the devil came again?

Immediately, my thoughts returned to my last visit with Joe Brady, the therapist I had seen for a year. On that visit, I had run out of his office sobbing after I asked him, "Am I an alcoholic? Just tell me the truth, even though I know therapists are supposed to help us figure it out. Please, tell me the truth."

Looking directly at me, Brady painted a picture like this: "Over the next few years, as your drinking escalates, you will stay in your current job, but soon, you will move on to another position with greater prestige or money. You will lose that new position because of your drinking. You are a blackout drunk and will be dead by age fifty-five."

That was why I ran out of his office. I could not even wrap my arms around Brady's statement that I could die in eight years.

Currently, I am only forty-eight. Despite Brady's warnings and my beginning to realize I might have a problem, I could not envision my life without being able to drink, going out with friends for a glass of wine after work, or drinking with friends at dinner parties, celebrations, and so much more.

Fortunately, I was due to take an administrative sabbatical (a short paid leave) from my position at the college. I decided to spend some of that time in New York with Joe over the upcoming summer months. He had been living with his brother, but now he was in his own apartment. It would be a perfect trial for me to see if what Joe and I had together was worth my quitting my job and moving back to New York or whether he might be coming out to live with me in California.

Through those next three months in New York, I decided to test some ideas about my drinking—I would not mix alcohol, hard liquor with wine. I would drink water between whatever alcoholic drinks I was having. I would make sure that I had eaten something before having a drink. I tried all sorts of various tests, but the reality was—it did not matter. After the first drink, I kept drinking— like a real alcoholic.

This time together in New York helped us look at our relationship, and we decided we wanted to be together. Joe felt he could quickly get a job as an editor in California, as he had a great resume in publishing. His biggest issue was that even though he was divorced and living independently, his two children were still in high school on the East Coast. His wife had made it nearly impossible for him to see their children. He was mostly allowed to see them for only one hour during the week at a diner near their home. I felt that leaving his children would be an immense emotional problem. I did not know how he would handle that. However, love seemed to have conquered, let us say, almost all. Joe decided he would move out to California.

However, I had made a tragic trip as a speaker in Boston before he moved to California. It was the height of my career—I was the keynote speaker at a conference where Buzz Aldrin was the opening speaker, and Bill Clinton and I also crossed paths. For all the glitter of the evening, when I sat, hungover, with Maureen at breakfast the next day, she told me she had seen me in the lobby with a strange man's hand up my skirt. When Maureen told me that, the room spun around.

I started having flashbacks of the night before. Although I had no clear memories of that night, including seeing Maureen in the lobby, it all started to rush back. There was a pool table in a lounge off the lobby. My clothes were all over the floor. I was lying on the pool table. There was a man on top of me. I had no idea who he was. He was having sex with me—I could not say I was even there; instead, it must have been a dream. He was laughing.

After this image ended, I remember coming out of the bathroom and wiping my clothes. Someone helped me walk down a flight of stairs. Other than that, I remembered nothing. I do not know how I got to my room or about going to sleep.

No matter how horrified I was by what happened in Boston, I was still not done with drinking.

Like a perfect alcoholic, not ready to admit I had a problem, I continued trying to analyze my drinking patterns. I thought I was smart. I was sure I could figure this out so I could still drink yet know when to stop. That meant I did not ever miss work. I did not have hangovers. When drinking, I carried on conversations like a reasonable person (or so I thought).

I did not drink to get drunk. I did not have to have a drink; I only drank when going out with a friend or a group of friends and may or may not have had one night during the week or weekend. None of this is relevant because once I began drinking, I did not stop after that second drink, and some parts of my brain must have shut down too.

When talking with friends about how they handled their drinking, they said, "Well, I only drink beer," or "I only drink wine," or "I drink a bottle of water between my drinks," and on and on.

I thought, well, if others can do that, so can I. As I looked back on my life, trying to discern how my drinking had become what it was, the truth was that it began when I started working at the law firm in downtown Los Angeles that year. It started with martinis at lunch or dinner, leading to trouble. I felt horrible inside then, but I justified my affair with my boss due to alcohol. Yet at that same time, while married to Larry for the next dozen years, Larry and I rarely drank unless we visited his or my sister. Then it was still one or two drinks—a social evening.

Over the next twelve years, with my second husband, Donald, we started drinking a glass of wine with dinner or possibly a hard-core Scotch on the rocks on the weekends. We did not drink every night. After a sailboat race, we might go to the yacht club and have drinks with the crew or friends. But by the end of twelve years with Donald, my binge drinking had escalated, and I did not stop after the second drink. He could handle his alcohol, but I could not, so he left and never returned. Right after he left, I asked my medical doctor about blackouts. I must have known on some unconscious level that my drinking was becoming a problem. However, I did not acknowledge it or do anything about it then.

Later, after Joe and I met, I dined and drank at incredible restaurants across the country. He and I became heavy scotch drinkers. The point was, it was not how often I drank, but when I did drink, how much I drank, and how it affected my brain and behavior.

In December 1990, Joe drove from New York to California and moved in with me.

Joe and Marly After Marly's speaking engagement.

This move for Joe was the month after my trip and my horrendous blackout in Boston. Then, one day, sobbing almost uncontrollably, I told Joe about my Boston incident. We both made a promise to each other and decided we would never again have another drink. His agreement and sticking with me on our decision to stop drinking initially supported our sobriety.

The thought of what had happened to me while I was speaking at the convention at the Copley Plaza sickened me. I still saw the image of the pool table and my clothes lying around the room. I had no clear memory of the event. I was a blackout drunk.

I was thrilled that Joe and I were finally together in San Clemente. All my friends met him, and through many get-togethers, they got to know Joe. They thought he was delightful, and Joe and I had terrific times with them.

Early on, the problems Joe and I had to deal with when he moved in were 1) his guilt about leaving his high school- aged children, and 2) now he was without a job. We were both drinking a lot in the evenings and on weekends.

Immediately. his not having a job was debilitating for him. Plus, rarely discussed was his leaving his two high school–aged children. He did not talk about his feelings; we drank in the evenings and often on the weekends. Finally, we decided we needed to stop drinking entirely. Also, we wanted to tell my sister Connie and her husband, John, that we were both stopping drinking. I have always been very close to Connie and John. Joe and I have a great time with them and their small boys when we are together. We decided to fly to San Francisco over a three-day holiday to visit them.

The first evening with the Friels, we had our typical pre-dinner two double scotches on the rocks, and wine flowed at dinner. Joe and I began discussing with them that I have come to grips with and understand that I am an alcoholic and need to stop drinking. Of course, this conversation occurred while we were all drinking before, during, and after dinner, which did not have the positive effect it should have.

My sister said, "You are not an alcoholic but are taking Chlor-Trimeton daily, and you are not supposed to drink while taking that." Nevertheless, as the wine continued flowing, they both began to reiterate stories of many horrible things I had done while drinking with them and others over the past ten years. At one point, emotionally I felt crushed and awful atabout what they were saying about me. I needed a break from it. Dinner was over, and I excused myself from the dinner table to go to the bathroom. Then I went into the den where we were staying. Even though it was dark outside, I decided to get some air. As I put on my coat, Joe entered our room, wrapped his arms around me from behind, and quietly said, "No, do not go!"

He thought I would run away and never be heard from again. Maybe he was just sad about how the conversation went down at the dinner table. He gripped my arms from behind me and was not letting go of me. When he did not let go of me with my asking him to do so, I thrust both elbows backward to get released from his tight grip. Simultaneously, my head went back and unintentionally struck him in the nose. Now, blood was running down his face and clothes. At the same time, Connie and the boys walked in to see what was happening. She screamed at me, "How dare you do that in front of the boys!"

It was a gruesome scene. We did not want the boys to think we were fighting, physically or not, which it appeared had happened. Then I turned and went out of their front door. I ran, sobbing, up and down a few streets in their neighborhood. Finally, I found a little cement wall to sit on between two hedges. There, I sat and cried and cried. I was a horrible person. In a short time, John found me; and as he approached me, he said, "You need to come back to the house. Everything is fine, and you are not a bad person."

Joe and I returned home the next afternoon to San Clemente. After the unfortunate incident at Connie and John's home the previous evening, Joe and I went to dinner at a great restaurant on the beach to talk about what happened. At dinner, I said, "I knew before we went to see Connie and John that I would quit drinking. However, now, more than ever, I have made a firm decision: I will never drink again. I will not let the family curse of alcoholism take me down." That was November 12, 1990.

Poor Joe. That flip of my head backward when he put his arms around me broke his nose. The next day, I introduced him to the plastic surgeon who had rebuilt my prior ugly nose because of my deviated septum, and now he took care of Joe. After his surgery, he had a beautiful, manly Roman nose. Afterward, we laughed and said, "We should have done that long ago."

So how did I quit? For a few years, I had been afraid to deal with the fact that I had a problem with alcohol and that the family curse had snagged me. Otherwise, before I visited Joe in New York, why would I have asked Brady whether he thought I was an alcoholic? His response in my last therapy session was a dramatic wake- up call. I trusted him.

Joe and I talked about how we felt about each other and our issues around drinking. While visiting Joe in early November 1990, we agreed to quit drinking and continue seeing Brady.

TWO LIFE- DEFINING DECISIONS

Addiction is hard to overcome. As you might remember,
I drank too much at one time in my life.
—George W. Bush, 2008

I resumed individual sessions with Brady, the therapist, and Joe also attended separate sessions with him. During my meetings with Brady, I conducted a personal assessment of my drinking habits. The repulsive incident of the devil pursuing me on my blackout night in Boston had shaken me to my core. The reality was that I knew I had a severe drinking problem. I had to break the family curse.

Since my last session with Brady, what I had learned about being a blackout alcoholic was hard to listen to, but it seemed to describe me to a tee. Since my grandfather, father, mother, and older sister, Sharon, were alcoholics, I was highly likely to have some genetic predisposition for alcohol. Research studies show that a person's risk increases for alcoholism if born into a family with the following difficulties:

•An alcoholic parent is depressed.

•Both parents abused alcohol.

•The parents' alcohol abuse was severe.

•Parents' conflicts led to aggression and violence in the family.

Bingo! I was never lucky enough to get that many correct answers on any test before! Still, I could not imagine that Brady was right.

Brady suggested I meet with a particular woman, a psychologist he was counseling, who had similar issues. She was willing to go with me to an AA meeting. I agreed to meet with her.

My assumption about AA was that it was a bunch of lowlifes. I truly thought that most of these AA people were typically deviants and did not engage in society like the rest of us. Their values differed from mine and most mainstream people: skirting the edges, unemployed, victims of bad upbringings, high school dropouts, and prostitutes. They took drugs in dark, dirty alleyways, robbed innocent people, went on binges, and engaged in high-risk behaviors.

Finally, I met this woman Brady wanted me to meet and went with great trepidation to my first AA women's meeting with her. Much to my dismay, I discovered that most of its members were like everyone I knew. They were parents, children, friends, workmates, and sisters. They held down jobs, had friends, went to social functions, and enjoyed their weekends. Some were wealthy corporate presidents, teachers, stay-at-home mothers, psychologists, and every type of worker possible. Some were very successful people, and others were just everyday people who knew they had a drinking problem. Indeed, some failed to manage their addiction and became entrenched in a lifestyle that the stereotypes embody, but most did not. Addiction does not discriminate between rich and poor, young or old. I met one AA member who is considered one of California's top ten wealthiest men and women, aged thirteen to ninety-two. I only felt comfortable attending women's meetings. I was afraid to participate in mixed AA meetings and meet men I could potentially become involved with - someone who had the same problem I had— drinking.

I will never forget this one woman in my home AA meeting. Sandy was twenty-seven, beautiful, and had been in and out of AA since she was nineteen. She had destroyed her liver with her heavy drinking and was now on the waiting list for a liver transplant. Within about ten months, she received the great news that she could have the transplant surgery and was so grateful for a second chance in life. Everyone who knew her was thrilled, as we knew that without the transplant, she would die. One month after the surgery, she began drinking again; Sandy died within six months of her liver transplant! Unforgettable! That shocked me to my core.

The first year of my not drinking, I must admit, was difficult. Some call my feelings or behavior that of being a "dry drunk." That term describes someone who no longer drinks alcohol but, in many ways, behaves like they are still addicted. Emotionally, as a dry drunk, I was full of resentment and anger. I thought, God, why me? Wasn't being abused by the devil, my drunken father, enough? Plus, at this point in life, my menopausal hormones simultaneously had run for the hills. I cannot imagine what it must have been like to live with me. Had I been an everyday drinker - morning, noon, and night type of drinker, I would have most likely needed to go to a rehabilitation facility.

However, I did not have the DTs (delirium tremens), the rapid onset of confusion, or a severe form of withdrawal from alcohol, so I handled quitting alcohol—on my own. Quitting was a decision. When I decided to quit, I was done.

For me, quitting drinking may have been easier than for others because I was a binge drinker, meaning I drank occasionally, not daily, usually with friends. I did not think quitting on my own was easy then, but I refused to go to a rehab facility and leave my son and my work at the college. I was determined to beat the disease of alcoholism on my own. Not everyone has the willpower to quit cold turkey. That may be impossible for heavy daily drinkers, which I was not. But my quitting drinking was still a challenge.

I used to think I would never have fun again. How could I dance and be uninhibited on the dance floor? Initially, I felt self-conscious and subdued without alcohol under my belt on the dance floor. Picture this: the person who loved dancing so much was now afraid to go out on the dance floor sober. How sad. What else would be difficult for me to do? Gradually, I began to find confidence in how to live a full life without alcohol.

Is AA necessary to get sober? My answer would be that it depends on the person needing assistance, their work environment, family support, etc. My Thursday night women's meeting was a safe room where I could share what was happening with me through becoming free of alcohol.

To date, I have not had a single drink for thirty- five years. Brady's counseling of three years was the catalyst. I trusted him and learned a great deal from him about my behavior. He saved my life by helping me wake up. However, the fellowship of AA women from entirely different backgrounds and socioeconomic strata was a constant reminder that sobriety truly is "one day at a time." Some people attend meetings seven days a week because that is the kind of support they need; others attend meetings once or twice weekly. For some, it becomes purely social. The critical point is that there is help for us alcoholics by phone or meetings for the rest of our lives. Even in my travels, I discovered there are AA meetings across the globe. Even though I no longer drink alcohol, I will always be an alcoholic. It is easy to blame my addictions on my genetics or the damaging patterns in my upbringing. The reality is that addictions or dependencies are now being described as chronic brain disorders and not merely behavior problems of self-regulation involving alcohol, drugs, food, work, gambling, or sex. Two decades of advancements in neuroscience convinced the American Society of Addiction Medicine that addiction affects the brain's reward circuitry that governs control and judgment, resulting in the pursuit of rewards such as alcohol, sex, food, sugar, gambling, and more. I loved all those rewards. Some believe that addictive behaviors are a manifestation of the disease, not a cause. If that is true, then choosing recovery is like people with a heart condition choosing to eat healthier or begin exercising. It seems that the same regions of my brain that gave me my intense curiosity, obsessive focus, and ability to learn and memorize quickly also made me vulnerable to potential bad habits that I rapidly locked into them. Had I been aware of this information while in my alcoholism, I am sure none of it would have made any sense to me or caused me to stop drinking.

Being an Enabler

I loved Joe but soon realized I was the great enabler and had been my entire life. I provided Joe with all the comforts of home while he did not and sometimes could not reciprocate.

I would even have to ask him to take out the garbage. When he moved to California in 1990, we thought getting a job writing or as an editor would be easy for him. He applied for dozens of jobs. He was told he was either overqualified or unqualified. I realized how complex being in his financial position was, as he did not have a full-time job. His lack of income worsened because he had that sizable monthly alimony payment (for life) and child support payments, as his kids were still in high school.

It took me a while to understand why his alimony was so high. However, as expected, a story about paying alimony in New Jersey has a history behind it. It goes something like this: Joe told me he was the only one of all his friends who went to college. That was not the most unusual news. Instead, nearly all his neighborhood friends became members of the Italian American Mafia. As a result, growing up with these friends, he heard remarkable stories. He would love to tell our friends and me these tales and would go on forever telling them. They were fascinating accounts of the five families that controlled New York and Chicago's old-style patriarchy: the Italian American Mafia: the Bonanno, Colombo, Gambino, Genovese, and Lucchese. With that new knowledge, I now understood why, when Joe talked about alimony, he laughed and said, "In New Jersey, you either kill your wife or pay outrageous alimony." He did not want to join most of his childhood friends, who were either in jail or dead. When I visited Joe while living in New York, he drove us by the "clubs" and pointed out which Mafia group frequented each.

Luckily, at Saddleback College, where I was the Dean of the Business Division, there was a need for a person to teach part-time classes in Business English and Business Communications. Joe's background and his caliber of work experience in publishing made him a perfect faculty member for those courses. The students loved Joe. These part-time classes, at least, helped him pay his debts back East.

Several years passed since Joe moved out of New York, and I thought that he had settled into life with me in California. We were getting along great. He loved his teaching at Saddleback; my friends and family all loved him. Outwardly, he seemed incredibly happy. About eight years into our living together, something happened to him. The underlying shadow of his Catholic guilt for leaving his children in New York got to him. One day, when I returned home from work, he was not at home, but the light flashed on my phone's answering machine. Joe had left a message for me. It said, "I cannot handle life with what I have done to my kids, and I am going to end my life." I shrieked.

Oh my God. The despair and hopelessness in his recorded voice shook me to my core.

Immediately, I called his AA sponsor, who told me he would look for him. Then I got my three best buddies, who knew him well, to come to our house. They listened to his voice message. Then we started the search by driving all over Orange County. Pretty crazy thought process as to where does one go to find someone who is going to kill himself?

Also, as I have used various psychics my entire life, I called Linea, a psychic in Temecula. She listened to Joe's message. She responded, "He is okay. He is sitting near the water's edge around Carlsbad or San Diego but cannot go through with what he had planned."

Later that evening, another male friend from work came over to help me figure out where Joe might be. As Joe's bills were on his desk, my friend called the credit card companies shown on Joe's bills, pretending he was Joe, and said his son had taken his cards. He wanted to know if any charges were on them during that day. Sure enough, a couple of gas charges between where I lived and San Diego. There were 7-Eleven purchases, probably for food, and a strange one for a rental car with Rent a Dent. That charge seemed weird he had a rental car because he had left our place with one of our two vehicles.

On the sixth day of Joe's disappearance, I made an appointment to see Joe Brady, the therapist. When I drove to his office, my jaw fell open as I saw a yellow car with Rent-a-Dent tags. I approached the car and glanced through the driver's window, spotting three photos—his son, his daughter, and mine—alongside his worn copy of Paradise Lost by Milton on the dashboard. My mind was spinning. I went into Brady's office and saw Joe sitting with Brady, now looking at me, grinning ear to ear. Joe never apologized in Brady's office or ever - for putting me through this strange kind of hell. He was clueless about the emotional trauma he caused for me. We left Brady's office and went to our cars outside the office.

He proudly showed me that he had a hose and rags in the rental car trunk as he planned to gas himself. He had been on the beach near San Diego to carry out his plan and had given his remaining money in his pockets to some vagrant. It was interesting that he rented a car on the way out of town as he did not want to die in my car. Wasn't that thoughtful? I followed him in his little yellow rental car to the Rent-A-Dent agency, and he returned the vehicle.

We drove home together. When home, he functioned like nothing was unusual and seemed happy to be back. At that moment, I recognized that Joe was truly experiencing significant emotional distress. For me, I felt like I was always holding my breath, living with a time bomb. I am not a therapist, but his behavior and lack of expressing any feelings of sorrow for the consequences of his actions told me, "I have a serious problem on my hands." I should have had him move out, but now I was afraid this would push him over the edge, and he would commit suicide. I did not want to feel responsible.

He was not paying bills but just throwing them all in a box. Nothing for him had changed. However, I had changed. Now, my radar was up because I had always heard that if someone attempted suicide once, they would do it again. I loved him and did not know what to do. So, for the time being, I did nothing.

Then a few months later, it happened again. A recorded message from Joe was on my answering machine. This time, the message he left said he was no good for me and was planning to end his life. Oh my God. Not again. Pure, stark terror. I called Brady, who said there was nothing I could do about it. I should not feel guilty because Joe must face his demons.

This time I called his two elder brothers, Sal (Salvatore) and Tony (Antonio), who loved and adored Joe, their little brother. They were distraught and wanted to know what to do. I told them they could do nothing, but I wanted them to know I was very concerned. If he committed suicide, I did not want to call without forewarning them.

While Joe was gone, physically and emotionally, I was a wreck—waiting for the other shoe to drop. At the same time, one night, while upstairs working on the computer for about three hours, I was also washing clothes downstairs. I finally realized I could hear the washing machine still running.

I ran downstairs and stepped into about three to four inches of water throughout the house's main floor. The hose on the washing machine had broken. I called a company that comes out 24/7, the Water Restoration Company. They arrived at about 3:00 a.m. Meanwhile, I was shoving water out the back door into the garage using this giant garage broom. I remember saying aloud, "God, I guess this is another test, but I am wearing out."

Joe returned home five days after his second suicide message, showing no remorse. When I asked where he had been, he said, "I had driven to an area near the Mexico border and saw a small chapel where a wedding was taking place. I drove up to the chapel and went in and sat in the last pew." Whatever Joe felt sitting in the back of that chapel near Mexico triggered his need to return to the Mission at San Juan Capistrano. There he saw a priest, and for the first time since he moved to California, he took confession with a priest at the Mission. Great! What can I expect now that he has been absolved from his sins?

Well, Hallelujah! I only wished his faith had removed my pain and emotional trauma. I did not expect him to get down and beg for forgiveness. However, I soon realized he was oblivious to how he had impacted me or anyone else. He was furious that I had called his brothers. I realized that Joe was sad, nearly penniless, and shut down emotionally. He could not understand his emotional impact on loved ones. He showed no feelings of compassion or remorse for how he impacted so many people.

After these events of Joe leaving his suicide recordings and disappearing, I became less receptive to living with him. However, I did not talk with him about it. The residue and emotional trauma of his failed suicide attempts had worn me down.

Someone was listening. My prayers were soon to be answered. One of the full-time faculty members, Peter, in the Business Division at the college where I was the dean, was going on a sabbatical for a year in Europe. I asked Peter if he might like Joe to house-sit for him, and he was delighted with this idea. Perfect. Peter called Joe and asked (without mentioning our prior conversation) if he would house-sit for a year. Yes! In a few months, Joe moved out of my place entirely and into Peter's house. He was so happy to be helping Peter. He did not think twice about how it may or may not affect me. That is how our relationship of eight years ended. He was clueless about why that was happening, but he did not question it. I believe Joe only thought he was helping a friend, Peter.

The weekend Joe moved out, the Band of Four, Don, Maureen, Angela, and I, drove to Santa Fe. I could not stand to be around while he was leaving.

The Band of Four: Maureen, Don, Angela, and Marly.

His departure from my home truly devastated me because I deeply loved Joe but knew I could not save him. I cried the entire time I was with my friends, which I guess they expected. Joe had been the editor for Don and me on several of our books, so Don, too, felt very close to Joe and was deeply concerned about Joe's well-being.

After Joe moved out, we remained good friends. Occasionally, I would see him at Saddleback College, where I was still the dean. I was often at the college in the evenings when he was there teaching his classes. Seeing him always tugged at my heart.

Several years later, I had moved to Northern California for another position at DeAnza College, and I heard from one of Joe and my close friends that Joe had a terrific, loving relationship with a woman named Angie. I was incredibly happy for them. I learned they had lived together for several years and that he was a very loving partner and helper in raising her children. As significant, he had reunited with his children from back East and two brothers who visited him in California.

THE FALL OF GORBACHEV, COMMUNISM, AND THE USSR

*Let us step into the night and pursue that
flighty temptress, adventure.*
—J. K. Rowling

During his college years, Christen traveled to Moscow for two summers to study at the Pushkin State Russian Language Institute. He studied political science and Russian for his bachelor's degree and felt this language immersion would greatly benefit him. So off to Moscow. Chris had a family connection in Moscow where he could stay in a room with them in the institute's dormitory tower. The tower was a whitewashed, fifteen-story building made of prefabricated concrete slabs, not a very welcoming place to stay. Christen alternated staying at both, depending on the time he finished his studies and work each day. His Russian family consisted of a son, a daughter, and their mother.

The following summer, Christen was asked if he would manage the Institute, continue his studies, and they would pay him to do so.

At the end of Christen's second summer of study at the Institute, he invited me and my co-author/traveling friend, Don Busché, to attend the graduation ceremonies from the Pushkin Institute in Moscow. Once again, Don and I decided to take this opportunity to attend his graduation and visit the USSR to see a country we might not have previously considered.

Before we left, Christen wrote to me, asking, "Would you please bring some items that my friends and Russian family need?"

I said, "Of course. What are they?"
He responded, "Bring twelve pairs of
blue jeans in these sizes, bring as many cans of fruit as possible for you to carry because my friends never get fruit in Russia, and please pick up at least six or eight dozen condoms."

"What?"

"Mom," he said, in a calm but imperative voice, "my friends here do have sex, and their condoms are the size of garbage bags and do not work, and they do not want to get pregnant—so please."

Picture this: I am now inside Costco and have loaded my cart with all these items Christen requested I bring with me. I am still unclear how I will carry all the canned fruit in my luggage. Soon, I was in the checkout line at Costco: The checker was a young man who scanned the jeans. Then, the few dozen large cans of fruit went through the scanner. Finally, he began scanning the eight dozen condoms. The checker was now staring at them. Up to this point, he had not looked at me. Now, it was all he could do—not to see who was buying these dozens of condoms. When he finally looked up at me with curiosity and squinting eyes in disbelief, I did not crack a smile. I said, "It is going to be a jam-packed weekend." His face turned bright red, and he could hardly wait to get me out of there. Oh, I have such fun sometimes.

On Our Way St. Petersburg

In June 1991, Don and I began the USSR trip in Leningrad (a month later, the city name reverted to St. Petersburg, named after St. Peter, a name given in the early seventeenth century). It is a coastal city located on the eastern shore of the Baltic Sea. The sky always seemed overcast and left a gray pallor over the city's gray structures. We took taxis through their wide streets. We visited a few famous sites: the Hermitage Museum, the Imperial Palace, and the Church of the Savior on Spilled Blood (which has several names).

In the Hermitage, we were overwhelmed, as in jaw-dropping, by the incredible opulence and grandeur of the architecture of historic seventeenth and nineteenth-century structures. Many of their interior walls were covered with gold and filled with centuries of fine art collections. Catherine the Great wanted to ensure her city had more palaces than any other European city.

Never before I had seen the vast number of stunning treasures and jewels displayed within the Hermitage; they were indescribable. One could spend weeks exploring this magnificent museum. It holds over a million works of art and archaeological artifacts. We could have spent days just touring this amazing museum.

The people of St. Petersburg loved our U.S. dollars, so they wanted our dollars in this city even though we had picked up some rubles, their currency.

St. Petersburg was the initial stop on our trip, and it did not show us the poverty and misery I was expecting. Before the trip, we learned that the USSR's economic conditions were rapidly deteriorating. Russia is a nation fraught with economic inequality. In this land, the rich get richer while the poor descend further into poverty. We soon heard that food rationing occurred in many Russian cities for the first time since the 1940s and that St. Petersburg had received humanitarian aid from abroad.

Odessa

Soon, we left St. Petersburg for Odessa, Russia's most important port city on the Black Sea. Our hotel had a bevy of beauties always hanging out in the lobby, waiting for their next customers. Here, Don and I decided we would go to a ballet performance at the renowned Odessa Opera and Ballet Theater. The performance was a beautiful display of incredibly talented artists. Several great world ballet artists have begun their careers at this theater, such as Mikhail Baryshnikov, Anna Pavlova, and Rudolf Nureyev, to name a few. I felt privileged to have watched Nureyev perform in the United States. In Odessa, we watched with great excitement and admiration the precision and beauty of these beautiful precision dancers. Occasionally, I felt transported to the stage, enjoying the thrill of the dance. Too soon, it was over. Then an interesting phenomenon occurred during the evening as each performance ended; the local people clapped in unison.

There were no taxis when we left the theater. It was pitch dark—no streetlights. Don was always up for a walk and said, "It is not far. We will not have any problem—come on."

As we headed out on this trek back to our hotel, all I could hear were the last words of the hotel desk clerk saying, "Do not walk alone at night." What were we doing? Walking alone at night on streets with no streetlights! Soon, behind us, I could hear at least two people walking. I could hear the clop, clop, and clop of their hard-soled shoes. We walked faster. They walked more quickly, and it felt like they were getting closer. I was in high heels, trying not to fall in the dark and into the cracks on this broken old sidewalk.

"People are following us," I told Don.

Being very pragmatic about most things, he said, "You're just imagining it. No one is following us."

I said, "Then let's cross the street now and see what happens." Quickly, we crossed the street.

The two people following us crossed the street.

Now, we were walking as fast as we could without breaking into a complete run, which I could not do in high heels. A few blocks into this near run, I looked down the road to the upcoming intersection that would be where we would cross the next broad street. Then an oncoming car appeared to the right of the upcoming intersection and seemed to have a man driving with a small person in the vehicle. I said to Don, "Let's stop that car."

Despite my high heels, Don and I broke into an all-out run down the middle of the street directly toward that car. I stopped in front of the car's path without really thinking until it stopped.

I cried out, "Puljalesta, Puljalesta. The Black Sea Hotel." The nice man let us climb into the back seat. With the man and his child in the front seat, he drove us safely to our little hotel of whores.

Kyiv

Having survived Odessa, we set off for Kyiv, the capital and largest city in Ukraine, located in the north-central part of the country on the Dnieper River. The number of residents was close to 3 million, making Kyiv the eighth most populous city in Europe. Kyiv is an important industrial, scientific, educational, and cultural center of Eastern Europe. It is home to many high-tech industries, higher education institutions, and world-famous historical landmarks.

Our guide in Kyiv knew about the nuclear power plant the government had built outside Chernobyl. We asked our guide to tell us about the Chernobyl reactor explosion in 1986 and its impact on Ukraine's people. It spewed two hundred times the radiation released in the bombings of Hiroshima and Nagasaki. Approximately eight hundred thousand firefighters and emergency workers came from the former Soviet Union to extinguish the fire. These people worked for over two years to put out the fire and bury the radioactive equipment, homes, storage facilities, etc. The government built a tomb around the plant to contain the radioactive material that had collapsed into the reactor. Many workers are now dead, disabled, or have committed suicide. Soon after the accident, the government evacuated the people living in Kyiv and the surrounding area. Evacuation procedures were chaotic. People had to leave their homes, some with just the clothes on their backs, and many never returned.

Our guide had sent her family away so they would not be in danger of the explosion's fallout and the aftermath. Over three hundred fifty thousand people resettled in existing communities or new communities built especially for evacuees. Over 7 million people were affected, mainly in Belarus, Russia, and Ukraine. Sheep in northern England and reindeer in Lapland died as they had been exposed to radiation by the winds wafting through their countries. Over sixty-three thousand square miles of land were affected. Four to five million children and adults still live on contaminated soil, growing food on contaminated earth and eating poisoned food. Generations later will feel the impact of this disaster.

Moscow—Meeting Up with Christen

Finally, our last stop was Moscow. We had agreed to meet Christen at our hotel. We had to go through lengthy discussions and inspections at the entrance of our hotel. Once inside, I saw Christen wildly waving his arms. My heart was pounding with excitement. I was thrilled to see him. He wrapped his arms around me and said, "I love you, Mom. I am so happy to see you." Don did not get the same greeting, but we all laughed as we began to tell the stories of our trip, mostly about what was in our suitcases.

Christen's blond hair was longer than usual, and his new manner of dressing resembled other Russian men his age. However, that was the only similarity. The nicest Russian men often tend to be gruff and slightly off-putting. I was relieved that my son was still the gentle, humble, soft-spoken man I had raised. We spent a few hours together hearing some of his past three months' stories and then gave him some of the "goods he requested we bring" in our suitcases. He did not want to carry luggage as he was on foot and asked us to bring it by taxi when we visited his Russian family for dinner. We agreed. Chris had to get back to the institute. We said our goodbyes. Then Don and I went downstairs in our hotel for dinner (a couple of cold pieces of salami, a hard-boiled egg, and a crisp baked potato).

Don and I knew we would not see Christen for a few days, so we had some time to tour Moscow. A few days passed, and now Don and I are out of rubles and US dollars. We did not think that was a big deal, but soon discovered that no one would exchange our American Express checks. You know that old American Express saying, "Don't leave home without them"? In Russia, it was "Do not leave with them because they are no good here."

Our hotel concierge told us we could cash our American Express checks at a particular bank, for which she wrote down the address for us. The following day, we went to that bank and stood outside it for about two hours, waiting for it to open. While waiting, this time was exciting because four lines of soldiers with rifles guarded the entrance. Shoulder to shoulder, they stood. They blocked all bank access, even on the steps leading up to the bank. We did not know who or what they expected, but they seemed prepared for an unsolicited takeover. We wondered if we were unaware of something going on in Russia's government leadership. The presence of soldiers everywhere was a little disconcerting, but we waited patiently. We waited about an hour for the soldiers to let us move up the steps near the bank's front. Once the bank opened, we had to wait patiently at the front door until we got a nod from a banker that it was okay for only one of us to proceed into the bank. I approached the seated female banker. You guessed it. The bank would not take our American Express checks. She told me to go to a particular address where someone there would accept our checks, wrote the address on a piece of paper, and gave that to me. Our lack of usable funds has become a dangerous situation. No dollars or rubles were accessible to us except for what little we had in our pockets for another three days.

We left the bank, hailed a taxi, and attempted to pronounce the address we wanted the driver to take us to. We showed him the address the banker had given me without getting anywhere with our inadequate Russian language skills. Don and I were nervous as the driver drove us around in circles. Soon, the driver abruptly stopped the car and let us off (or maybe he yelled in Russian, "Get out!" but we certainly would not have known the difference).

He pointed to what looked like an apartment building. By his motions, we thought this must be it. We paid him nine rubles as were shown on the meter. We had no idea where we were or if it was anywhere we wanted to be. We got out of the taxi and began walking down the street. Suddenly, we heard sounds nearby of someone speaking English. It seemed to be coming from a building doorway near us at the top of some stairs. Quickly, we went up the stairs and into the building. We followed the sound and immediately came upon a lovely gentleman from England. After telling him what we needed, he said, "Come with me."

He led us to a van nearby and said, "Get in, please." In hindsight, that could have been the biggest mistake of our ignorant lives, where a person ends up alive in a bathtub of ice without a liver. It was not. The English-speaking man explained that he was in the lumber business and could not take rubles or dollars out of the Soviet Union, but he could carry American Express checks. We exchanged our American Express checks for his US dollars and felt relieved.

Moscow is a major metropolitan city. It is one of the largest and, in 2019, considered one of the most expensive cities to live in the world. Walking within the city center, the air that day felt heavy and dirty. Every building had a rootlike grayish, dark tone to it.

The streets consisted of old, worn, dirty brick and/or stone. The size and feel of Moscow seemed like being in New York. The immediate difference was that Moscow's people appeared grim, mirroring their city's worn gray look and feel.

In a few days, we left the hotel and found a taxi to take us to Chr

Christen's Russian family and friends entertained Don and me.
-1991

Christen wore jeans, a long-sleeved gray shirt, and a dark black sweater for this family dinner. His attire was like that of his Russian guy friend—both were about 5'10" with similar slender builds. Christen's demeanor is always gentle, humble, and soft-spoken, yet with a hearty deep-felt laugh. The mother greeted us with a big smile and a firm handshake, although she seemed nervous. During the early 1990s, very few Russians entertained Americans in their homes. She wore a short-sleeved dress with a floral pattern on the skirt, which her apron covered. She had made a special effort to look nice for us. Everyone was talking at once, trying to communicate with each other. Christen was interpreting as needed. Sometimes it just took gestures to talk with one another. What an event! The mother, two children, and a neighbor friend Christen knew were about the same age. Soon, all of them were treating Don and me like family. Everyone was grinning, laughing, and talking with animated gestures to ensure we understood. They had squeezed into their tiny living room a smooth wooden door to use for our dinner, which functioned as our dining room table on two benches.

The meal was excellent and consisted of four items: (1) borscht (a sour soup cooked from pickled stems, leaves, and umbels of common hogweed, bone stock, beetroots, cabbage, carrots, onions, potatoes, and tomatoes), (2) knish (mashed potatoes, ground beef, onions, and cheese filled inside thick dough pastry and deep-fried or baked), (3) sweet-and-sour cabbage cooked in red wine vinegar, applesauce, butter, onions, diced apples, sugar, with bay leaves and cloves added on top, and (4) finally, a dessert called blini, a thin crepe-like pancake made from unleavened dough, filled with minced apples and powdered sugar—a delicious meal. We were overwhelmed by the meal's preparation and extent, considering they had little or no money to support themselves.

Looking around the room, I noticed bookshelves lining most of the walls. There were no books on the shelves but instead rationed goods. The mother explained, "If the ration slip were for sugar this month, we would get all the sugar we could afford because you may never see it again." The same was true for all the other staples one uses to cook and eat. As we ate and talked through the evening, it became apparent how much Christen's Russian mama and two teenage children cared about him. I felt this by how they spoke with him and occasionally would affectionately reach over and touch his arm or shoulder—as a family does. As Don, Christen, and I left, waving goodbye that night, we talked about our gratitude for this beautiful family and how they gave so much and had so little.

Invitation to Dinner at Another Russian's Home

The following evening, Christen, Don, and I went to Yuri Synakov's home for dinner. In 1988 I met Yuri when I entertained him and three other Russians visiting the US on a People-to-People program. While he had been in the US, I had invited Yuri and his three Russian friends for dinner and drinks at Christen and my home in Dana Point, California. At that time, Yuri worked as a television producer for Yeltsin.

Now, arriving at Yuri's address in Moscow, we paid the taxi driver and looked at the dozens of tall, look-alike, whitewashed apartment buildings. Yuri lived on the third floor of one of these buildings. After a ride in a sketchy elevator to the third floor, we found Yuri's apartment number and rang the doorbell. We could hear Yuri say he would be out to get us. Then the strangest realization was that there were three steel doors we had to go through to get to his apartment's main entrance, each of which Yuri bolted behind us.

We were excited to see Yuri again and meet his wife, Anna. She served a fantastic five-course meal. Yuri could not understand why I was not drinking because we drank a lot when he visited us in Southern California. I did not want to offend him and his wife by not accepting a drink. I told them I was an alcoholic and had to stop drinking if I wanted to live much longer. He did not believe that I was an alcoholic. Young people in Russia begin drinking vodka early, just as people in France drink wine. Don took some polite sips of what appeared to be vodka. Later, Don said it was sour and so intense that it felt like the alcohol had removed the enamel from his teeth.

We had a wonderful evening, and as we were about to leave, Anna and Yuri presented me with a gorgeous amber necklace. It never crossed my mind what the value of this gift might be, but rather how kind it was for them to do that. It was their way of thanking me for the fantastic time I had shown Yuri and his friends during their recent visit to the US.

I must say that the amber necklace has caused me a few challenges. When we went through customs leaving Russia, they searched our baggage. I did not claim the amber necklace, as it was a gift.

I thought I only needed to declare "my purchases." I was held in a private room at customs, where I was then body searched by two large female Russian attendants. I had no idea what was going to happen next. Finally, I was released with a fine that I paid of around $189 US.

The Amber Necklace

A few years after my trip to Russia, I wanted to apply for the TSA/ Global Entry pass as I planned to travel to other countries. This pass allows one to access customs and security check-in points more easily at crowded airline terminals. I drove to a location where I could have the required in-person interview to obtain my TSA/ Global Entry System approval. The man interviewing me had my application. I was seated across from him as he entered something into his computer. Then he just sat there staring at his computer for a long time. It seemed like this went on in silence for maybe ten minutes. Then he turned to another man working beside him and asked, "What do you think?" Now, they are both staring at one computer screen.

Finally, I asked, "Is there something I could help you with in my file?" Then he began to interrogate me about my travels. As I had been to twelve countries in the previous ten years, I could not remember the exact dates of each country I visited. Ultimately, the TSA agent said, "Your fine of $189, leaving Moscow, was because you had not claimed a $4,000 necklace.

This TSA program is a trusted traveler identification, and we only want people to have it whom we can trust." I had no idea of the value of that necklace.

I told him about my life, my work, why I visited these countries, why I was given the necklace as a gift, and why they should trust me. The TSA agent finally approved my application. A few weeks later, I received the card in the mail. When I use it, I usually bypass long lines and sometimes a lengthy inspection by TSA security (opening bags and pat downs), especially when going through customs.

After our two very different and beautiful evenings and dinners with Christen's Russian family and Yuri and Anna, Don and I eagerly anticipated joining Christen at the Pushkin State Russian Language Institute. He had spent the past two summers perfecting his prior college study of the Russian language. While in Moscow, he used that visit to learn more about Russian culture, literature, and civilization or took a course in business Russian (communication and correspondence). I was so proud of him. The institute management invited Chris to manage the institute for his second summer, which paid for his travel, tuition, board, and room. He was involved in many tasks, including helping lead the other students and meeting and lining up all Russian businesspeople and politicians speaking to the group.

Christen had invited us to visit the Pushkin Institute for his graduation of the summer's attendees.

We dressed in our best clothes with great anticipation and took a taxi to the institute. We found the designated room and anxiously paced around looking for Christen among a place of excited strangers looking for Christen. Everyone in the room was talking and laughing. We could almost feel their excitement about graduation and the end of their time at the institute. As educators, Don and I knew that the students and teachers had worked hard all summer, and this graduation meant a great deal to all. Then we spotted Christen, who was engaged in conversation with someone. They both were talking animatedly, using lots of hand gestures. He caught our eye and immediately brought his friend over to us. He introduced us to Maxim, one of his instructors. We expressed our pleasure at attending their graduation and meeting Christen's teachers and friends. He kept introducing us to everyone in the room. The instructors and students were from all over the globe. His teachers were pleased to meet us. They and the students had terrific compliments about Christen's efforts at the institute. I was so proud of him.

We all sat down for a light meal, and I had fun getting to know a few of Christen's friends. Then the institute president announced each graduate's name. They walked forward, were given a diploma, and shook the hands of several instructors. The president called Christen's name. I had tears running down my cheeks. I thought my heart would burst. I was so full of love and pride for this remarkable young man.

What an accomplishment—Christen had successfully conquered learning the Russian language. Since learning Russian, he has used his Russian language skills in some of his business dealings.

Don and I laughed as we discovered that the Russian language has ten vowel letters (as in the English language), а, э, ы, у, о, я, е, ё, ю, и . There are six exact sounds and look-alikes (A, E, K, M, O, T). Many other Russian letters are like their English counterparts in appearance or sound. Don and I tried to figure out a few words while wandering about but found it impossible.

The Russian alphabet comes from the Cyrillic alphabet. The Cyrillic alphabet was developed at the Preslav Literary School in the First Bulgarian Empire in the ninth century. Moscow is not like European cities where most people understand English and are happy to assist or communicate with a few words in their language. Not so in Russia.

I asked Christen if he had ever found himself in a difficult situation with people on the streets. He often walked some distance between the institute and other places. He indicated, "One time, in particular, five guys decided to gang up on me looking for rubles. My well- honed years of taking Aikido helped me fend off these guys until others came along to help me out."

Aikido is a Japanese martial art that relies on using energy to control the opponent or throw them away from you. It places great emphasis on motion and the dynamics of movement. When he was a child, about five or six years old, I started him in a self-defense program because I felt everyone should know how to defend themselves. Later, after years of studying Aikido from various dojos, I was thrilled and proud to know that Christen held the high honor of a triple black belt in Aikido, 3 Dan.

He has had great joy in leading groups in the instruction of this martial art and continually learning. The day after the institute's graduation, we met Christen at breakfast for our last time together. Later that day, he would be off for his flight back to the US, and I think he was happy to return home.

I never could stand goodbyes with him, and this one was no different. The days I could spend with him since he graduated from high school became fewer and fewer. I know that is how it is supposed to be as one's children grow up, go away to school, get jobs, get married, and so on. Still, I never liked his goodbyes and do not know how that will ever change. Any time I had with Christen was just a great pleasure for me. When I returned home, I knew that Chris would be around for a short while and then soon back to college. He shook Don's hand, and Christen and I hugged. He is so sweet to me and always gives me such an enormous hug. He said, "How can I ever thank you for all you do for me?"

I said, "You can continue to be the best that you can be. I love you"

With tears running down my cheeks, he gave me another big hug and a kiss on the cheek, said again, "I love you, Mom," and waved goodbye as he left.

One day after Christen left for the US, Don and I walked through Moscow's streets. No one was on the streets other than armed soldiers.

The people seemed nervous and would instantly turn away from our gaze. Walking on the streets and shops in Moscow, we sensed a strange, disquieting feeling. The shops we entered had maybe one or two items on a shelf. Armed soldiers walking everywhere made us feel trepidation that something was about to happen. It was very unsettling. Christen's friends had told us that there was an internal struggle within the government for power. This strife was the apparent cause of the nervousness of the people we saw. That week, hardly anyone was on the streets other than armed soldiers or women and children sitting in the streets begging for rubles.

Russian architecture has a beauty all its own.

Russian Woman and Me

Mother and Child begging for Rubles

The Russian Train

The following day, we headed toward the Moscow railway station, the renovated Pavlensky station, for our journey to Berlin. Amid the Russian people's tremendous poverty, I was shocked as we entered the Moscow railway station. The station was immense, and its beauty was hard to believe. Immediately, we were amazed by the highly sculpted ceilings with gorgeous, enormous chandeliers hanging throughout. The crystals hanging from them sparkled brilliantly. The station was spotlessly clean, despite multiple beggars quietly trying to survive.

A Russian Woman Selling Flowers

We boarded the Russian train around 5:00 p.m., and an elderly woman led us to our first-class car, or private sleeping enclosure called a compartment. She seemed to be in control of our space.

Missing photo of Russian woman Railroad conductor checking my ticket and helping us find our compartment on the train

We wanted a first-class sleeper on this train; otherwise, we would have to share one small nonsleeper compartment with six to eight people. Ours had bunk beds that dropped out from the wall above a bench on each side of the area. They were attached to the wall with a small bracket. The beds seemed small. I opted to sleep on one bench seat below an upper bed. We had so much luggage that it did not fit under the benches. One bench had to hold two of our bags. Watching Don climb up on the bunk above the luggage was interesting. Luckily it held Don's weight as I was sleeping beneath.

Our compartment lady often visited our small space to see if we wanted "tea or tay," which we drank frequently. She would usher us to the correct doors to use for the nearby bathroom and point out how to find the "dining car." The most frightening people approaching us were Russian soldiers in all their army regalia who, with rifles in hand, inspected our passports, luggage, and compartment. They went through this same inspection process not once but three times during our overnight ride to Berlin. They lifted everything not nailed down in our compartment each time they entered. They went through our luggage and always looked at our passports as if they had changed since the last time they inspected them. Even sleeping, they would startle us by banging on the compartment door. The soldiers would motion for Don to crawl down from the top bunk, and then they would go through everything again and again.

Going to the dining car and eating was a unique experience. First, we did not dare leave our compartment in the passenger car unattended by one of us. I decided to be the first one to go to the dining car. Bravely I set out on this new experience, pushing my way through the cumbersome heavy doors of about nine cars from our compartment. I was intimidated by having to jump across the train's moving outside gangway connectors to reach the next car. There was nothing to hang on to between the jostling cars. I just held my breath and did it.

People sat in booths next to the windows on both sides of the narrow dining car. I determined that the very robust woman walking around in the car with a pad and pencil might be the waitress. There appeared to be only one open space in a booth occupied by five others. I motioned to this group of five and asked if I could join them. They said, "Da," and stood up so I could squeeze into one side by the window. When the waitress came to take my order, I just pointed to the items these people had on their plates, and she brought them. I received my bill of ninety US dollars, or around 6,380 Russian rubles, when I finished. I believe they may have "stuck it to me" and I probably paid for the entire group of meals for those who sat in the same booth. I returned to our compartment.

Then, Don left on his dining excursion and only bought an apple.

During the middle of the night ride, the train came to a screeching stop. Then the most bizarre thing occurred that I was not aware would happen.

Separately, railroad workers lifted each car on the train using some hydraulic pump or jack. Then the car would rock, lean, lurch, and seem to fall as each of the wheels on the train was removed and changed. At one point in European and Russian history, the size or gauge of the track was intended to be different in Russia than in Germany. I learned this was an intentional design to stop the rapid troop movement between Germany and Russia. The changing of all of the wheels on the train took about two hours as each of the cars on the train jolted, jerked, and rocked. At one point, I got off the train and walked around on the station platform. Don did not think that was a good idea, as he was sure the train would leave or was possibly hoping it would leave while I was wandering.

After we returned home from Russia, we learned that what caused the unsettled atmosphere on the streets and shops during our visit to Russia was about to occur in the next few months.

Our walk around Moscow felt like we were witnessing the precursor to the decline of the Russian Empire. Gorbachev was still the president of the USSR, and in 1991, he promoted many peaceful international relations. Gorbachev was awarded the Nobel Peace Prize on October 15, 1990, for his excellent leadership and contributions to world development and overall betterment. His policies set the stage for the country's collapse. By trying to reform the ailing communist system, Gorbachev unleashed forces that ultimately destroyed it. However, the way it ended was very abrupt.

Shortly after we returned from Russia, Boris Yeltsin became president of the USSR. He has been given credit for ending the USSR with a flailing Soviet economy; Gorbachev's anti-communist chief rival had entered the scene. Yeltsin, a dynamic former Communist Party member, emphasized radical economic changes. Gorbachev's generals warned him that he should send Yeltsin far away. He responded, "No, it is impossible because now we live in another society. We must be human." That decision Gorbachev lived to regret as a mistake he made in his assessment of Boris Yeltsin. Gorbachev only demoted Yeltsin, who staged a political comeback in 1991 when he ran for president of the Russian Republic, becoming the first popularly elected leader in Russian history. Real power still rested with Gorbachev and the Communist Party. Nevertheless, the attempted coup by Communist hardliners in August 1991 changed everything.

Yeltsin's bravery in facing the coup leaders transformed him into a national leader. Mikhail Gorbachev resigned as president of the Soviet Union on December 25, 1991, not long after our return.

Yeltsin set about dismantling the Communist Party, and all fifteen of the Soviet Union's republics moved to secure their independence.

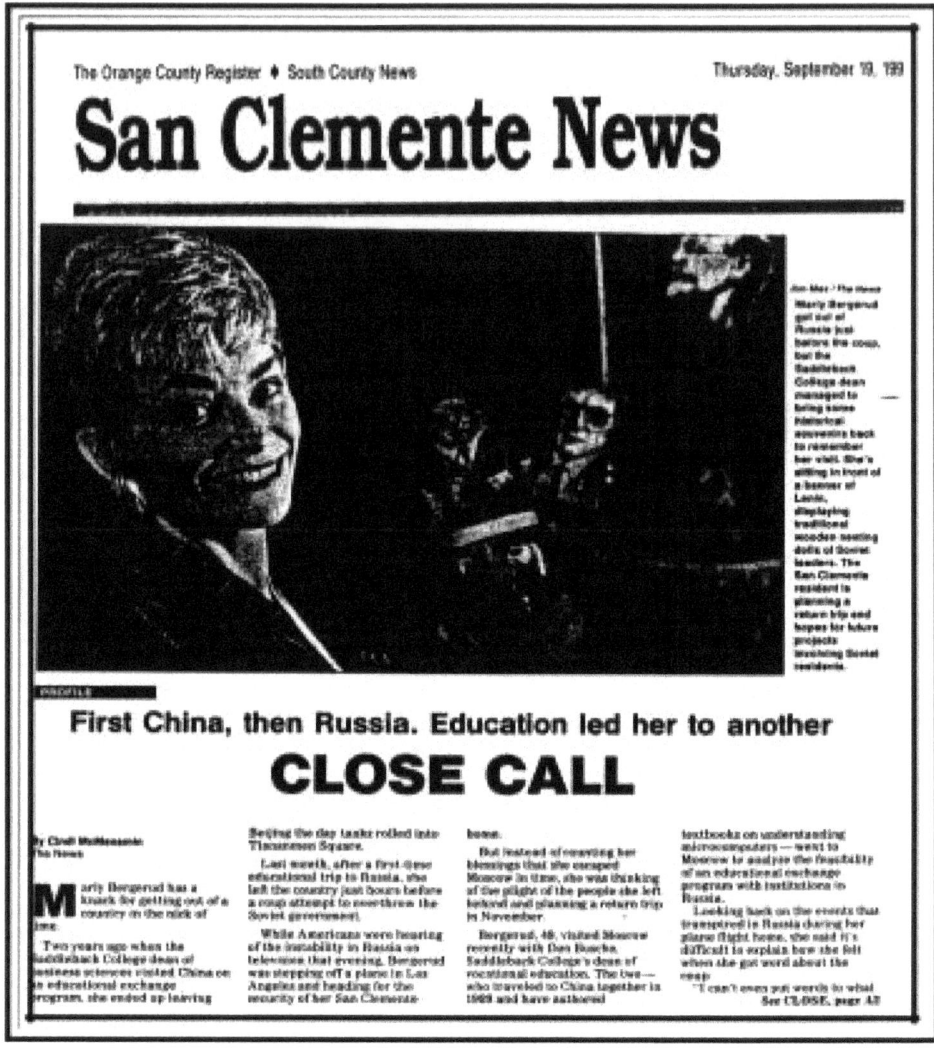

*CLOSE CALL: First China, then Russia.
Education led her to another.*

The recent and continuing war in Ukraine by Russian forces deeply saddens me, especially the destruction of its people and its beautiful cities: Odessa, Kiev, and more.

THE FALL OF GORBACHEV, COMMUNISM, AND THE USSR

The death of any loved parent is an incalculable lasting blow.
Because no one ever loves you again like that.
—Brenda Ueland

The relationship I had with my father affected me in many ways. Child abuse caused emotional blockages still endured. Nevertheless, this father-daughter relationship had a positive and negative impacts. I developed tenacity, strength, perseverance, and resilience, influencing my ability to achieve many things in life. As a strong woman, I have learned to love, forgive, walk away, let go, try again, and persevere, no matter what life throws my way. The most pertinent negative impact was my generational predisposition to alcoholism from my grandfather to my father to me, and in the past twelve years, the devil brought the cancer gene from my mother to me to take its toll.

In 1993, about a month before our father, Winton, died of cancer, he and I were on a walk in Mesa, Arizona, where he and our mother had retired twenty years prior.

He told me, "You need to take care of your mother because she has cancer and a drinking problem."

I responded, "Of course, I will care for her." Then we talked about all the alcoholism in the family. I said, "I, too, had been an alcoholic but quit drinking a few years ago."

He appeared shocked to hear this. I reminded him of that.

Our family: Marly, Sharon, Connie, Florence, and Winnie.

"When my sisters and I were growing up, and I was around twelve, you and Mother had severe drinking problems, resulting in raging physical fights. Your alcoholism and brutal physical rampages caused my mother and me great physical pain. I suffered physically and emotionally when trying to stop your horrific drunken battles with our mother."

He tried to hide the tears running down his cheeks as he listened. I said, "It was in my mid-thirties, during a conversation between you and Helen, when I understood that a significant part of your internal anger originated from your experiences with your alcoholic father, who was physically abusive."

Silently, I believed that in addition to the consequence of child abuse Ernest's children incurred from him, that part of our father's "devil rage" or temper came from nearly being burned alive as a young boy. That is something he never talked about with me. I thought he might have suppressed that incredulous pain and emotion from his excruciating burns at age twelve. His grueling two-year recovery and the limited use of his legs may have caused him psychological and social issues as a young man.

Those horrifying conditions of his youth were no excuse for his behavior as a father. Still, a better understanding of where his rage may have emanated empowered me. It permitted me to release my anger toward him and feelings of "not ever being enough" into an inner strength that helped me survive and become a strong, successful woman.

I told Father, "I am not whimpering about my childhood with you. Instead, I want to let you know I had become an angry alcoholic, like you, for about ten years. However, I did not repeat your abusive treatment of me, as I did not beat Christen. I swore I would never do that to him."

This news appeared to shock him.

Father said with tears in his eyes, "I am so sorry for how terrible I had been to your mother and you. I had no idea how it had affected you ."

I hugged him and said, "I forgive you. I do love you." Thank God for therapy. Thank you, Joe Brady.

At that moment, I felt I could forgive all the men who had broken my heart. Plus, I could not forgive myself for letting them.

I realized I was stronger for it.

A few days later, during this same visit with our parents in Arizona, I sat at a table in their living room and was writing something.

Father said, "Marly, what are you writing?" I answered, "Your obituary." "Oh, great!

Can I help you?"

Well, we started laughing so hard that we were in tears. "Could you have a Shriners' parade for me?" "You have got to be kidding."

"No, I am not. You remember the kind of parade where the Shriners ride on their motorcycles with a sidecar carrying another Shriner? "

My retort was, "I suppose you want a band too?"

"Yes, that would be terrific."

"I am not sure that I could pull that off."

We laughed a lot, but I think he meant it. Then he asked me, "Would you please go down the street and get Digger O'Dell to come to our house?" That was the nickname he gave to his good friend, who used to be an undertaker. Father did have a sense of humor.

Digger O'Dell came over. Father asked, "Would you please take Marly Kay to one of our three local funeral homes and pick out a casket for me?"

"Oh, my God. Are you kidding?"

He was not. Soon, Digger O'Dell and I drove off to visit the three funeral parlors. When we entered a large room filled with open coffins, the reality of our father's imminent demise suddenly struck me. I gasped as we entered this room.

I told my father's friend, "Just put me in that pink satin one over there, close the lid, and let's call it quits."

Shortly after visiting my mother and father at their home in Mesa, they flew to San Francisco to spend time with my sister Connie and her husband, John. Father's prostate cancer worsened, and it had metastasized to other organs. Soon, Connie contacted the hospice organization, which came in to assist him in his final days. Cuts or sores on Father did not seem to heal, and soon he had ghastly-smelling gangrene on his lower right leg. We all took turns trying to clean his leg and keep him comfortable. He knew he was dying.

Our mother did not know what to do. I gave her The Tibetan Book of Death and Dying; she flipped through it without seeing the pages. Soon, Father was on a morphine drip to assist in keeping him comfortable. He was bothered by the oxygen nosepiece, the feeding tube, and the catheter since he had not been able to get out of bed for some time.

While sitting in his room, occasionally, he would twitch and wince in pain. As I sat there, I thought about our painful past. Suddenly, his head seemed to be slipping off the pillow, and I went over to help prop him back up. This movement startled him, and he yelled, "Get me out of here!" Get me out of here!" They are grabbing at me!

I asked, "Who is grabbing you?"

"They are all around me and pulling at me."

"Father, you were a badass quite a bit in this life, so you will just have to fight your way past them, but you can do it." He tried to smile as he knew I was always straight with him.

Soon, he looked at me with his eyes begging to end this painful demise. Suddenly, I could see him as an ordinary young boy on a hot day long ago on the farm. In a moment, his friend dropped a lit cigarette, and he was ablaze, on fire and burning, running, screaming. Again and again, I saw it. For a moment, I knew it all over again. I felt it. I could see it. I heard it. I was in the field with him, running with him, the gasoline smell, my lungs burning, crying, desperately wanting it to stop.

He cried out again, "Stop them!"

I felt the flames eating away at my skin. I tried to get this young boy out of the fire. His clothes burned and burned me, and my mother and all his clothes were burning.

Tears were running down his cheeks on the bed in front of me. Mother was sobbing. I cried. I reached out, and the fire that burned him still burned me and our family. I saw his father before him in the heat of the blaze. He screamed again, "Let me go! Let me go! Let me go!"

I looked at my mother; her face was a bloodless mask. As she began to slip to the floor, Connie and John grabbed her and took her out of the room.

I cried again. "Father, I love you."

"No, I loved you! Stop them! Stop them! Please stop them!

Help me! "

I could see the orange flames as he was burning and hear his screams. Tears ran down my cheeks as I thought of his drunken father beating him. I trembled as I stood there, remembering my mother on the floor in her pretty gown, my father strangling her. As I recalled my mother's screams, my whole body shivered. I saw myself in the room, young and helpless. His face was enraged. Yet I knew I would miss this man who, at times, was very generous, often a hilarious man, who at parties would put on his friends' hats, scrunch them, and possibly get on the floor "listening to hear if the Indians might be coming" while telling great stories and making people laugh.

Long ago, I knew that my inner strength and success were due to his pounding into my head, "You can do anything if you work hard enough!" He was a self-made man, and I exemplified his work ethic. I had spent a lifetime trying to please him, and the love-hate relationship was ending.

I stood next to him as he cried out again, and I looked at the drip of the morphine.

My mother,Connie, and John came in.

He opened his eyes. I looked at him.

He nodded.

It was easy now, relaxed as another drink of whiskey.

I love you, Father. Finally, he could never hit me again.

He cried out again, and a doctor turned up the drip, and in one last scream, he said, "Help me!" We did, and the flames burned out.

As the monitor flatlined, I looked at him. It was as if, at long last, peace and calm came over his face—almost a smile as if he was about to tell a joke. I felt I could see his soul soar. Finally, it had ended—this great love-hate relationship. He had suffered such incredible pain in his life.

We had a memorial service for our father, Winton, and all three of his daughters, Sharon, Connie, and I spoke at the service. Our sweet mother, Florence, agreed to everything we planned for this service. His sister, Helen Rose, came from Palm Springs, as did Christen. Mother seemed to go through the motions, always attending to everyone else's needs, seemingly lost about what she would do without her mate of nearly seventy years.

When our parents owned the clothing store for nearly sixty years, our mother lived under constant work demands placed on her by our father. She dealt with his alcoholic abuse. They retired during the last fifteen years of their lives, and at age sixty-five, our mother took up the game of golf. Father used to laugh and say she used to cook; now, she goes to play golf. Our father dominated her for all those years, and she finally found an escape. She loved him, but she loved golf.

The year following our father's death, Florence, our mother, was beginning to shine.

Florence, Age 80

She spent about three months visiting each of her three daughters, Sharon, Connie, and me. When she stayed with Joe and me in San Clemente for those summer months, it was a miserably hot summer in the high 90s and low 100s. Her visit would have been good, but we did not have air conditioning, as the temperature is usually in the mid-70s. We bought a big metal tub, filled it with a few large ice blocks, and the temperature was bearable with a fan blowing at high speed across it.

One memorable evening with my mother was when I surprised her with tickets to the Segerstrom Center for the Arts in Costa Mesa, row 4, middle orchestra seats, to see Phantom of the Opera. She was thrilled to go out to dinner and then to the theater, a great night out for her, as Mom and Dad never attended the theater during their retirement. Toward the end of the play, there is a scene where the six-hundred-plus-pound stage chandelier drops several feet.

When that occurred, it seemed like it stopped falling directly above us. We both let out a muffled scream at that point. It was fantastic to enjoy these special moments with my mother.

After spending one month with each of her daughters, she was happy. She died shortly after visiting each of us. Our father always required her to tend to his needs when he was alive. I was heartbroken not to have had more quality time with just her after our father died.

A CRITICAL AMEND (1993–2003)

I have learned about forgiveness, and I have reached out to family and friends to make amends.
—Marly Bergerud

Most parents probably wonder what kind of relationship they would have with their children as adults. I was no exception. Toward the end of this traumatic time living with Joe, my internal radar had elicited some feelings about my times with Christen that I needed to resolve. They were those gut-level thoughts parents often get when their children have gone to college or moved away from home.

At one and a half, Christen had endured my leaving his father and then Donald years later. Donald was in our lives for most of Christen's growing-up years. He was seventeen when I became sober, so I was always concerned about the impact it may have had on him. As a result, during the past fifteen-plus years of my sobriety, I have, on occasion, asked Christen about how my drinking affected him when growing up. He always said that my drinking did not impact him. But I thought it must have. How could it not?

I did not physically abuse him, thank God, but I yelled a lot—which, to a sensitive person, can be as bad as physical abuse. I always felt underlying guilt that my drinking had negatively hurt him. However, he continually denied it and told me not to worry.

After graduating from college in 1993 and moving with friends to New York, Christen seemed to love his work and new social life. His occasional contact indicated he was excited about the companies he was dealing with through his work. He loved all that New York offered. At one point, he invited me to join him at a friend's home in New York for Thanksgiving dinner, which I quickly accepted and enjoyed immensely.

However, even before Christen graduated from college, he was beginning to open some distance between us, which I felt was normal for him as a young adult and out on his own. We had a wonderful visit in Russia, but that was the last of our real closeness for a long time. It was enough distance that I was pleased that he supported me by attending both of my parents' funerals in late 1993 and 1994. Nevertheless, there was already something happening between us that did not feel right.

I was sober by then, and Christen was the most important person in my life. But I felt a schism open between us that I had no way of understanding.

Soon after my parents' funerals, it became painfully apparent to me that he wanted or needed to disengage entirely.

I had no idea when this disengagement began that our separation would last a long, painful ten years.

It was not the kind of detachment that all parents have when their child leaves home for the first time. That had occurred when he went to college. I kept rationalizing this new, more profound distance as his need to assert more independence.

However, it was not that.

He needed to distance himself from me completely. I had no choice in it. During this time, I would call him, leave messages that I loved him, and hoped all was going well. Occasionally, we would talk. I internalized and felt sure that this must have to do with my drinking's impact on him during childhood. I always thought that we had such a close relationship. I found this estrangement intolerable. My life went on. I was preoccupied with Joe, my friends, my sisters, and my work.

But underneath it all, I was grieving for my son as if he had been lost.

Then, around 2001, during a typical holiday gathering in Northern California, which we always spent with my sister Connie and her husband, John, their children, Jonathan and Brian, and others, I noticed something entirely different in Christen's interactions with me. He was now thirty, and I had not been an active participant in his life for the past ten-plus years, other than for a family holiday or graduation. In this holiday get-together, it seemed our interactions were stiff. Sometimes I felt he was rude to me and that his responses were inappropriate and hurtful, but I did not react.

I could not understand why he spoke to me in mean, angry tones. At one point, he said in an angry voice something about "abandonment." I immediately responded that I could not control what his father did or did not do. Little did I know that his abandonment issues were from me.

During this time, when we saw little of each other, he had never been actively hostile toward me, only seemingly distant.

Over the next few months, I let my feelings about this interaction settle down; but I felt there must be something brewing deep within him, causing him to act out in this way. Finally, I decided I would make a serious attempt to understand what was happening between us. I called him and left a message. I asked him if he could pick some weekends when he would be available so I could come back East to see him. Soon, he returned my call, and we decided on a date.

I arrived in New York late on a Friday afternoon, and Christen picked me up at New York's LaGuardia Airport.

I was incredibly excited to see him. His broad smile indicated he appeared happy to see me too. Christen always greeted me with an affectionate hug and a kiss. His sparkling blue eyes stood out against his blue plaid shirt and jeans. We drove into Manhattan, where he lived in a small apartment overlooking New York Harbor and the magnificent Statue of Liberty on Ellis Island. Surrounding his apartment were green grassy knolls and beautiful granite benches, a ten-minute walk to those magnificent structures and to buy my half-price theater tickets for that day's performance.

The following day, we woke up to a beautiful day. It was exhilarating to look out and see the Statue of Liberty. We decided to take a walk. Soon, we sat on one of the benches near the Twin Towers.

At different times, I had asked him what was most challenging about growing up when I was drinking. Previously, he had always said there were no problems; do not worry about it! This time, it was a different conversation. My sensitive, gentle son and I had a heart- wrenching conversation.

 I felt that my relationship was on the line with him. With great difficulty, I began, "I wanted to see you as I would like to understand a few things I have observed when we have been with each other recently. During the past couple of visits with our family, you have seemed particularly angry with me."

Now, I am trying hard to control my emotions. My voice was a little unstable. "I am your only mother, and my actions warrant. I do not feel I deserve the way you have talked to me. What is happening, or can you tell me what you are feeling?"

When he began to talk, his lips began quivering; and with tears in his eyes, he said, "When I was about five years old, I could hear you yelling at Don and believed that since you had left my father, it sounded like you were going to leave Don, and I knew you would eventually leave me too. I decided then that you could not have it both ways, saying I love you one minute and then leave me the next."

Now, I was sobbing. This is unbelievable! I was the one who created abandonment issues for that precious little child to trust a mother's love, which embedded in him unresolved anger and distrust of me. It was not about his father, which I thought when he had yelled something at me in that prior angry conversation that had brought me to New York. It was about my abandoning him. At that moment, I could not describe my gut-wrenching feelings of devastation. I cried; he cried.

I asked him, "I hope you can please forgive me. Thank you for telling me." I added, "I hope you can get to know me as a sober, loving, compassionate mother." We hugged with tears streaming down our cheeks.

Christen has been nothing but an incredible, generous and loving son. Occasionally, he needs to discuss events from his early years that have contributed to various emotional challenges. Sometimes this has been very difficult for me to hear, but I listen, try to understand, and ask for forgiveness.

A DRAMATIC CHANGE
FOR ME (2000)

It is confidence in our bodies, minds, and spirits that allows us to keep looking for new adventures, new directions to grow in, and new lessons to learn, which is what life is all about. —**Oprah Winfrey**

One summer, the Saddleback College term had just gotten underway. My friend Don told me of a college administrator position opening that might interest me. It was as a vice president of De Anza College in Northern California. I quickly read up on it and discovered that it was a great opportunity; at least, I thought so at the time. I applied for the position. The week I submitted my application to De Anza College, I went on a long-planned ten-day trip with three of the six Good Ole Girls.

Cruising with Good Ole Girls (2000)

This vacation was my first cruise. It began in Venice, Italy, visiting the Piazza San Marco, riding through canals in a gondola, and marveling at this city in the water and its seemingly endless bridges over the canals. We stopped in Dubrovnik along the Adriatic Sea for a short tour. I was unfamiliar with how much the Croatian War of Independence had ravaged this city. However, the bullet holes in the building walls were still evident. Another stop for a few hours was in Corfu, Greece, a unique Greek island with whitewashed houses and many churches. I told my friends, "Let's get off the ship, rent a jeep, and tour the city in the hills."

The Good Ole Girls

Off we went, with me driving an open-air, stick-shift jeep. It was wonderful. After what they called a dangerous ride up the winding road, we arrived at a small village in the mountains. It was just as you might see in a travelogue about Greece. The local men were dressed in sleeveless white T-shirts, gathered around a table outside a bar, drinking ouzo and talking. The women were picturesque, with their bandanas wrapping their hair and aprons covering their skirts as they swept the cobblestone streets with a large handmade broom. We meandered through the curving streets and took in the sights.

From Corfu, Greece, the ship cruised around the "boot of Italy," visiting ports on the west coast of Italy—Portofino, Livorno, Monaco, and Nice, and a little village, Martigues, on the southern coast of France. In this picturesque small village, I wanted to go off on my own because each stop with four women, who all wanted to shop or try on everything they saw, was not what I wanted to do. So off they went one way and I, another. Soon, it was time to head down the mountain back to the ship. I went to the location where we had decided to meet. The Good Ole Girls were not there. I stood there for some time, afraid to stray from sight. Pretty soon, my three buddies came storming up the street, simultaneously yelling at me. As it turned out, I was at the wrong corner. They had waited until it was time to board the bus to return to the ship. When I did not return to the bus, all three got off the bus and said they were not leaving without me. They were happy to see me but furious that I caused the scare. The bus had returned to the ship, and the next task was that we had to find a taxi in this tiny village. No shops were open on Sunday, and the streets were quite deserted. Joycee went off alone to try to solve this dilemma while we sat and prayed for her success.

The other two were not in a good mood and preferred not to talk to me. Soon, a cab arrived. We barely got back to the ship before it was time to depart. When the taxi stopped at the ship's loading dock, my three dear friends got out of the cab and said, in somewhat miffed disdain, "You handle this." It was a $60 ride down the mountain.

Once aboard, the ship soon turned around and went south to Rome. After visiting these ports on the Adriatic, it was time to leave for Los Angeles. I have beautiful memories of being with three of the six Good Ole Girls.

I returned home after this splendid trip with my good friends. I had a message on my answering machine to call the De Anza College District's personnel office.

The personnel director indicated that I was a finalist for an interview in two weeks for the Vice President position for which I had applied before I left on my trip. I was so excited to hear this. I read all that I could about economic development in the region. My job would be working with other colleges in the area and many industry partners in Silicon Valley. I was thrilled. Emotionally, I was torn as I had lived most of my adult life in Southern California, raised my son, and owned my home. That was where all my close friends resided. I thought, why not interview? What can I lose? Either I get the job, or I do not.

On a beautiful, sunny September day, I flew to San Jose, rented a car, and drove to the college. I vividly remember the drive.

As the trees began turning their beautiful autumn colors, as I drove to their campus, my stomach churned with anticipation, like I had felt before going on stage to perform one of my clickety-clack tap dance routines.

I arrived at De Anza College and parked. I wanted to be at least an hour early. Walking through this large campus, I heard many languages and found it quite refreshing. Silicon Valley is extremely ethnically diverse. The college where I was a dean in Orange County was, at that time, composed chiefly of English-speaking Caucasian students.

Soon, I located the building where I was to interview and sat outside the conference room. I waited, nervously fidgeting with my presentation materials. I felt confident that I had dressed the part for this interview. My blonde hair was perfectly coiffed and set off by my navy-blue suit with a starched white pointed-collar blouse. My earrings were small silver hoops, not flashy, and I wore flesh-colored nylons and three-inch narrow navy heels. Confident in my outfit, I needed to wow them with my knowledge and expertise. After over thirty years in the field, I also felt relatively optimistic. That was about to be challenged, and not in a small way.

The conference room door opened within ten minutes, and I went inside. At that moment, my stomach lurched. I was about to dance before a large and hostile crowd. Inside the room, there was a team of twenty-one members who would ask me questions individually. Each member did a self-introduction with a brief explanation of their position at the college. Then my dance began.

I was ready. My steps were timed and perfect. I put into action all my skills in performing except without tap shoes or a sequined costume. The eye contact of the committee members showed interest, and their nods indicated acceptance. It felt like my presentation was just what they wanted. Previously, I had rehearsed the fifteen-minute presentation several times to keep the timing exact. It consisted of my vision for establishing a high-tech center on campus in collaboration with the surrounding colleges, universities, and industry partners.

The committee members seemed impressed with my answers. I noted their recognition of the twenty-five textbooks I had published. After their questions, I was escorted out of the room and told that they would contact me after they finished their interviews in the next two weeks. I was pleased. The group interview for this new position felt like a beautifully executed dance.

As I was in Northern California for the interview, I spent the weekend with my sister Connie and her husband, John, who lived nearby in Aptos.

I will never forget that weekend because of the unbelievable tragedy of 9/11 occurred. We were sickened at what was unfolding before our eyes.

I was terrified because the most immediate, critical issue was that I could not contact Christen. Since completing college, he has worked in downtown Manhattan near the Twin Towers. I remember he had told me that that day he was meeting a colleague coming into the city.

While trying to grasp the unbelievable reality of what happened in our country, Connie, John, and I needed to escape the television. We had been watching the horror of 9/11 for hours. We decided to get out of the house and drive to take our minds off what had just happened in New York or possibly look at potential apartments for me.

We drove around feeling as if in a semiconscious state about what had just happened. The apartments we looked at in several nearby cities, all surrounding the college, were costly. The demand for living space in Silicon Valley was high, and there were few available apartments.

Later that evening, Christen called me, and I cried with relief. He told an incredible story of being near the towers and meeting a work colleague. At first, they thought a plane had accidentally hit the tower and started walking rapidly to escape the area because debris was falling from the tower. Then immediately, they heard the second plane coming in. They began running as it was about to hit the second tower. They ran as fast as they could from the area for blocks, and blocks with debris pouring down and spewing everywhere. Finally, they caught a train to get out of the city and to Christen's home. He said everyone on the train was covered with debris and dust, staring quietly into space, trying to grasp what had happened.

A couple of weeks after my interview, I received a call from the president of De Anza College, offering me the position. I was thrilled—not only about this new position but also about a move to Northern California.

This position in community college education was considered a "step-up, "moving from dean to vice president, even though my salary would be less than my current position. Nevertheless, I thought it was the right move. In October 2000 I accepted a new job as vice president of workforce and economic development in Northern California at De Anza College.

Immediately, I sold my home in San Clemente, packed everything, and moved to a small town near the college. I was afraid to rent my current home as I had never done that before. Selling it seemed to be the right thing to do. My excitement for this move was palpable.

When I moved to Northern California for this job, I knew only three people: one girlfriend, Leslie Larrabee, and my sister Connie and John, who lived forty-five minutes away. My sister's home was "over the hill," as they called Highway 17, between San Jose and Santa Cruz. Leslie was in a different direction from my sister and was located about the same distance from me as where they are.

I was happy she lived nearby, as I did not feel I should mingle socially with people from the workplace, not for the first year or two. Leslie lived in a little town called Dublin. I had met her years before at an education conference when she was an administrator at a college.

Leslie Larrabee

Twice a week, Leslie would drive down to where I lived in Campbell to attend Pilates classes with me. Pilates lessons were great for strengthening my core and multiple body areas for my starting ballroom dancing. My knees were not loving Pilates exercises, but I needed these lessons as I still wanted to start taking some ballroom dancing lessons.

Finally, I decided to do one meaningful thing for myself on this "stint" in Northern California, where I knew very few people other than at work. I enrolled at the Fred Astaire Dance Studio to take ballroom dancing lessons.

The lessons were not until 9:00 p.m. A couple of nights each week, I worked until five or six every day. This time slot made it challenging to get excited at night to go dancing when, instead, I was ready to get into my pajamas and enjoy a good book.

I took ballroom lessons for three years. My instructor, Kim, was my dance partner, and we competed in local competitions, dancing one or more special routines: the rumba and the waltz.

This type of dance was entirely new for me, and in practice, I realized that I was using back and leg muscles that had not been fully utilized for many years. This reboot required working hard to rebuild my physical strength. Kim asked one female instructor to show me how to "swivel my hips," making a figure-eight shape to understand a rumba dance movement. My prior hardcore tap dancing did not require the body movements used in either of these ballroom dance routines. Below, performing with Kim in a competition: on the waltz, and right is the rumba.

Both routines were sometimes challenging, as each required body movements that were entirely new for me. However, it was great fun and required much practice.

I grew to love ballroom dancing and performing, but my arthritic knees were starting to give out. I had tortured my knees all those years: tap dancing, sliding on them across the stage floor, waterskiing, and water ski jumping. They now turned on me and were taking revenge.

My Position—A Commitment to Trying Something New

I was one of four vice presidents who reported to the president. I was on the management team, or so they said. The first day on the job coincided with a De Anza College gala that same evening. My sister Connie and her husband, John, accompanied me to this lavish affair. As a new hire at De Anza, we were a late add-on to this huge evening event and were placed at a table by ourselves on the edge of a vast, very packed ballroom. The rest of the management team was at a table with Chihuly, the famous glass-blowing artist. Honestly, I recognized that someone had made seating arrangements for this event far in advance; the president's table of senior managers was full, and there was no room for us. Irrespective, we felt they could have moved a few people around to at least have us closer to the management team's table. I thought sadly, "I hope this is not what is to come."

Unfortunately, my treatment that night was just a taste of what would occur. I had taken a pay cut for this new management position and was thrilled to be there.

In retrospect, over time, I felt I was possibly filling a temporary "ding" the college may have received on a recent accreditation report for not doing enough in the workforce and economic development arena. Perhaps they hired me to clear up that "ding" to keep their accreditation status, but not because they genuinely supported workforce and economic development.

Nothing about the job felt right from that first night at the gala. This move of mine to Northern California was extremely unfortunate for me. Professionally. I have always been treated with great respect. In eighteen years, I achieved an incredible reputation as the dean of business in my previous college position.

My former president used to refer to me as her "dream dean." She respected me for all I had done for Saddleback, its teachers, students, and programs. Plus, she appreciated my publications' recognition, consistently bringing in visitors from across the globe.

I soon began to regret the sale of my house in San Clemente.

Being in Silicon Valley from 2001–2004 was a stimulating environment in which to live. There was an undercurrent of excitement in the local news and business chatter in restaurants. Everyone seemed to be "making deals" with some aspect of new technologies. I found this part of my new surroundings to be exhilarating.

I joined a few organizations within the business community. I began trying to make inroads into how to make a difference for my new college. I connected with some brilliant people at Carnegie Mellon West (CMU-West). I began collaborating with them to build a high-tech center near their NASA Ames Research Center site in Moffett Field. CMU-West was working on creating a focus on project-centered learning with various new approaches to education. Great! This engagement with NASA Ames and Workforce Development is what I felt De Anza needed and what I was hired to do.

I was fortunate to review Carnegie Mellon's excellent summer high school robotics program. Their program evolved into an Office of Robotics Education to help educators, students, and parents interested in robotics get connected. Specifically, it promoted the ideas I had presented in my interview about developing a high-tech center for education. I proposed the creation of a center that would provide high-end technologies no school could afford independently.

Instead, this center would be a location where all school children from K-12 could use high-end technologies, expanding on the concept like the Tech Museum in San Jose but using the ingenuity of NASA and Carnegie Mellon West. It would allow students to use technology such as virtual and augmented reality to assist in moving students into STEAM internships in the surrounding business and industrial environments (Science, Technology, Engineering, the Arts, and Mathematics).

Moving to Northern California, in many ways, had been an exciting change for me. However, after three and a half years in what should have been an excellent position at the college, I sensed I could not make any headway with what I felt was my job. I did not believe I received the support from management that my position needed to be most effective. Previously, as a dean in senior management, I threw my soul into supporting those who worked with me. This job and its support did not feel right—I felt like I was waiting for the other shoe to drop.

Sure enough, in May 2003, before the legal May 15 cutoff date when educational institutions needed to "let go of employees," my boss, the President, called me in and said I was just "not a good fit for the position." Flabbergasted does not even begin to explain how I felt. What the hell just happened? I could not figure it out. I asked her if I could spend the weekend thinking about my written response. I was mortified.

The following Monday, I talked with the President again. She agreed that she would tell the Board of Trustees that I had decided to retire. I contacted my retirement system office and came up with a date that would be most beneficial for me financially from my thirty-eight successful years in education— January 4, 2004. That meant, devastated as I was, I had to smile and be happy on the job for the next eight months with my peers, the other three vice presidents who knew I would soon leave and why. Seriously, I could not figure out what had happened. Emotionally, I was devastated.

Eight months later, the President took me out for a Christmas "goodbye lunch." There, she told me that the three managers who reported to me had misled her about tales of my performance. In reality, these managers had never been responsible for reporting to a line management person before being assigned to me. For many years, they had managed their areas however they felt like doing. They preferred not to have their performance or budgets reviewed. Therefore, it is unclear what was said about me; they achieved their goals regardless. Hearing this revelation from the President was a little late and no consolation. My dream job was a bust. As a lifetime professional, dedicated, hardworking career educator, this was the worst professional defeat I have ever felt: me—the "dream dean." Even now, I shake my head, still in deep emotional pain when I think about it. I had never experienced a defeat in any aspect of my professional life - until now.

Now, I needed to figure out where I wanted to live and decided to move back to Southern California. However, during this move, I felt the desert calling. I moved to Palm Desert, about one and a half hours from Orange County, where I had spent most of my adult life and where my good friends of forty-five years still live. Today, Palm Desert is a busy city in the Coachella Valley's educational, retail, and cultural hub, one of Coachella Valley's nine cities. It is one of the most desirable places to live in California.

The next bombshell soon hit me. Just before my move back to Southern California, a good friend, Mike, a great guy I had been dating, shocked me by saying, "I think your memory is going fast." I remember him angrily saying, "You know you have asked me that five times. I do not know if you are into early dementia, have Alzheimer's, or do not give a shit, but you are irritating me."

I was astonished when he said that to me. I started to cry. I was horrified. I heard the words but did not know what to do about it. Seriously, I had no clue. I felt sad, distraught that he would say that to me.

I asked my sister, Connie, if she had noticed that I had a memory issue. She said, "Yes, I have noticed that you sometimes repeat yourself about certain things." Was I into early dementia or something worse? I was anxious to get settled into my new home and see a doctor about this issue.

I was sixty-four years old at this stage of life and had never had to deal with advancing age issues. In fact, up to this point, I never thought much about aging at all. This news about my "memory" was a wake-up call.

When I was in my thirties, life seemed perfect—a new baby at twenty-nine, a great job in education, writing and publishing textbooks, super physical condition—who thinks of aging?

In my forties, the world was my oyster, and one might say, a new marriage, a great son, and a fantastic job as a college dean. In my fifties, I began traveling with friends Don, Angela, and Maureen to places around the world that I had always wanted to visit: China, the USSR, Africa, Australia, South America, India, and Japan.

I have a fantastic son and twenty-five successfully published books. I must say that, except for my two failed marriages and all that goes with that, I have had a spectacular life. Who thinks about aging?

Now, I am encountering the horrible possibility of dementia or Alzheimer's! I do not know what to do. I felt overwhelmed. First, I needed to concentrate on my move to the desert.

Next, I have to prepare for my upcoming trip to Africa with my friend Don and his daughter Tiffany. Maybe my memory issues were caused by being stressed about leaving the VP job and returning to Southern California. Based on what my friends and family have said, I do not know whether my remembering is severe or just a temporary blip on the radar.

In the summer of 2005, once again, I packed up my life and moved back to Southern California and into my new home in Palm Desert, where escrow had just closed. Then I quickly packed and was ready to go on a safari with my writing buddy, Don, and his daughter, Tiffany.

WANDERLUST IS PART OF ME: AFRICA (2005)

Travel isn't always pretty. It isn't always comfortable. Sometimes it hurts; it even breaks your heart. But that's okay. The journey changes you;
it should change you.
—Anthony Bourdain

Within days after I moved into my home in Palm Desert, my friend, coauthor, and traveling buddy Don, his daughter Tiffany, and I went on our trip to Africa.

African Baobab Tree

Flying between African Countries

I conjured up two types of images when I thought about Africa. One image is what I have seen on television, and it represents war, famine, poverty, pestilence, and peril—or the other is the "good" Africa: safaris, colorful tribes, mostly what I have seen or read in National Geographic.

On this sixteen-day trip, a group of sixteen of us and our guide visited countries within southern Africa (Botswana, Zimbabwe, Namibia, and South Africa). This part of Africa's continent is often called the Rainbow Nation to describe the country's newly developing multicultural diversity in the wake of segregationist apartheid ideology. In talking with Africans along the way, I was shocked as I began to assimilate and understand the conditions that the beautiful people of this country have spent a lifetime enduring.

Africa had a significant impact on me. I will always cherish seeing the big five game animals: the lion, leopard, rhinoceros, elephant, and Cape buffalo.

Elephant Herd Approaches Our Jeep.

The beauty of these animals living free and roaming was thrilling to see. However, what I found to be most valuable was meeting the children and people of this country.

Before taking this trip, I thought hippopotamuses were just giant, piglike animals with cute little round ears. I was looking forward to our ride down the river on a pontoon boat. Once we boarded the river pontoon boat, it became surrounded by about twenty or more hippos, often called a bloat.

A Bloat of Rhinoceros

Immediately, our guide whispered, telling us to "move to the center of the raft slowly, and do not talk or make any quick movements." Suddenly, I learned that hippos are aggressive and considered very dangerous. In about twenty minutes, we disembarked the pontoon at a village down the river. Only then did our guide tell us how hippos could take down a pontoon boat with one or two swift chomps of their massive jaws. They weigh about six thousand pounds and can run over nineteen miles per hour on land and five mph in water. These gigantic creatures were not something I ever wanted to encounter.

I was deeply touched by the native people I met in Africa. It truly pained me to witness firsthand the way of life for many people in this country.

I felt their innate desire to rise from under their living conditions.
At one point during the trip, we visited a school.

Grades 1-12 Meet in One Classroom

We observed and talked with many children in the school, particularly those in a first-grade classroom. They were clean and beautifully dressed, and most did not have shoes. They sat on a dirt floor and only had a little handheld chalkboard and chalk for something to write on. The teacher had one textbook per grade level — the children had none.

The children and their schools received funds for providing tours for people like us. The teachers and children seemed excited to meet us and were well- prepared to speak with us. One beautiful little girl wore a pink organza dress and spoke perfect English. She told me she wanted to become a teacher. She walked four miles to school each day in her bare feet. The children received a pint of milk for lunch, which might be their only daily nutrition. The tour agencies have an impact on the lives of these villages in positive and negative ways. The villagers had learned to put on a show for the various tour groups, and their pay from the tour agencies assisted them in many ways.

We were outside in their play area during the children's recess. They all wanted their pictures taken and asked us to send them back through our guide so they could put them on their dirt walls at home. Despite their poverty, the children were well-dressed, good- looking Black children and seemed happy.

Marly and one of the boys in their schoolyard during recess.

A seventeen-year-old African boy in one village had an opposite reaction to our presence. He told me he was miserable living there as he had seen tourists like us who would visit his village.

A Typical Looking Village, Botswana, Africa.

He had talked with the many visitors about the cities where they lived and worked. These interactions had given him the incentive to get out. He yearned for life elsewhere. He said with tears in his eyes that he had learned so much about the world by meeting visitors like me. As a result, he now felt trapped in the poverty of this little village.

The African children and families we visited on our tours were good-looking, friendly, and wanted to talk with all of us. Throughout our visits with the many African individuals, I felt this gnawing internal pain as my father's bigotry floated through my mind. Those thoughts made me sad. I realized the dichotomy of thinking between my father and me was so different on numerous issues. His racism was genuine. I could not understand its origin.

His negative feelings about Africans or Black people may have come from his deep commitment to two organizations: the Masons and the Shriners (the Masonic society established in 1870) and their original history of being racist.

Don and I were the only two educators traveling in our group of tourists. Our guide had allowed us to linger for some time, talking with the children and their teacher. We returned to our busload of travelers and asked them to please donate some money so Don and I could buy the children's books in the local village. We spoke with the school's headmaster and asked him what they needed for their classrooms. From our tourmates, we collected a few hundred dollars. Then our guide, Don, and I drove our van into a nearby town and bought the teachers many books. The students and teachers were thrilled with their books, and we felt fulfilled, as we had at least done one little thing for them.

Marly is on safari, waiting for lunch to be set out.

On this tour in Africa, we also visited a family home in another village. The family seemed proud to show us their home, but it was on a "tour show." It was a domed hut with thick walls made from mud, hay, and sticks. Seat-like benches along the walls became their beds. They prepared their food in one large pot that sat over a fire in a deep hole in the ground or burned kindling in the same pit to keep them warm. Large sticks and mud framed the entrance to the hut. Outside was a wooden door that they laid over the opening to keep out the weather. The women used blankets to wrap their babies and carry them on their backs. We noticed one mother walking barefoot with a baby on her back, balancing a massive pot of water on her head.

Astonishing. She brought water back from the water hole a mile from the village. I learned about the tremendous survival skills the people of these villages developed and their sustainable living environments.

At one of our lodges, Don, Tiffany, and I attended the usual "sundowner" where the guests have a drink and visit with each other about the day's events while watching the animals come to their drinking hole. On this day, my tour mates greeted me with a Happy Birthday song and a chocolate-covered birthday cake from the guests and staff at our camp. There was no flour available, so my instructions were to cut the cake, but it would be more complicated than cakes I might have been used to cutting. With my very sharp knife, I began cutting, or maybe you would say, sawing into this round cake. Soon it became evident that it was NOT a cake but a joke, a chocolate-covered elephant dung.

The guests and I laughed at that and were then provided with another tasty birthday dessert.

Marly Celebrating her Birthday

After visiting these two villages in South Africa, I was soon to experience one of the most meaningful moments in my life. We visited Robben Island and walked around inside the initial prison cell and solitary confinement of Nelson Mandela. He was a lawyer and leader of the movement to end South African apartheid, arrested and imprisoned in 1962 and sentenced to life imprisonment for conspiring to overthrow the state following the Rivonia Trial. Mandela served twenty-seven years in prison, split between Robben Island, Pollsmoor Prison, and the Victor Verster Prison community. He could meet with a visitor only once a year for thirty minutes.

For just a few minutes, I could stand inside this initial cell he had occupied. It was eight by seven feet with a straw mat to sleep on. I still remember the pungent odor of wet dirt that permeated the space. While standing there, as hard as I tried, Mandela's survival in this space seemed unimaginable.

While incarcerated, Nelson Mandela had written on a scrap of paper the poem "Invictus" by the English poet William Ernest

Henley (1849–1903). He used to recite this poem to the other prisoners. This poem inspired him and his other prison mates to stay put and endure the hard times. I only recently read his poem, and the words touched my heart. The poem, condensed, means, "I am the master of my fate, the captain of my soul. We must strive to make each day a good one, no matter what our circumstances may be. How we think determines how we feel." These words continue to resonate with me in all that I do.

The people and views within South Africa deeply impacted me. I found it emotionally painful to witness such devastating conditions of life impacting countless people in this country. The eyes and words of the people with whom I spoke often told me of their innate desire to rise from under the conditions in which they lived.

Another stop in South Africa was our visit to Johannesburg. First, we visited a tech employee, Dave Lockwood, whom I met on Skype through a software company I did some work with, and he resides in Southern California. He agreed to take us for a quick look at one of the shantytowns in J-Burg, one of several names for Johannesburg. J-Burg is also called the City of Gold, the Rainbow Nation, and more. Dave told us that for him to take us anywhere near the shantytown was an extremely dangerous stop, and we could only get out of the car for a minute or two.

Nothing prepared me for what I was about to see. Before our eyes, there were thousands and thousands of connected metal-like rooftops, sitting side by side, as far and wide as the eye could see. Families lived in these handmade huts, each composed of four posts holding up a roof-like tin covering, possibly eight by six feet wide. Poverty—as far as I could see.

About a third of Cape Town's 3.7 million residents live in slums or informal settlements with limited access to essential services, such as water, electricity, and toilets. Candles provide much of their light at night, often leading to fires. These slums, often called townships, were built by the apartheid-era government to segregate people by color and ethnic origin. Twenty thousand to fifty thousand people could live in each of these shantytowns.

Our last stop on the southwest coast of South Africa was Cape Town before our trip home. Although we saw great poverty in South Africa, this city has beauty, diversity, and a feeling of vitality. It is on a peninsula beneath the imposing Table Mountain, one of its breathtaking destinations. The city's Cape Dutch architecture is quaint and has everything from cliffs, forests, beaches, Winelands, and wheat lands.

For the final part of this adventure, we stood at the southernmost tip of the African continent. This spot, the Cape of Good Hope, is the dividing line between the Atlantic and Indian Oceans. The wind felt like it was blowing a gale.

Hanging On at the Tip of the Cape of Good Hope.

The wind was so intense that I hung on to a stationary sign so I would not be blown over. Having raced sailboats with my husband, Donald, I thought it would be an incredible challenge to navigate in this region. Historically, the cape is known to sailors as a significant hazard on the traditional ship route. Our guide told us that a sharp drop in the ocean floor could cause rogue waves big enough to sink the sturdiest ships, even today's modern yachts. We flew home from Cape Town through London to Los Angeles the next day. I was not ready to leave. There was so much more to see.

Once I returned to my home in California, everything looked and felt the same. My chest did not pound as I walked around a corner, fearing that a pride of lions might be sunning themselves or a wildebeest might be staring me down. There was no longer an emotional edge of fear driving my car as it had been while riding in our open-air jeeps in Africa. Yet those rides were so very stimulating. Everything I saw and visited renewed my spirit. I enjoyed those precious moments of meeting people who often appeared happy living in squalor, as did those who lived well. Sometimes their living conditions broke my heart, but I always learned something from them.

At one point, when trudging in knee-high sand, carrying all my trip belongings on my back in a soft-sided bag, I was sometimes unsure I would make it. However, when signing up for this trip, I knew that part of the journey would be walking across this heavy, deep sand to the pontoon boat that might be surrounded by hippos or riding in a jeep through a herd of massive elephants. The excitement of having experienced visiting new countries and meeting people of many cultures is always invigorating. These adventurous trips ground me, and I feel present, at peace with myself, and even more grateful for my life.

FACING MY MORTALITY
(2005–2014)

Our memory is our coherence, our reason, our feelings, even our actions.
Without it, we are nothing.
—Luis Bunuel

The rationale for returning to Southern California from my short time in the northern part of the state was that I had lived most of my adult life in various Orange County cities. I had many close friends living there. However, I did not want to return to the overcrowded cities and the freeway traffic of Orange and Los Angeles Counties. I bought a wonderful home in Palm Desert on a beautiful golf course with a breathtaking panoramic view of the luscious green fairways and snow-capped mountains in the distance. The openness and view of the desert, the vivid green golf course, and the mountains in the distance were exhilarating.

I was thrilled to be moving to the desert. The desert does have extreme heat for three or four months out of the year, which can sometimes be difficult to handle. However, the cool evenings are remarkable. Like any inclement weather, people dress for it or stay in their cars, homes, restaurants, or shopping malls.

In the desert, people learn to always take water with them. The extreme heat of the desert reminded me of similar issues and precautions I took while living in the horrid -30 degree cold of North Dakota—the opposite end of the weather spectrum from the desert.

My Short-Term Memory Is Shot

On the trip to Africa with Don and Tiffany, I began to fear and consider that I might have a severe medical issue. The strangest darn thing started happening to me while on this trip. I sat in the safari jeep's front seat next to the guide, and five others were seated behind us. Later that day, Don told me that I would ask the guide a question during our safari trips, and he would answer it. Then I would immediately ask him the same thing again. As I listened to Don, I did not know how long this went on; but at some point, I remember one of the travelers saying, "Okay, Marly, now try to stay with it. You can do it." She kept razzing me about what I was saying. Finally, when we returned to camp, I told her I did not appreciate those comments because I did not realize I had already asked the question. Don told me later that my asking the same questions continued throughout our trip to Africa. This behavior is what Mike must have been trying to tell me. I did not know it was happening.

After the trip, I visited my internal medicine doctor in the desert. She listened to me for a few minutes, did not examine me at all, then gave me a box of pills and said, "Take these for a month and see how you feel, and then we will meet again."

When I got home that day, I looked at the package of pills the doctor had given me. It was Aricept. Quickly, I looked it up. It is the only treatment initially approved by the FDA to treat all stages of Alzheimer's. What?

I was crying hysterically. The possibility of slipping into Alzheimer's scared me to death. I shrieked as I fell into a heap, sobbing on the bathroom floor. I could hardly catch my breath. Oh my God, what if it was true? My mind was whirling. I did not know what to do. What caused this? How far back does this go? Maybe this memory loss had happened to me while I was at De Anza and was why I was no longer there. Was it the real reason my job ended at the college? I could not stand thinking that this memory issue may have happened to me while I was there. I imagined what my colleagues must have felt if I could not remember names, repeated myself, or possibly did not remember things I was supposed to do and maybe did not do. I could not stop sobbing for some time. I was scared and horrified.

As soon as the medical offices opened the next day, I decided to see another doctor to get a second opinion and immediately get an appointment. When we met, the doctor asked many questions, specifically about what other medications I was taking. My primary care doctor knew what they were doing and did not even discuss those with me when she handed me the Aricept medicine for Alzheimer's. When I told this new doctor that a doctor had prescribed Lipitor for me for cholesterol six months ago, he suggested that I stop it for three months and see if there is a change.

He indicated he had had another patient who experienced memory loss, and they determined her memory loss was from Lipitor.

I returned home and immediately tossed out my Lipitor. I gave myself three months, and soon, my "loss of memory" was no longer an issue. In researching my medications, my new doctor told me I was "one in a million" with an allergic reaction to Lipitor. Thank God my friends still love me and travel with me. No wonder Mike thought I was losing it. I was, but at this point, it seemed to have been caused by Lipitor. As I reflect on my time with him, I remember one evening. We were on a boat on San Francisco Bay, looking at all the beautiful lights and homes decorated for the holidays. I must have said "wonderful" and "beautiful" a hundred times. He yelled at me, "Can't you say anything but 'wonderful' and 'beautiful'?" and acted like he was ready to throw me overboard. I was clueless that I was doing that.

Three or four months after quitting Lipitor, I did various things to test myself. I would write a question or list items on paper and put it in my desk drawer. Then a day or so later, I would try to recall what I had written on the paper by writing down what I remembered. Soon, I felt reassured that my memory was intact and that I was not in immediate danger of losing it.

A CALL TO WORK IN HIGH TECHNOLOGY (2007–2013)

We are changing the world with technology.
—Bill Gates

A couple of years after my move back to Southern California and now living in the desert, I received a call from the president of EON Reality, a high-tech company located in Orange County, Southern California, my former stomping grounds. He wanted to meet with me to discuss his ideas regarding building their education market. We set a date, and soon, I drove an hour and a half to meet him. The president wanted me to develop their education market across the U.S. For colleges and universities to implement their interactive visual simulation technologies.

This proposal was a fascinating idea because I love working with technology. I was thrilled at this opportunity and told the president that I would think about it and write up a contract for him to consider.

I contacted an intellectual property attorney in San Francisco, and she created a contract for me to review. It was between me, as a contract employee, and EON Reality. As a contractor, they would pay me commissions and expenses through my small consulting business, Strategic Alliance Solutions, LLC. I agreed to work with them in this capacity only if I could report directly to the president. I did not want to become an employee of their company. The president took my contract to their attorney and then called me when he was ready to sign a contract that we both found to be acceptable.

At home, I began studying the company's complete product line of software and computer systems. The technology tools they have created are brilliant. EON Reality provides technologies to improve communication and transfer knowledge in business, education, and research anytime, anywhere. How did this happen? People use Eon Reality's software to create realistic experiences or applications, turning words or actions into augmented and 3D images using AI (Artificial Intelligence), AR (Augmented Reality), VR (Virtual Reality), and IoT (Internet of Things) where the collective network of connected devices and the technology that facilitates communication between devices and the cloud, as well as between the devices themselves, come together to propel human-computer interaction to new levels.

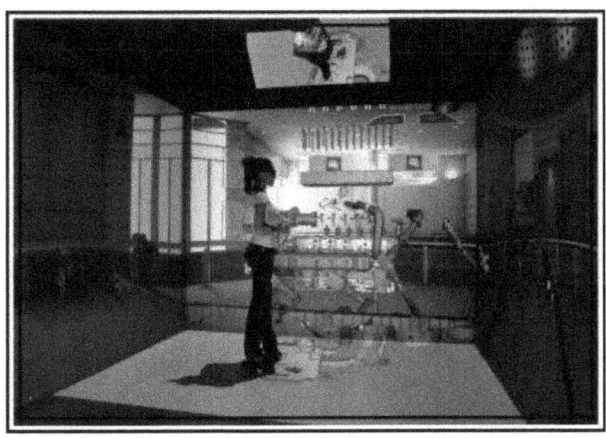

An example of someone working on a virtual piece of machinery:

EON's technologies (software and hardware) provide a process for changing learning from telling (teacher in front of a classroom) to showing (visually demonstrating using interactive objects). Traditionally, in schools or industries, if I wanted to teach a person in schools or industries, how to repair a car engine, I would have to acquire a car for students to disassemble. Then they would have to put it back together to repeat the process. With virtual software and integrated computer systems, the students could create a visual replication of an engine and display it on multiple screens using computer hardware. The graphic representation of this engine, designed within the software, was now a digital image object. This image may appear to float before a person wearing special 3D glasses.

An example of someone working on a virtual piece of machinery:

The person viewing the virtual object and wearing a special headset could use their hands to take the visual engine apart and virtually put it back together. The learning applications were endless, especially for medicine, engineering, and education. Today, more than ever, 3D, virtual reality, visual simulations, augmented reality, and artificial intelligence have become more commonplace in homes, industry, and education.

For me to reach the United States education market in colleges and universities, I needed assistance to track all the customer data and hired a good friend, Colleen Reynolds. We worked from my home in the desert. Together, we made significant inroads into building a U.S. client education list of over three thousand colleges and universities. During this time, I commuted between my home in Palm Desert and Irvine, sometimes three or four times a week, often staying with friends overnight in Orange County.

When visiting educational institutions and demonstrating these high-tech products to educators, administrators, and boards of trustees, their acceptance was terrific. At the onset of a meeting, I always described my extensive background as an educator and college administrator. The attendees seemed to relax and not look at me as a salesperson trying to sell them something. I honestly cared about assisting education administrators and their faculty in changing how people learn.

I worked as a contractor for EON Reality for about six years. I was at the top of my game as a salesperson of their software and computer hardware. I found this type of work to be stimulating but very intense. Every transaction ranged from several thousand dollars to $1.25 million. This journey's reward was observing the joy of students and educators using virtual reality or visual simulations. Today, virtual reality has become commonplace and has many applications in business and education.

The sales aspect was challenging. Its intensity reminded me of my feelings on the speaking circuit for six years in the 1980s.

During that time, I worked full- time in education and had a young son at home; nearly every two weeks, I traveled on a Friday night, spoke to a group on Saturday, and returned home on Sunday. Those weekend seminars involved talking to and teaching educators about word processing and all the new technologies that had entered the workplace. The most significant difference from my long career as a teacher or educational administrator was that now I was in an entirely new arena: the high-tech industry.

I had always been immersed in learning the latest technologies, as had Don, which is why we wrote many textbooks to assist others in learning how to use them. Nevertheless, I accepted this career change because I knew I would still impact learning by working with educators in colleges and universities across North America by providing them with technologies that would assist in changing how people learn.

During this time, Jamie Justice, other educators, and two software engineers with EON Reality and I felt that the company, EON Reality, needed to deliver a software manual with any of its software sales. The company's president gave us the "go-ahead" and I assisted this energetic group in creating and delivering a 726-page, four-color book that explained their extraordinarily complex software within one year after the color book. The ambitious team I worked with virtually was from Australia, Kentucky, London, and California.

Soon, the freeway trek from my beloved desert home to Orange County was getting to me. It was 258 miles per round trip. I decided to lease a house closer to work. A realtor in the desert found someone to rent my furnished desert home for two years. Her name was Celeste, a beautiful multilingual young business-woman from Europe. She had a sales position with a prominent international company that wanted to capture the West Coast market. They agreed to pay a two-year rental lease, and she wanted to move in immediately.

We signed a contract, and I got busy finding a place to rent in Orange County.

Immediately, I found a perfect home to lease near the beach in Orange County. It was close to the corporation where I worked as a contractor. Plus, shopping, the airport, and my good friends of many years were within minutes of where I would live. I was excited and delighted not to drive back and forth for work. Plus, I could now concentrate full-time on work.

For a few years, everything worked out beautifully in my exciting role in implementing virtual reality in colleges and universities across North America, except for one crucial piece. At the close of the sixth year of working as a contractor for EON Reality, my commission payments owed to me suddenly stopped. This situation had become very stressful as I had many business expenses to pay (over $100K in travel expenses, rent, and more). I counted on my commission checks, and this violated our contract. I refused to continue to work for them as a contractor, not knowing when I would get paid, if ever. I loved working with many of my clients. Unfortunately, it took my hiring an attorney and two and a half extremely stressful years to reconcile this situation.

During this same period, late one evening, I received a call from Schoree, one of the Good Ole Girls. Schoree said, "Joe is in the hospital dying, and if you want to say goodbye, you had better get there soon." Immediately, I called the hospital to see if Joe's brothers or his children were there.

The nurse indicated that they were not. Then I asked the nurse to please contact me with whoever was visiting in his room. She did, and Angie, Joe's girlfriend of the last ten years, came to the phone and said to me, "Please come to the hospital so you can say goodbye to Joe. He always loved you, and he does not have much time." I threw on my clothes and drove to the hospital.

I arrived at the hospital near midnight and located Joe's room. Joe was lying there, his mouth open and laboring to breathe. I could not tell if he was conscious or not. Angie and his AA sponsor were in the room. The three of us talked by his bedside for an hour or two about Joe, the good times, and the three very different relationships each of us had with Joe. Angie said that Joe discovered only three months prior that he had pancreatic cancer.

Finally, I asked them if they would mind if I said my goodbyes to Joe. They both left the room. I walked close to his bed, held his hand, leaned very close to him, and said, "Joe, this is Marly. Can you hear me?" I almost gasped out loud. Immediately, Joe closed his mouth, appeared to have difficulty swallowing, and slowed his heavy breathing.

Joe Tinervia during a happy time in his life in California.

I felt rushed because I did not want him to die while they left the room. He was listening to me. I continued, "Joe, I want you to know I loved you very much and will always love you. We had a wonderful life together. I am sure you do not want to leave us, but your parents are waiting for you to be with them again."

I did not want to quit talking with him, but I felt that getting Angie back into the room was urgent. I walked out and thanked her for asking me to come to the hospital and for how much I appreciated it. When I found my parked car, I got in and sat staring blankly out the window, and then I sobbed almost uncontrollably for some time.

There were three memorial services for Joe. One was filled with his AA "sponsees," the men Joe had sponsored over the years while he was in AA. Another service was held by members of the Business Division at Saddleback College, where he continued teaching for several years after I left my position there as Dean of the Division. Angie held another service for him. At this service, I remember seeing his tattered and worn copy of Paradise Lost lying at the base of the altar. He read that book constantly, marking up pages and rereading them repeatedly. Joe loved that book. One of his favorite passages was when Satan tells Beelzebub that "the mind is its own place, and in itself can make a heav'n of hell, a hell of heav,n."

Joe had lived through his very own kind of hell.

After I quit working with EON Reality, I remained in Orange County with my home in the desert still rented. I knew I needed to establish new and regenerate old relationships. I wanted to collaborate with industries and the primary colleges and universities in Orange County to build a high-tech learning center.

In reaching out, I met many new, incredibly bright people in all business areas and education. The plan was to create a Digital Innovation Center for the Arts, Sciences, and Technologies as a collaborative venture of educators from all nine colleges and universities in Orange County, as well as with area businesses.

Finally, one businessman who was president of the Orange Council Business Council, a group of business leaders, became interested in my project. For a few months, we talked over all the options. In late November, he called me and asked me to come to his office to meet with him the next day. I was excited about this meeting but very nervous. I took extra care to prepare for this meeting that day, wearing my best navy suit over a crisp white long-sleeved shirt. I could hardly contain my excitement.

At this meeting, he indicated that his organization would put together $300,000 to pay me and for me to hire a couple of people to start working with me to get my project off the ground. The funds would be available by January 1. Two of his organization's four missions were education and technology, so their involvement seemed a good fit. I left his office on an enormous high. I was so excited about this opportunity and anxious to get a team to build this high-tech center.

I began meeting with architects and the owners of the property I hoped to lease. I started assembling a team of county-wide educators. Carefully, I chose a group of educators who were movers and shakers working in Orange County. Their educational institutions were the nine California community colleges; the University of California, Irvine; and California State University, Fullerton, plus many other private colleges and universities. January 1 could not come fast enough to get this project up and running.

THE UNFORGIVABLE (2012)

*Sadly enough, the most painful goodbyes are the ones
that are left unsaid and never explained.*
—Jonathan Harisch

Addilyn was the most caring and compassionate friend I have ever known. We talked about everything, I mean everything—in depth. After spending the day with her, I realized it was 11:30 p.m. I told her I needed to leave and go to my rental because I had an early drive to my home in the desert in the morning. She wanted me to stay longer, so I stayed well beyond midnight, and we continued talking about everything imaginable.

The following morning, as planned, I returned to my home in Palm Desert after spending a terrific few days working and visiting the Good Ole Girls. I was looking forward to a beautiful weekend in the desert. My cell phone rang as I turned the key in the front door of my desert home. I remember having trouble digging the phone out of my purse. Finally, I was able to answer the call. It was from one of the Good Ole Girls, Margie. She was sobbing hysterically. I could not understand a word she was saying.

As I walked into my home, I had to yell at her, "Stop, stop! I cannot understand a word you are saying!"

Margie settled down, choking back her tears as she said, "Addilyn died!"

What do you mean she died?" "Her heart stopped. Her daughters called me and asked me to let the Good Ole Girls know. There will be a service next Saturday at her church."

In disbelief, I told her I could not assimilate what she said and that I would call her back. I thanked her for calling and hung up.

My legs buckled, and I collapsed onto the floor in my entryway and sobbed. How could this be? The day before, I had gone with Addilyn to her favorite church, a quaint little chapel. During the service, I remember she grabbed my hand and squeezed it. Hers was trembling, but that had occurred before. I remember thinking her trembling seemed to be happening more often since her big eightieth birthday bash six months ago.

After the church service, she said she wanted to light some candles. I waited outside. She was in the church for some time. I thought she might be lighting every candle in the church. Soon, she met me outside. She indicated where she wanted me to meet her for brunch.

We drove separately to a restaurant nearby. Our brunch conversation that day was like all our chats were. I remember her telling me how much she loved Cameron, her second husband of ten years. I laughed and said, "Do you realize that all I ever hear you say is, 'He is such a nice man'? Before this moment, I had never heard her say that she loved him."

As friends of hers walked by us in the restaurant, Addilyn chatted with them. Then she seemed extremely excited, telling me about the trip she and Cameron would go on the next day. They were flying to England to visit one of her daughters. Then they were getting on a ship for a two-week Western Mediterranean cruise, including ports in Spain, Italy, Morocco, and Tunisia. Their trip sounded delightful. We hugged and said goodbye, and I drove back to the desert.

This news of her death was incomprehensible. It was shocking. I could hardly stop crying. I truly loved Addilyn and our beautiful friendship. She was a very cherished close friend. I had often stayed with her and Cameron when I only had a house in the desert or lived in Northern California. Even after she married Cameron, I often stayed there, enjoying the company of both Addilyn and Cameron. I had a few surgeries at various times, and we laughed that her home was my rehab place. She loved to take care of me as she did all her friends.

The Good Ole Girls did not know if she was seriously ill. In the previous six months, we had noticed that her hands were shaking a great deal, but we did not want to question her about her "shaking hands" because we did not want to make it worse—whatever was causing it.

My parents and others close to me have passed away, but this death has devastated me. The Good Ole Girls, now five, gathered in our grief and attended the church memorial service for Addilyn in the same little church where I had sat with her the prior week. Also, at least two hundred people were standing at the doorway of this tiny chapel but could not get in for the service. Addilyn was a devout Catholic. As I am not Catholic, why there was no mass never occurred to me.

After the church service, there was a gathering at a local hotel of about three hundred of Addilyn's friends and family. She was loved by so many. I talked with all her grandchildren, her nephews, and her two daughters, whom she adored. Everyone appeared bewildered and seemingly just stared into space. Such sadness I have never felt.

A couple of weeks later, Marg, a Good Ole Girl, called and asked if the Good Ole Girls could come to her house. We all showed up and sat down, waiting, wondering. Why was this urgent gathering needed? It was unusual in the way it occurred. With bated breath, we waited to hear why we were together again. Finally, Marg said, "Addilyn's daughters had called me to their home and said they wanted the Good Ole Girls to know the truth about Addilyn's death." We all looked confused. She took a deep breath and said, "She killed herself."

We all cried out with gasps and gaping mouths, "That is not possible!" We all sat in disbelief and sobbed as if the news we had heard ten days ago when she died had not been enough. Not one of us could put our minds around this as being the true story of her death. And thirteen years later, I still can't believe it.

Our grief over her death was now forever altered. How could Addilyn and the Good Ole Girls all be such close friends, with me being the last of the six of us to see her and not have a clue? I was angry with myself. I was outraged at her. What could we possibly have done to help her? Was she on drugs? Have they done a toxicology report? How is Cameron dealing with this? How could this be?

That image of Addilyn taking her own life was incomprehensible. All I want to believe is that she must have known she had some horrible disease that she did not want to deal with or have her husband or daughters needing to handle it. She was always the strongest, most rational of the six of the Good Ole Girls. She loved life, Cameron, her daughters, her grandchildren, and all her friends.

The only other thing that made no sense to me, which led to how she handled her exit, was that maybe there were no drugs in her system. She may have intentionally stopped taking her five prescriptions and just mentally flipped as she was coming down off these medications she had been taking for some time. Possibly, she did not realize she had not taken the five drugs that stabilized her.

The toxicology report returned in three weeks, and we were told, "Addilyn had no drugs in her system." I knew she was on Xanax, Paxil, heart medicine, and three others. The only reason I could fathom that may have triggered her action was that she knew something about her health condition that no one else did, not even her daughters. Stopping suddenly all five needed prescriptions most likely had to have helped push her over the edge. There were other reasons, possibly, but we will never know.

Since her death, this comment kept coming back to me: "There were no drugs in her system." I know little about Xanax, Paxil, high blood pressure medicine, and the other drugs she had been taking. However, I read in the literature about Xanax—it only takes five hours for Xanax to be cleared out of your system. Also, one of the possible symptoms of someone taking Xanax is severe tremors. Of course, that makes sense. She had been trembling uncontrollably. In retrospect, we, Good Ole Girls, intentionally did not interrogate her about this type of thing because several months before, she had said she needed a heart valve replacement. Vehemently, Addilyn had said, "I do not want a pig valve in my body!" As a result of her terror of having that valve replacement done, the Good Ole Girls did not want to question her about what she was taking and upset her about anything.

We asked her daughters if they knew about any diagnosis their mother had received. They knew nothing. We tried to think of every possibility for what may have caused this horrific tragedy. Maybe a family member possibly struggled financially, so perhaps she thought she should help them out now?

Her hand tremors could have caused her to think that she was very sick, which may have given her the courage to do what she did. Possibly, she wanted to escape from a hopeless health condition that only she knew about or felt would be an intolerable health condition. Suicide might have been the preferred solution to a disease or disability, which she may have feared worse than death.

Addilyn's death again triggered the horrible feelings I had gone through during Joe's failed suicide attempts. After Addilyn's death, her daughters talked with the doctors to see if there was anything she did not want them to know and were told, "No, she had no terminal illness." But the HIPAA laws provide protection for you of your health information.

The Good Ole Girls will never know "the reason our dear friend felt the need to die, especially the horrible way she chose." Often flashes of Addilyn's beautiful face, smile, and laughter come to mind. I grieve for our friendship, our great conversations. I feel I let her down somehow. I will always feel that the remaining five Good Ole Girls missed or ignored something that maybe could have helped her.

THE DEVIL CALLS AGAIN (2013–2014)

*Anything can be a blessing, a miracle, an opportunity if you choose
to see it that way. When you see life through a lens of hope,
everything can change.*
—Oprah Winfrey

It was a week since I learned I would receive the funds to launch
my project. I was thrilled.

The phone rang.

"Is this Marlyn Bergerud?" "Yes ."

"This is John Smith, the radiologist from the Breast Care Cancer Center at Eisenhower Hospital. I am calling with the results
of your breast needle biopsy."

As with most women with a family history of breast cancer, the
usual procedure every year was to get a mammogram, possibly
an ultrasound, or an MRI; but this time, I also had a needle biopsy.

Barely taking a breath, he continued in his monotone voice, "You have two breast nodules in your right breast that are cancerous, and you need surgery as soon as possible. So, find yourself a surgeon and take care of this immediately. Do not wait. Your mother had breast cancer, and so did her mother. Did you hear me?"

"Yes," and we both hung up.

I started shaking uncontrollably, which I never do. I could not even cry. I was stunned. After catching my breath, I did call my sister, Connie, and her husband, John, and my elder sister, Sharon. They commiserated with me and agreed I just had to find the right doctors and get it done. With breast cancer in my family history, I always knew that getting cancer was possible. Nevertheless, hearing those words that I had cancer was as if a bomb had dropped on me.

My mind was whirring. I must take some action. I was avoiding what I had just heard, but it was already 5 p.m. on a Friday, and today I could not begin to solve the problem. Also, the next day, I had the remaining four Good Ole Girls over to celebrate the holidays and our Christmas gift exchange. We usually had this get-together at a restaurant, but I thought having it at my little house in Orange County would be fun. Next, I stood up on my shaking legs, went downstairs, and started baking rum cakes for our lunch. Taking action was always good for me, rather than sitting and stewing over things. I was dazed, feeling nothing—just functioning like a robot.

This news was a big deal: cancer. I now know I have the genetic gene, BRAC2, from my mother.

My dreams and plans for creating the high-tech center would

take a back seat. Was the cause of my cancer my push and stress to find the funding for the tech center? Or was it the stress of my eighteen years working in management at the colleges? Was the cause possibly the debts I had incurred that I was constantly worried about? Or the two-and-a-half-year lawsuit with EON Reality to get the money they owed me? Or was it just pure genetics?

The next day, December 5, the four remaining Good Ole Girls arrived. I had managed to temporarily set aside the trauma of the news that I had cancer. Yes, I was fearful but not crying about it. Unfortunately, my seemingly stoic inability to weep was a carryover from childhood traumas.

The four Good Ole Girls arrived, and we sat down to a beautiful lunch at my exquisitely decorated holiday table. We talked and laughed nonstop, as we always did. After lunch, we moved to the living room area for our gift exchange. Our friendship of over forty years has always made our time together precious, even more so since our recent tragic loss of Addilyn. Before they left, I said, "I have to talk with you about something." They looked afraid, only considering eleven months prior, when Marg had revealed the truth about Addilyn's death at a similar gathering.

They cried. It was as if I had said I was dying tomorrow. "I will be fine. "This surgery is just something that must happen." My sweet friends listened for a while. Each had a great need to tell their relatives' or friends' cancer stories while continually reassuring me that I would be fine. Of course, neither they nor I had any clue.

On Monday, after my gut-shattering Friday phone call from the radiologist, I began searching Orange and Los Angeles Counties to find the best breast surgeon and plastic surgeon for the implants for restoration. I asked doctors I had gone to for years which surgeon they would go to if they or their daughters or wives needed this surgery. One name kept coming up: Dr. Alice Police. I called her office and made an appointment for the next day. At our first meeting, after her examination and review of my scans and biopsy, Dr. Police immediately got the surgery scheduled for three weeks from that date.

January 3, 2013, one month after the phone call with the news of my cancer, I had the first of three surgeries. One of the Good Ole Girls, Schoree, took me to the hospital because my sister, Connie, could not get there until after the surgery but was waiting for me in my room. I heard her voice. She kept saying, "On a scale of 1 to 10, how do you feel?"

I would respond with "3." Then I asked the nurse for a cup of coffee and took one sip, then immediately fell into a drugged sleep with the coffee spilling all over me. My sedation from the surgery had not worn off, so nothing I said or did seemed to make any sense. Then I vaguely remember telling Connie, "I am freezing."

Shortly after that, I passed out. Much to my dismay, the nurse on duty had given me the wrong medication through my intravenous tube. She gave me medication for high blood pressure. I have low blood pressure. My sister said that immediately there was a flurry of people and activity. Nurses moved my legs and arms and got me up to walk, tubes and all, to bring my blood pressure back to normal.

After that debacle, Connie was afraid to leave my room and

go home. She slept in the hospital room that night to ensure no other screw-ups. In a few days, Connie drove me to my little leased house in Newport Beach. I had long drain tubes with bulbs coming from each breast. Connie was quite the trooper. She had to continually monitor and empty the bulbs and record the amount of fluid from each bulb. This process went on for three weeks. I was propped up in bed with pillows onto both sides to prevent me from turning over on my side. I never sleep on my back, which makes this a little uncomfortable, but one can get used to almost anything.

Connie stayed with me those initial three weeks of recuperating, doing exceptional "hands-on care" day and night, getting me through my initial most challenging weeks. Christen asked me several times if I wanted him to come over, and I told him, "No." I loved him dearly, but I did not want to see anyone. It was as if all I could do was accept what I had just been through and to begin to deal daily with healing before my second surgery, three months out, weekly preparing with the plastic surgeon to get implants. It was not a complicated process, just time and patience. At first, I took the prescribed pain medication but did not want to become addicted, which would have been easy. Three weeks after surgery, I eased off the pain pills. When recovering from surgery, the advice is always, "stay ahead of the pain," meaning do not wait until you are in pain before taking something for it.

As for the dream of creating a high-tech center, the following week after my call from the radiologist, I called my biggest business supporter, who was ready to give me the funds, went in to see him, and sadly had to tell him about my new project: cancer.

Three weeks after the surgery, I began a new procedure with the plastic surgeon, Dr. Bradley Strawn, who had worked alongside Dr. Police. During the operation, he placed two ports into the two newly embedded breast expanders. Then, weekly, the ports were injected with fluid to expand the skin as much as he thought it could bear. We did that procedure until the skin finally stretched to a point where we decided to stop. Three months after the initial surgery, I went back into the hospital for another surgery to have the plastic surgeon remove the breast expanders, and the actual implants were placed under the skin. Then the healing process began all over again.

As it turns out, the BRAC2 gene was fed by estrogen. Therefore, a year after this surgery, for the next five years, I took the drug Arimidex, known as an estrogen depletor, to keep the gene from taking off in the wrong direction again. My chance for cancer recurrence was 7 percent.

Despite its many pitfalls, I believe cancer taught me to slow down, de-stress, put off building a high-tech center, and have fun and take care of myself. Honestly, I do not worry or think about cancer as something that will recur. My attitude is, "If it does, it does." I do the checkups and struggle to avoid one of my remaining addictions—sugar.

I do not think silence about the disease of cancer, or our eventual death, serves any of our interests. Nor did I feel we should be silent about domestic abuse, child abuse, or alcoholism. As a result of having breast cancer, a double mastectomy, and breast implants, I wanted to do my part to change the conversations about cancer by describing my journey with cancer for you.

As I was recovering from my surgeries, I had plenty of time to think long and hard about what I wanted to do next. Did I want to start working again? Did I need to keep working? After thirty-eight years of working hard and contributing to the California State Teachers' Retirement System, I was fortunate to have a valuable pension. I often thought I would probably be a "bag lady" without it, as I always seemed to spend every penny I made. Was I ready to hang it all up and retire?

I lived most of my adult life in various Orange Country, California, cities. I always loved wherever I lived, and my very close friends of so many years are still living there. There are excellent shopping centers, incredible theater performances, and beaches and mountains nearby. But in the forty-plus years I had lived there, the downside was that the area had become densely overpopulated. The four-lane freeways were jam-packed with drivers racing at 80+ mph.

My friends of more than forty years, the Good Ole Girls and the Band of Four, lived in various cities in Orange County, California. Yes, I did enjoy living near them again and spending time with them these past few years. It was interesting adjusting to being retired. All the Good Ole Girls are married, have full lives, and enjoy their grandchildren. As a result, their availability to spend time with me was limited. It was unlike our available time many years before, even though we were all working then. During this last location for me in Orange County, one of my very best friends and traveling companions, Don Busché, was always very attentive. At that moment, I had nothing but time on my hands. However, no matter where I lived, I always got together with these beautiful close friends for special occasions (birthdays, weddings, funerals, and babies). After all, Palm Desert was only a short drive from Orange County for our get-togethers.

Celeste recently moved out of my desert home and was in San Francisco to take advantage of what she thought was a great business investment opportunity. She was an excellent tenant, renting the house and belongings with great care. Initially, when Celeste moved in, I introduced her to my desert friends. She soon spent time with them, and they enjoyed her. She had also become a good friend of mine—almost like the daughter I never had.

Because Celeste had moved to San Francisco and was no longer paying rent that covered the mortgage on the desert home, I needed to decide what I wanted to do and where I wanted to live. I chose to get rid of all my debt, including all my credit card debt and my desert home. I did not want financial stress any longer. Whether it is true or not that stress plays a role in causing disease, I felt I needed to make these new decisions.

During my time of recovery, I thought a great deal about traveling. My thought process on travel was that I had set aside traveling to European countries to visit later in life. I felt that many European countries would be more accessible than my earlier travels to China, Africa, Australia, Russia, South America, Austria, Sicily, and more.

At the end of about a year after my first surgery date in 2014, and living in Newport Beach rethinking how I wanted to spend my life, I moved back to the serenity of the desert. A realtor friend of mine in the desert helped me find a rental, a lovely home. It had a panoramic view of the golf course with the snow-capped mountains in the distance.

My sister, Connie, discovered the "jewel of the earth," John Philip Friel, and in 1973 they married and shared an incredible life together for 50+ years. Their children, my nephews, Jonathan and Brian, have been the significant "go-to family" for Christen and me. We have spent most of the family birthdays, holidays, vacations, and graduations together with the Friels. John was like the brother I never had, always giving advice when asked or helping me whenever called upon.

John Philip Friel

August 3, 1944 – March 21, 2024

John spent a lifetime in the healthcare industry, assisting in getting hospitals built and improving the healthcare system wherever possible.

Connie and John have two terrific, very successful sons who married smart and beautiful women: Jonathan married Alex, and they have two great boys, Owen and Jackson. Brian, their other son, married Melissa (Christen officiated their marriage on Catalina Island).

They have two wonderful children - beautiful Aira (very artistic and adorable,and Lego guy – Augustine ("Auggie"). I love spending time with all of them whenever I can.

Sadly, in 2024, John, the matriarch of the family, passed away after a courageous three-year battle with cancer, leaving a profound void in the hearts of all who knew and loved him.

ITALY ON MY MIND (2016-2017)

Italy is a dream that keeps returning for the rest of your life.
— Anna Akhmatova, poet

Now, I am retired, living in a beautiful home in Palm Desert where I meet and enjoy new and old friends. However, there is always an underlying desire to travel. Of all the renowned cities and countries I have had the incredible opportunity to visit, Italy is the primary one frequently on my mind.

My life changed the first time I met and fell in love with Italy. I truly enjoyed traveling with friends and family, but I learned to love traveling alone, seeing new places, meeting new people, experiencing new cultures, and embarking on adventures. Italy was an effective remedy for redefining how I wanted to live the rest of my life.

When traveling to Italy, the energy I feel when the airplane wheels touch down is like Cinderella when the glass slipper is placed on her foot. Why do I feel this way? What makes me feel so good, so aligned with myself, when my feet connect with Italian soil?

Even though living in the United States is terrific, I am enamored with Italy and feel like I am home when in Italy.

Since visiting Italy with Christen in 2010, he has shown his caring in many thoughtful ways, including a second trip for me to Italy in 2016. He provided a month's stay in an apartment in the center of Siena, the Piazza Il Campo, where I drafted this memoir.

Christen knew I needed time away from all distractions to begin writing this book.

I love the Italian culture, their museums, and listening to the locals tell stories from the old days. Cooking classes always teach me a thing or two about cooking. Looking into the future, I would happily spend half my time in Italy and half in California. I wish these two beautiful locations were physically closer. I do not discount living in Italy one day.

Siena is one of Italy's loveliest and most visited places in Tuscany. How ideal! Anna Benocci owns the apartment that Christen rented. It overlooks the Piazza del Campo. The history attached to the Piazza del Campo was from ancient times. Anna also has her apartment in the same building. She is someone I would rent from wherever she has space—she is a terrific lady and has become a wonderful friend I have had the privilege of getting to know. Her husband, Ricardo, is a kind, gentle man who owns apartments in Florence that he rents to others.

The apartment living room was perfect, a large open room encompassing the dining and kitchen area. It had a large sofa bed, closet, and drawer space for clothes and luggage. The galley-like kitchen was more than adequate. It held all the appliances/utensils/ dishes necessary to cook full meals and keep food fresh. One bedroom has a king-sized bed and an adjoining bathroom with a tiny shower. There was no television and no radio.

Best of all—the apartment was on the third floor, with each of the two large rooms overlooking the Piazza del Campo, the principal public space of Siena–one of Europe's most fabulous medieval squares. This center, Piazza del Campo of Siena, is the site of many public activities, festivals, and daily tours for tourists brought through Siena. There was usually some daily activity occurring in the Piazza.

Across the Piazza from my apartment windows was a tower connected to a long three-story building. I explored the tower and inside found a magnificent museum.

From my window, the Piazza del Campo.

I wrote daily, sitting at the dining room table in the morning, having coffee and fruit, and writing. I drafted this book on an iPad Pro from many handwritten outlines, notes, and filled yellow paper pads. Being very visual, I often wished for a printer to see my writing printed before me.

After a few hours of writing, taking a brief walk was always a new experience. I would walk down one flight, get on the tiny one-person elevator, go down another three floors, and venture out the enormous, old wooden double doors to the street, on the backside of the Piazza del Campo to Via di Citta, the main shopping street in Siena. Beautiful shops, restaurants, pastries, gelato, galleries, museums, churches, and groceries are all within walking distance from the apartment. Wandering down the side streets that were offshoots to the Piazza-like the spokes on a wheel, was always a new experience.

Usually, I went out for dinner between five and was home by seven. I was uncomfortable walking alone in the dark after 7:00 p.m. Restaurants abound in a half circle below the apartment in the Pizza. I visited them all. When dining out, I noticed no women were sitting alone. Usually, there were two or more women together, or families, or a few couples. Sometimes being alone bothered me as I missed sharing the joys of travel with others.

Nevertheless, I loved the solitude of writing. I found it easy to eat well and live a healthy lifestyle, away from the temptations of all the processed foods found in U.S. supermarkets. The great Italian weather gives its people many opportunities to get outside and enjoy their gardens. However, living in California provides comparable weather year-round. Every few days, I would buy fruit and bottles of sparkling water at a small market about a twenty-minute walk away.

Then, after shopping or strolling about, I would return to the apartment to write without distractions or excuses. I loved the solitude of writing.

While there, I wished I knew Italian, although almost everyone I encountered in Italy spoke English. At one point, I enrolled in a class teaching Italian with about three weeks remaining on the trip. After the first class, with an assignment of about three hours of studying, I came to my senses. I could not afford to spend my remaining time in Italy studying Italian and not writing. I still have the Italian lesson book in a drawer at home. Hmmm, maybe someday.

The exciting buzz of activity in the Piazza made meeting many people, locals and tourists, easy due to this fantastic location. One day, I heard many people gathering outside in the Piazza from my third-story window. Just as I looked out my window, I was astonished to see the Piazza packed with people. They were looking up. As I turned to look upward, I gasped as I watched three men separately parachuting from a small plane onto a patch of blue in the center of the Piazza.

Another day, I went into the crowd gathering in the Piazza to watch the selection of ten Contrade for the El Palio race.

This famous horse race is complete with solid local traditions tied to its 17 districts (called "contrade"), like counties in the U.S. Only ten horses are selected from the 17 contrade for the next Il Palio horse race. It is the biggest annual event in the Piazza del Campo, twice each summer. Similar races occurred in the 18th and 19th centuries astride donkeys or buffaloes. However, in the 19th century, the importance of the Siena Palio, governed by the 17 districts and its rules, made it the ideal joust.

Siena is a magnificent city extremely rich in history and art. If a traveler wants a tranquil location in Siena, this may not be your space. For me, I loved the constant activity in the center.

I marvel at Italy's considerable contributions to art, architecture, fashion, opera, literature, design, film—and more. Not to say anything about their food, which is remarkable. However, Italy has only been a country since 1871. I believe that Italian culture promotes the acceptance of everyone as they are, imperfections and all. The Italians I met seem to value all people, individuals, and the collective Italian family. The people are friendly, helpful to visitors like me, and appear to enjoy their country with a love of great food and wine. They are out late at night, 10:00–11:00 p.m., and later with their entire family, babies and all, enjoying food, drink, and friends.

JUDY AND MARLY IN TUSCANY

My very good friend, Judy, accompanied me on the initial leg of this return trip of mine to Italy, which began in Florence. There we rented an apartment for three days from Ricardo. As Florence is known as a city with the greatest concentration in the world of museums, churches, buildings, and artworks, each day we took in as many sites as we could. The weather was oppressive in the 90s+, and we were dripping wet as it was unbearably humid. Many European places do not have air conditioning.

After a few days, we drove to San Gimignano, where I had rented a place through my timeshare. Ours was a second-story apartment that we entered from outside the walled city of San Gimignano. All cars must park outside the city's walls. The city is known for its ancient 72 stone towers. We explored the main street for the first few days, which was a long walk from the city gate to the top of a hill with shops along both sides. Judy and I had lunch in the square at the top of the main street from the entrance to San Gimignano.

Judy in San Gimignano.

Because our apartment did not have air conditioning, we would leave it early in the morning. Then, we would begin our trek through the many villages and cities of Tuscany. Part of our reasoning was to find cool air.

We drove most of the day, every day. Some of the towns where we stopped were Arezzo, Lucca, Pisa, Livorno, and a unique beach town, Forte dei Marmi, where we stayed one night. That day, the heat was too unbearable to keep driving.

One of our last excursions was a drive to Assisi, in the region of Umbria, where we visited the Basilica of Saint Francis of Assisi. This site is one of the most important Christian pilgrimage sites in Italy.

These two weeks with Judy were packed with days of laughter, eating incredible food, and seeing Tuscany's many beautiful sights, especially loving the beauty of the rolling hills of vineyards in the countryside.

Marly and Judy enjoyed Tuscany.

Our apartment had a living room overlooking a busy street below, a separate bedroom, and a bathroom. Judy took the couch pullout bed, and I got the bedroom! Some evenings after dinner, we watched a movie on my laptop.

That was hysterical - the two of us crouched together, resting the laptop on our knees to watch movies.

When touring in our little rental car, we tried carefully not to get a speeding ticket, but it wasn't easy. The speed limits changed rapidly. We followed these limits: 50 km or 30 mph (cities and towns) to 90 km (55 mph) on single roads, to 110 km/h (about 68 mph), on dual carriageways, and 130 km (80 mph) on motorways. But, to no avail, we got a ticket when the speed limit entering one of the villages abruptly changed from 100 km to 80 to 40 in about one minute. Within months after our return home, Judy received the ticket and a large fine.

We stopped our self-made tour whenever we saw a quaint village or restaurant or to take pictures. Suddenly, we came to a screeching stop so as not to hit a motorcyclist and his rider. Quite shaken, we got out to make sure the motorcyclist and rider were okay – and they were. But when Judy slammed on the brakes, we ended up with a quart of water held between my legs, spraying us, the entire front seat, and the car dashboard.

After recovering from the fright of nearly hitting a motorcyclist and rider, we had to laugh because we were wet and had not planned to cool off that way.

Returning to our hot apartment each day, a lovely man residing in our apartment building found two small fans, which we each slept with one of them, blowing on our faces to help us sleep. After two very fun-filled weeks of touring Tuscany, we returned to Florence, where I left Judy for her return home to California. Then, I hired a driver and drove to Siena, a forty-five-minute trip from Florence.

I stayed in a hotel during my first few days in Siena, as my former apartment was unavailable until after the Il Palio Race. Then, I was fortunate to have been able to rent the same apartment from Anna for a month.

The Il Palio race was exhilarating. I thoroughly enjoyed watching the 40,000+ packed and standing individuals inside a ringed area in the center of the free zone of the Piazza del Campo. I would not have been able to handle five hours standing in that hot, packed crowd. I had purchased a bleacher seat ticket a year prior to the event, and it was located on the perimeter of the Piazza. Even though I had a place to sit, I nearly passed out from the heat sitting on the bleacher facing the blaring hot sun. At one point, I had to climb down and sit under the bleachers to cool down.

Thousands stand in the free, roped-off center to view the parade and the Il Palio.

While staying in Siena, I usually went out for dinner between five and came home by seven. I was uncomfortable walking alone in the dark after 7:00 p.m. Restaurants abound in a half-circle below the apartment in the Piazza. I visited them all. When dining out, I noticed that no women were sitting alone. Usually, there were two or more women together, or families, or a few couples. Sometimes being alone bothered me, only because I missed sharing the joys of travel with others. Nevertheless, I loved the solitude of writing.

It was a joy to have had the opportunity to spend time with Judy touring Tuscany and, finally, to see the famous Il Palio.

COCKEYED OPTIMISM IN
THE DESERT (2015–2017)

*All the world's a stage, and all the men and women merely players; they have their exits
and their entrances, and one man in
his time plays many parts.*
— Shakespeare

I met him through an online dating service, Match.com. It was a typical coffee date. After several emails, we decided to meet on a Sunday morning at a coffee shop in La Quinta, California. I arrived there early.

Soon, I noticed a man crossing the street and approaching the coffee shop. From the description I got from our phone conversations, I thought this must be the guy. He was wearing a light-colored sport coat. What can I say? No one wears a sport coat in the desert heat unless they are going to an exclusive restaurant or an occasion requiring it, but for coffee in the morning?

I called out his name, "Robert!" He recognized me from my pictures, waved at me, and crossed the street. I was peering at him over my sunglasses as he approached. It was too bright to take them off.

Robert was very talkative and asked many questions, unlike most guys who like to talk mostly about themselves on a first date.

We had our coffee. He was a good conversationalist. Then he said, "Let's walk." We talked as we strolled around the downtown streets of old La Quinta and went in and out of the quaint shops. He insisted on buying something for me as we wandered through the shops. He kept holding up clothes and asking if I would like this or that. I just kept saying, "No, I would not wear that." I finally acquiesced and came home with a lovely gift of exquisite olive oil and balsamic vinegar, which I appreciated. I joked that he would soon be broke if he did this on every Match.com coffee date.

There was an immediate attraction. Indeed, Robert was very handsome, but his smile and infectious laugh hooked me. Soon, I learned that he was a doctor. Then he proceeded to proclaim, in quite an arrogant way, "I am one of the best surgeons in the world, and maybe someday you will understand what I mean."

I responded, "I assumed all doctors were somewhat arrogant and thought that way." He just laughed.

We spent nearly every day together during our initial six months of dating. Soon, I accompanied him to a surgeon's conference in Taormina, Sicily, where he joined his colleagues from all over the world.

Robert and Marly, Taormina, Sicily, attended the MGB (MiniGastricBypass) Conference.

The doctors I met confirmed en masse that he was indeed a well-known surgeon. Robert had created a new bariatric surgical procedure, the Mini-Gastric Bypass, or MGB. He had trained these 28 or more surgeons from around the U.S., Mexico, and Europe in implementing the MGB. The success of his MGB and its immense value to his overweight patients was well documented and published in many medical journals. The surgery has succeeded in incredibly helping obese patients become thin and keep their weight off. There was also recent documented success in the MGB helping to eliminate diabetes.

Before his move to California, he had performed hundreds of such surgeries in Nevada for many years.

As a result of creating this surgical procedure, he was in high demand to train other doctors and speak at meetings worldwide. When I met him, he had traveled the globe by invitation for six prior years to teach his technique to doctors.

After dating him for about a year, Robert moved in with me. Living with him, in many ways, was one of my happiest times, except for most couples' usual little ups and downs. Robert's brilliance was not only in medicine; he was exceptionally well-read and had seen most movies, mostly old ones. Our early morning discussions were always lively, covering everything from politics to an old 1945 Joan Crawford movie we had watched the previous evening. He suggested I watch that film because the story of the star's alcoholism might help me with some aspects of my writing.

I called him Rob. He was generally a happy person. He had an energy I had never seen before, walking at least five to ten miles daily while listening to podcasts. Wisely, he liked his naps. He made me laugh and do healthy or good things for myself—like going to the hot tub almost daily for my osteoarthritis. There was much about him that was great. Specifically, he was intellectually stimulating, plus we laughed a lot. He was a great companion.

When we met, he worked in a clinic quite a distance away and stopped working there when he moved in. This decision was to concentrate on looking for a job that would better utilize his talents as a surgeon. Ultimately, I knew he would work again as a surgeon, but it might take time. Meanwhile, soon he seemed to have no funds. I had assumed that soon this situation for him would change. Later, we discovered why his getting another position as a surgeon might be nearly impossible, at least for some time, because of his lapsed credentials. He could not perform surgery until the American Board of Surgery provided a new date for surgeons to retake the certifying exam. The opening to retake the exam took three-plus years after I met him, which, in the meantime, was very difficult for him and me.

My success rate in selecting a suitable mate had not been high. Was Robert any different? No. Robert was a genius. Initially, I was just bewildered by some of Robert's behavior. For instance, returning to our second coffee date, we walked around a downtown outdoor market, and he said, "You are beautiful." I thanked him for the kind compliment. Then he proceeded to repeat those very same words about twenty times. I joked later, "Do you have Tourette's syndrome, or are you just very nervous?" He just laughed. As we began to see each other more and more, I discovered that some of his behavioral characteristics seemed to fit someone on the Asperger's spectrum. That means he had some unusual characteristics or behaviors in social situations that were often unsettling for me, my family, and my friends.

Robert would do little things that made me a little crazy, but I had not lived with a man for nearly twenty years, so I figured I needed to adjust. The most significant conflict was that I had convinced him to quit that excellent-paying job at a clinic because he had the night shift. We thought it would be easy to find him another position. Finally, a director of medical doctors at a nearby facility shocked me by saying that if Robert had been out of the country for six years with a lapsed credential, it might be years before he could perform surgery again. A couple of years later, the American Board of Surgeons finally allowed surgeons with a lapsed certification to retake their boards to be recertified. He did, passed it, and was ecstatic about getting started doing surgery again.

During our time together, the landlord of the beautiful home I had leased for three years decided he wanted to renovate the house and move in. This news meant we had to move out soon.

I began looking at other homes to lease and a few to buy. No one wanted to give me a multi-year lease.

I called my son, Christen, and asked him if he would consider loaning me the down payment, and I would pay him back. He said when I found something to let him know the details. Soon, I called him and said I had found a house. He came from Colorado to look at it, and we put it in escrow. My worries were over—what a jewel. I put a down payment of $25,000 in escrow to hold the house, and my incredible son, Christen, paid the remaining amount in cash for the home. He has always been extremely generous and took care of me, allowing me to live in this house. I will be forever grateful.

Robert viewed this move into a home I now own as a permanent place for me, not him. He said, "I love you and will miss you." Our three-plus years together were my best, but your buying a California home was your way of ending the relationship. If you were in a partnership, you would have included me in the decision to move into a permanent home." What? He did visit the house, along with Christen, me, and the realtor, and exclaimed, "This is a great home."

Immediately, Robert packed his worldly belongings into his car and left for a city in Southern California to hopefully start working with a doctor friend he had been talking with for several months. That statement from him stunned me. We talked about his sharing in the expenses of where we lived and that he would share when I did find something else. He agreed. At one point, we had talked about possibly having two homes, one near where he works and the other in the desert.

Since the move to my new place, I asked him if he thought I should have gone with him, moved from hotel to hotel while he was trying to find a job, and lived in an entirely new city where neither of us knew anyone, and for me to leave my friends and family. I believe he felt he should have been considered more in the final decision to buy the new home. Truthfully, my biggest disappointment was that he did not help me pack up the house we had lived in together for three years. He said, "You can hire someone to do it." What? Well, that was quite a send-off. He got into his car with all his worldly belongings and drove off. Oh my, maybe one day I will address my deep-rooted enabling issues.

Despite my continual and obvious enabling issues and other matters of learning to live with Rob, he was, in many ways, an intellectually stimulating companion. I loved our early morning coffee and discussions about politics and everything happening worldwide. Robert was always happy, funny, and complimentary toward me, influencing me to take better care of myself. He listened to dozens and dozens of books on his walks. He was a constant supporter of this book, and he had many suggestions for my writing. Robert consistently supported my writing, and we discussed other writers and this book at great length.

Unfortunately, and with great sadness, I must tell you that Robert Rutledge was diagnosed with cancer, left for Punjab, India, to be with his best friend, Dr. Kuldeepak Kular, and there he transitioned in April 2025. Over the years, I feel privileged to have read dozens to hundreds of remarkable letters from his formerly obese patients thanking him for dramatically changing their lives of obesity.

THE GREAT ENABLER NO MORE (2017–2021)

Enabling is the mortal enemy of consequences.
—D. C. Hyden

There was a knock at my door. It was late in the evening. That was strange. It was 10:00 p.m., and I was not expecting anyone. Before opening the door, I asked, "Who is it?"

She answered, "Celeste!"

I opened the door, and Celeste fell into my arms, sobbing hysterically. "What happened? What is wrong?"

She spoke through her sobs. "Rondelyn threw me out, tossed some of my clothes in my car while I was at work, and expected me to sleep in the car."

I thought there must be more to this story, but I ushered her into the living room, where I tried to calm her down. One of the Good Ole Girls, Joycee, from Orange County, had just arrived for the weekend; my guest room was in use.

No problem. While Joycee talked with Celeste and made her a cup of tea, I brought out the air mattress and readied it in my office for Celeste to use. Soon, she crashed for the night. I felt it best not to ask too many questions until morning.

This woman was the same beautiful French businesswoman I had met several years before who had rented my previously owned home in the desert. At that time, she was a highly paid marketing executive for a European company. She had been assigned the Coachella Valley and everything west of the Mississippi as her territory. Previously, when I had moved to Orange County in 2010 to be near the company I worked for as a contractor, I had introduced Celeste to my female friends, especially those still in the workforce. One of these friends was Rondelyn.

A couple of years later, when I discovered I had cancer, I needed to sell my home in the desert. In her late thirties, Celeste graciously moved out and moved in with Rondelyn for a few years. They got along incredibly well, but there were very few job opportunities in the desert for this multilingual French beauty. She decided to set out for San Francisco, packed most of her belongings into her car, left furniture and household goods in storage, and headed out.

Soon, Celeste invested all her savings into a failing jewelry business off busy Market Street in San Francisco. She was confident that she knew retail sales and marketing and could make a go of it.

However, the $7,000 monthly lease in this very high-end part of town was a tough nut to crack each month. Much of her jewelry was on consignment, plus she had taken out loans to buy other merchandise.

During the next few years, Celeste barely survived in her jewelry business. One day, a handsome man, Dylan, came into her store. Dylan, outwardly a sophisticated man about twenty years older than Celeste, was looking for a gift for his girlfriend. They chatted about his girlfriend's clothing and jewelry taste and whether she wore more gold than silver. Finally, he picked out a pair of beautiful gold earrings. Celeste wrapped them, and off he went.

A few weeks later, Dylan returned to Celeste's shop and, after a long conversation, asked her if she would meet him after work for a drink. She did meet him and discovered that the girlfriend who had received the gold earrings was history. Also, he had been married twice and had grown children about ten years younger than Celeste. She started to date Dylan, and it seemed they were in love.

At one point, Dylan asked her to marry him. He was a good-looking man but a big drinker. As the story goes, Dylan drank whatever anyone put before him. Celeste rarely imbibed in any alcoholic drinks before meeting Dylan. She came from a family where her father was an abusive alcoholic, like mine. In her evening together at Dylan's home, she had tried drinking. She did not like the wine he offered her and hated the hard liquor; his favorite was scotch, but she seemed to enjoy drinking beer. Their romance had its ups and downs, much fed by alcohol.

One evening, Celeste and Dylan were drinking, and she screamed at him, "You treat your daughters better than you ever treat me!" Celeste grabbed his car keys and ran out of the house. She was sobbing as she drove into San Francisco and had a car accident. Celeste was French, meaning she would talk very fast when excited and go between French and English, waving her hands in frustration. At the scene of the accident, Celeste was understandably flustered. She told the police that she did not do anything wrong. She had no evidence to show the officer that she was permitted to drive Dylan's car. She was handcuffed and taken in a police car to jail. Even though Celeste spoke fluent English, she kept hysterically proclaiming, "Jen, ai rien fait, ou me prenez-vous?" (I did nothing; where are you taking me?) She was booked for her first DUI (driving under the influence) and spent several hours in jail until Dylan picked her up. This event ended that relationship.

The loss of Dylan was a crushing blow to Celeste emotionally, mentally, and physically. I was shocked when I saw her. This beautiful blonde woman had lost over twenty-five pounds and was not eating, apparently only drinking. This behavior was not that of the charming, vibrant friend, Celeste, whom I met, got to know, and loved when she first came to the United States, who lived in my home in the desert. What had happened? Was it just alcohol?

Her jewelry business was not doing well, and she could not turn it around. The location was set back just enough from the "main drag/Market Street" that it was not a draw. Celeste tried various marketing techniques to push sales, but she was barely surviving financially. One day, she locked up the store to go around the corner and inside the hotel to use the restroom, as there was no restroom in her shop. While she was gone, someone threw a brick through the window, came in, and stole most of the jewelry. That action truly put Celeste over the top.

After the theft incident at her jewelry store, Celeste called her good friend Rondelyn, crying hysterically. Rondelyn carefully laid out a plan for Celeste. After handling the police and insurance reports, Celeste filed for bankruptcy in the following days.

At that point, Rondelyn told Celeste, "Put everything you can fit into your car, drive down here, and you can move back in with me." That was October 2017. The knock on my door with Celeste sobbing was in March 2018.

The Next Morning

What happened? Celeste sat across from me and was crying. "What am I going to do? I am forty-three, single, with no family, boyfriend, money, or a decent job! Here I am with an MBA and a temp job earning $12 an hour."

I tried not to be too offensive. "You do not realize it does not matter if you have an MBA or five PhDs. What matters is that you are qualified to do the jobs you are applying for. Be happy someone hired you and is paying $12 an hour." You must eliminate your superiority attitude as it will get you fired."

 Later that week, she was fired. Within a few weeks, her excellent prior work background, beauty, the allure of her French accent, and outgoing personality helped land her a management position in a clothing store in a nearby city. She and her new boss, Peter, got along famously. They began interviewing dozens to fill the many positions necessary to open a new retail store, hiring everyone from stock people, salespeople, floor supervisors, and more. Within a couple of weeks after hiring their workforce, the day came for the store to have its grand opening. The store instantly became a new smashing retail success in the desert. Every day Celeste and her excited team exceeded the sales goals set by the corporation. She was thrilled working with her team and loved her new job. Her conversations with upper management made me feel she was on an upward trajectory to corporate responsibility.

Within two months of beginning her new job, Celeste exhibited a strange behavior pattern. She would call or text me saying she was on her way home, and sometimes we had planned to go to dinner together. What should take twenty-five minutes to get to my home from her work became one hour, two hours, five hours. Soon, this was a regular pattern. Ultimately, after many text messages or unanswered phone calls to her, I would eat. Then around 10:00 or 11:00 p.m., I would go to bed— still, no Celeste.

Where I live in the desert, there is always an attendant at the property gate entrance. When someone enters and comes to my address, the attendant at the gate issues them a pass and automatically sends me an email. Sometimes the email indicates that Celeste went through the entrance to the property at 10:15 p.m.; now it was 12:30 a.m., and she was not home. What in the world was she doing?

The attendant at the gate told me that Celeste would enter and leave again shortly after that. Why? I later learned that she would sit outside the property and drink beer. Once, the gentleman attending the gate called me and said, "I am assisting your intoxicated guest in finding your property. We are outside your house. Would you please come out and get her?"

Immediately, I opened my garage door, and the gate attendant stood beside Celeste and her car. I was shocked to see her in a near- unconscious state. I am not sure she knew who I was. I helped stabilize her as she stumbled out of the car. Her speech was slurred and incoherent, and her eyes dilated and rolled backward. I helped Celeste maneuver her way into the house. She was belligerent and did not want any help. She collapsed as soon as I let go of my firm grip on her arm. Sprawled out on her stomach on the floor, Celeste squirmed around until she finally used a chair to pull herself up and get both legs under her. She managed to stumble about thirty feet into the guest bedroom. I did not dare go in there until later. She had passed out on the floor where she slept.

Recognizing the difference between the Celeste of 2010 and the Celeste of 2018 was complicated. It was like knowing two completely different people. She was still a beautiful, multilingual, bright, educated woman, but there were changes. Now, she was perimenopausal, with her hormones seemingly out of control. She took prescribed Prozac with the appropriate doctor's warning of "do not drink" while taking this drug, yet she was drinking daily. Unknown to me but driven by deep-seated emotional issues from childhood beatings, Celeste drank most evenings immediately after work, supposedly to drown these memories.

Several mornings after Celeste had gone through an evening of apparent drunkenness, we would have a pleasant conversation about what had happened the night before. Being compassionate and, unfortunately, a great enabler, I believed her stories. As time went on, the tales became ludicrous. Once, she told me this story when she had not come home the night before: "I was parking downtown and bumped a car behind me as I pulled in. A police car nearby saw me bump into that parked car, looked up my license number in his database, saw my previous DUI, handcuffed me, took me to jail, and had my car towed away." Did I think that bumping into another parked car puts you in jail overnight? No, I did not believe this story. I later discovered this was DUI number 3 with an alcohol content of .032 (the legal limit for blood alcohol concentration is .08 percent). She was more than three times over the legal limit.

Soon, I realized that these three months of her living with me were causing me immense stress. At night, my stomach was in knots. I felt like a mother waiting for her kid to be out, drink too much, and hopefully not get in an accident, killing herself or anyone else. What helped me understand that I was suffering from stress was what I did next. I provided timeshare weeks to Celeste near her workplace. I told her that being closer to her work would allow her to stay closer to her work for three nights at a time—which was true. And being closer to work would give her more time to look for an apartment. Celeste had always said she would get her own place to rent after getting employed. Those nights were heaven for me. She did not like packing her clothes and making these temporary moves.

Then the strangest thing happened. One evening around 8:00 p.m., We chatted about her work that day. She indicated she was excited to meet some of her company's corporate people the next day. Her company had been discussing a possible corporate spot for her. I was so excited as she had a tremendous background. It sounded like a terrific opportunity for her. As she was tired, she said, "Bonne nuit" (Goodnight), and we both went to our bedrooms and shut our doors.

Around 3:00 a.m., my phone rang. Half asleep, I answered and said, "Hello?"

On the other end, Celeste said, "Marly, Marly, Marly. Marly, Marly, Marly."

"What? Celeste, where are you?"
"I am on the highway, very high up on a nearby mountain."

"Are you drinking?" That was stupid.

Of course, she was.

"Yes. Marly, Marly, Marly."

"Well, please just get in your car and come home. I'll wait up for you. Do you want me to come and get you?"

She hung up. I tried to reach her again, but she did not pick up. I was worried sick about what she might do.

The following day, after another night of not sleeping for fear of what might happen to her, Celeste had not come home. I quickly got dressed and left the house for a doctor's appointment. I called Celeste on the way. There was no answer. Before arriving at my doctor's office, I called one of my best friends, Judy, and said, "I cannot make any calls while at the doctor's office. Would you please call the local hospital emergency room and try to locate Celeste? If she is not at the hospital, try the morgue." Within about twenty minutes, Judy texted me. She said, "Celeste is okay and in the emergency room at the local hospital." We agreed to meet there in half an hour.

In driving to the hospital, I could not imagine what I would find in the emergency room. I parked my car near the ER entrance and walked in. There she was, lying on a bed in an ER cubicle. I asked her, "Are you okay?" What has happened?" Celeste started to cry. "Mais oui, I have ruined my life. I have destroyed everything."

The company manager fired me yesterday because of my drinking. I drove off a cliff to end my miserable life." She was driving a small loaner car since her car was in the shop. Somehow Celeste managed to leap this little car over the twelve-inch V-shaped barrier edge on the highway and luckily only bounced to the bottom of this steep, rock-filled hill. At the bottom, she hit a boulder, and the car burst into flames. Celeste does not remember how she got out of the burning vehicle. The highway patrol report indicated she was dazed, wandering along this busy highway with her purse on her shoulder.

Someone driving on this mountain pass must have seen her and called the highway patrol, as she was brought into the hospital by a highway patrolman.

Because this accident was an attempted suicide, after she was stabilized, the doctors transferred Celeste to another hospital for up to three days for a psych evaluation. Two days later, in the evening, I received a call from an attendant at this second hospital who said, "Celeste is ready to be released and go home."

"Please come and pick her up now."

I was shocked. "Celeste cannot come home. She is mentally unstable."

The attendant talking with me said, "She is perfectly calm and ready to be released."

"You have not seen her manic stage. No, she cannot come here tonight."

"We will hold her overnight, but you must pick her up at 9:00 a.m. tomorrow."

"Okay. "

I hung up the phone and was not sure what I should do. Then my adrenaline kicked in. Immediately I called five of my friends and asked them if they could please come over that evening to help me pack Celeste's belongings. We packed Celeste's clothes into her two large suitcases and a trunk, except for her heavy coats. Rondelyn, the friend who initially took Celeste in when she moved to the desert from San Francisco, got on the computer to find a one-way ticket to France for Celeste. She purchased a $987 ticket from Palm Springs to Paris, France, leaving the following day. We all agreed that she needed to return to France because, as a citizen of France, she could receive the medical treatment they would provide.

Rondelyn and another friend, Jaimee, arrived at the hospital at 9:00 a.m. and picked up Celeste. She was surprised and hurt that I did not come. She was distraught and tried to escape the car while it was moving. Jaimee had to put the "child locks on," so Celeste could not get out as she tried to open the doors. When the three arrived at the airport, Rondelyn and Jaimee sat with Celeste until she boarded her flight. Finally, there was the last call for her to board. She sobbed as she clung to Jaimee and Rondelyn, saying her goodbyes. She did not want to leave the US. All three of them cried.

I could not be there to say goodbye. It would have hurt terribly to have Celeste sobbing in my arms, begging me not to send her back to France. I might not have been strong enough to see this through. I always looked at her like the daughter I never had. I truly cared about her and her well-being. Nevertheless, she desperately needed medical and psychological attention, which would be available in France as a French citizen.

Now, several years later, we talk by phone. Celeste has apologized for all the pain and agony she caused Rondelyn and me.

I hope and pray that Celeste remains happy and well.

In September 2022, my generous son, Christen, provided for my eightieth birthday an incredible weeklong river barge cruise in France for me, my significant other, Bill, my sister Connie and her husband, John, Donald Hucker (my second husband), Christen, and his delightful wife, Amber. The fantastic trip began and ended in Paris.

Celeste met Connie and me for a beautiful lunch before the cruise and returned a week later to spend one evening with all of us before we left for the U.S.Celeste is now very healthy and happy, is a successful college teacher of management and marketing courses, and is setting up an international business program for another. Her education and expertise as a highly successful global salesperson provide her with a terrific background in teaching.

Previously, when Celeste had been living with me, she had dreams of having a stable relationship, marriage, and family and was shouting that this had not yet become a reality. Yet, after significant trauma, she has had most of her dreams come true, including her recent marriage in France to Jean Davy Barthelemy. I only wish for her happiness.

THE DANCE WITH THE THREE DEVILS HAS ENDED

Writing this book has allowed me to release former pain, recognizing that inherited family trauma helped shape who I am and that I needed to end the cycle. It has assisted me in reflecting deeply on my life experiences—the good and the not-so-good.

One significant accomplishment was recognizing why and how I functioned much of my life as an enabler: as a young teenager trying to hide the trauma of abuse in my home, being the best I could be, craving the love I needed from my parents, giving money to people who asked to borrow it but never getting it returned, and caretaking others. I likened my unfulfilled dreams, shattered relationships, and alcoholism to Celeste. As a sober alcoholic, I assumed I could function like an AA sponsor for her, as I had for others. However, honestly, I was a perfect enabler for Celeste and others, especially the men in my life. Often, I prioritized their needs over my own. Learning about my behavior as an enabler has taken a lifetime of experiences. It was most likely rooted in abusive childhood experiences of a one-sided, emotionally destructive, and abusive parental relationship.

Why did I not pursue my dancing? After fifteen years of studying dance, I hoped to become a great performer on stage and screen. That part of life did not turn out as I had hoped. I let that dream disappear after getting married at the early age of twenty-one. Why? Why did I not pursue this dream when Larry and I moved to California? My initial excuse was that I did not have to work full-time. Did I escape my life in North Dakota and do anything that would take me away? Was it that I dared not pursue what I had always wanted? Years later, at the age of sixty-two, I commenced competitive ballroom dancing and thoroughly enjoyed participating in competitions until I experienced knee issues.

Now, after a knee replacement, I have thoughts of starting to tap dance again. There is a group where I live of six women called "The Tappers."

 I used to have this deep internal emotional pain that I believed was my disappointment and disillusionment with who I was and what I should have become. What was missing?

Was it the feelings of trauma from physical abuse as a child, the Boston incident, the lack of follow- through with my talents, or the disappointment in my male relationships?

I had an extremely successful career in education.

I have an incredibly generous, loving son who has created a beautiful life for himself.

I have two wonderful sisters (one passed in 2016)

I have many terrific nieces (Stacey, Kristi, and Wendy) and nephews (Jonathan and Brian) and their wives (Alexandra and Melissa) and children (Owen, Jackson, Aira, and Augustine).

I have published twenty-five computer textbooks.

I have had great male relationships and many caring friends.
I live in paradise on earth in a beautiful home.

I married Larry at age twenty-one, and Christen was born when I was twenty-nine. Christen and I left Larry when Christen was 1-1/2, and then we divorced at thirty-five. I had a terrific twelve-year marriage with Donald, but it ended because of my rage when I had too much to drink. I soon met Joe and had a fantastic time drinking, dancing, and working on some of my textbooks. That relationship ended because I could not help him heal his emotional issues. Did these relationships end because of me? Was I not emotionally available, or did I have a "poor picker," as my sister Connie called it?

After two drinks, I would often become a blackout drunk. I frequently prayed for many things in my life to be different, but God did not intervene. Finally, after the Boston incident, at age forty-eight, I stopped drinking with the help I received through therapy, AA, my angels, God, and the therapist, Brady. With great joy, I have been sober since 11-12-1990 (at this writing, thirty-five years).

I find dramatic beauty in the desert. The community I live in has created an impressively designed and well-established gorgeous desert landscape. In the springtime, especially if there is rare rain, the variety of plant life seems to dance in unique and colorful blooms. People look healthier here, although some have been overcooked in the sun. On the flip side, I must admit that getting used to the cruel sun beating down for a few months out of the year takes some time. Plus, the sky does not cooperate with a wisp or two of clouds to lessen the severe heat rays. Even the lizards take shelter under rocks where the sand or cement is not hot enough to bake them. Some days, the air seems hot with each breath, almost like swallowing burning coffee. However, we are blessed with evenings that are total bliss.

Now, how do I spend my time back in the desert? I re-engaged with friends I knew from having lived here and have met many new friends through the organizations I am involved in. We attend fabulous theater events at the McCallum Theater, frequent excellent restaurants for delicious bites, and take in the latest movies.

I joined a few organizations I had previously been a member of when living here before. Soon, I became incredibly involved on the boards of the Palm Springs Writers Guild (PSWG), the Steinway Society, and the World Affairs Council of the Desert, all nonprofit organizations. For the PSWG, I was their director of education and later president for two years.

These organizations are terrific groups of energetic, creative people who work hard as volunteers to create tremendous success for their organizations and to benefit students and people within our communities. I have many new friends within these organizations. Plus, after Palm Springs Writers Guild meetings (before COVID), I had the excellent opportunity to entertain various professional speakers who are movers and shakers in the writing and publishing world.

People my age and younger often talk about their bucket lists. I have never had a "bucket list" - only the dream to become a professional dancer. That was my bucket list, and you know how that turned out. For some people, a failed ambition, such as mine, becomes the cause of depression and intense dissatisfaction throughout one's life.

Honestly, I have enjoyed a vibrant life through my careers, cherishing my son, birth family, loved ones, sailboat racing, writing textbooks, speaking tours, amazing friends, remarkable travels, and now, writing.

People ask me, "Why are you writing this book?" I need to do so to express myself, and it seems natural for me to write. For centuries, writing has helped shape the world in many ways. Going back to 3200 BC or possibly earlier, writing has been humankind's principal technology for collecting, manipulating, storing, retrieving, communicating, and disseminating information.

Writing textbooks was a satisfying experience in the early years with my coauthors, Jean Gonzalez and later Don Busché.

We knew the textbooks helped educators and students.

For some people, the written word makes the bad bearable, as it can take us to a place we may never see or experience. I hope my words bring courage to other women and men, to action and compassion, and to become their best selves.

As I am now in what I accept is the last quarter of my life, do I think about dying? I have made plans so my son and remaining family members will not have to worry about all the pieces for that part of my exit. I have my medical directive, my trust is current, and a Trident policy for cremation exists. My instructions for the party are ready.

If I know my death is imminent, I will have my family and closest friends over. We would have farewell conversations and toast our lives together—tears and laughter with piano music playing in the background from the 1960s. Hopefully, when the time comes, I can legally ingest drugs to assist my departure and avoid pain.

Recently, when Christen asked me what I wanted to do for my "big" birthday, I said I wasn't having a big birthday until he reminded me that I was soon reaching the milestone age of eighty. My response was that I would love to travel somewhere with him. Within a few months, he devised a River Barge cruise in France for me, Bill (my dear friend), Connie, John, my ex-husband, Don, Christen's wife, Amber, and himself. We had a fantastic flight in and out of Paris and an unbelievable weeklong cruise on the Seine. Toward the end of the cruise, the barge cook escorted the seven of us to a terrific restaurant in Paris, where he selected everything we should eat that evening—another incredible meal.

We were shuttled back to Paris after the barge cruise was now over, where we had a night at a delightful little hotel.

My sweet friend, Celeste, took a three-hour train ride from her hometown to spend a wonderful evening with all of us and stayed overnight at the same hotel. I loved seeing her and catching up on her life. I am thrilled at how well she is doing with her health and success in her work life and education. She is always very thankful that we sent her back to France, where she received the medical attention she needed at that time.

Today, I no longer have the same feeling of unlimited time left as most of us do in our forties and fifties. I worked ridiculously hard for forty-two years. I raised an incredible son and co-authored and published twenty-five computer textbooks during that time. There have been remarkable, loving men in my life. I am thrilled to have loved and spent precious time with them. Yes, I should have played more and been less stressed, but some did not grasp that until our time had passed.

Writing about my life has caused me to reflect on my successes and failures, look them in the eye, and see what defined me. Much of my life was improvised, dependent on luck and being in the right place at the right time. I could have made different choices at different times; without a doubt, part of my life would have changed.

My family and friends are incredibly caring and thoughtful.

They are always there for me in so many ways.

Life for me has been a limitless dance. I was blessed to have a terrific son, Christen. He is a caring, thoughtful, and generous person who has been the greatest gift in my lifetime. My amazing, sweet sister Connie and her husband, John, have always been a loving, supportive family whom I have enjoyed whenever possible.

She has always been my best friend and there for me during tough times and the good times. I have great fun enjoying them, their children, and their grandchildren. I miss our parents, who died in their eighties. Sharon, our elder sister, passed away suddenly a few years ago; I miss her terribly. I am fortunate to occasionally spend time with her grown daughters, my nieces, Wendy, Stacey, and Kristi, and their families.

Wendy, Stacey, and Kristi

I live closest to Stacey, so I am thrilled to spend time with Stacey, her husband, Matt. Their son, Colin, who is in this high school graduation picture with his parents, is now away at college in Charleston. I am fortunate to see Kristi and her daughter, Samantha, occasionally on a quick trip to my place from their homes in Arizona.

Stacey, Colin, and Matt

Throughout my work life, I have enjoyed incredible successes. I have traveled the world. My religious instruction growing up was Sunday school and many church sermons. But what do I believe? I do believe in God and Jesus Christ. Was there a Big Bang theory? An Adam and Eve? Is there heaven and hell?

Do our souls live on after death? My experiences in this life have led me to believe they do. As many do, I believe that all that exists on this earthly plane consists of energy or particles of dust spinning in the Milky Way. Someday I will know if this is true—or not.

What has been most important in my life? My birth family, my son, two marriages and divorces, and the men with whom I have enjoyed my life, as well as wonderful friends. Becoming a mother caused me to no longer think about how horrific or significant past incidents affected me but how they would affect my son. I decided that going skydiving was no longer essential, but seeing my son grow up took priority. My two marriages and divorces were significant in Christen's life. But, from Christen, I learned that his hearing my alcoholic arguments with my second husband and the pressures or expectations he felt I placed on him in his youth were much more problematic and impacted him more than I ever realized.

Sometimes our lives are understated or uncomplicated. My son's life has sustained me with lasting pleasure. His thriving as I decline reminds me that my life as a mother was completed long ago. The early days of his childhood, our outings with just the two of us, our trips together, and his successes evolved as they should – all beautiful memories.

Connie, her late husband John, and their family are a constant joy in my life and in Christen's. They support me in all I do and pray that they do not have to help me move again. Whenever there is a small or significant crisis, like my prior breast cancer, they both have had my back, as I do theirs. I will see my sister Sharon, plus wonderful John and many family members on the other side.

I am happy I can spend time with Sharon and Connie's children.

What will I miss? I will miss my incredible sister and extended families and knowing how my son Christen and Amber's lives turned out. That is what I will miss most: their faces, voices, and laughter. Christen is a brilliant, kind, and generous soul. His actions have shown me repeatedly and in many, many ways. I am overwhelmed by his love and generosity. Now, he is a middle- aged man whose computer company was acquired; what will he do? He may help computer start-ups, like he once was, to grow and flourish. Not surprisingly, several years ago, he bought and renovated a warehouse in a small mountain town and turned it into a beautiful aikido studio near his prior home. Christen is a fukushidoin, a dojo-cho, and was a senior instructor to teach his favorite martial art, aikido, and passed it on; he holds a Sandan rank (third-degree black belt). In his youth, he was a karate practitioner.

I am thrilled to report that recently Christen married a wonderful woman, Amber Cooney. Their incredible wedding ceremony was in the beauty of the outdoors of Colorado. It was an unbelievably wonderful, multiple-day occasion in a gorgeous mountain setting. It could not have been more perfect. I am blessed to have a fantastic, loving, and generous son and now Amber, a beautiful, thoughtful, and accomplished daughter-in-law. My greatest wish is for their happiness.

Chris and Amber   *Marly and Christen*   *Bill Lewis and Marly*

My family at Chris and Amber wedding.

I shall miss seeing the snow on the beautiful mountains, the sun, the desert, the wind, the rain, the blue sky with wispy clouds, the ocean, and everything else in my world.

I feel my life has been a dance of many routines. There have been serious impacts on my recognizing the devil that arose from my father's fire and his being burned, plus the devil that my father became at night when drinking. Then, there is the devil that came to me in the form of my breast cancer in 2014 which I thought I had conquered at that time. But, unfortunately, it returned in 2024 in the form of bone cancer starting in my lower back, but at this writing, it is under control. I am continuing to manage my hereditary health issue of cancer. I am treating it with a type of chemo pill, Lynparza, and shots to strengthen my bones, as well as doing exercise weekly with weighted machines. I am under the care of a tremendous oncologist, Dr. Amy Law.

I feel blessed to have achieved enormous success in my career in education, in the writing of many computer textbooks, and in my leadership roles. I loved implementing VR technology in the early days of 2007–2010, which changed and is continuing to change how people learn. I will not miss knowing what happens next in this changing world. I say that as our political system in the US and world dictators may destroy our climate, humanity, and the earth.

My experiences traveling the world, both alone and with friends, have been diverse and a very important part of my life. The support and friendship of my friends, parents, sisters, their children, and Christen and Amber have greatly enriched my life.

The face of the devil was in the fire that burned my father when he was only 12 years old; it was in the eyes of my father when he was beating my mother and then me in an alcoholic rage. Now, the face of the devil has returned to me again, bringing my breast cancer back to me in the form of bone cancer.

I have fallen many times throughout my journey, but those lessons have shaped my path by providing me with not a punishment but a difficult preparation for strength and purpose. I learned that even in my darkest places, the only victory that mattered was the one I claimed for myself, and that was not to let the darkness win.

THE END

www.ingramcontent.com/pod-product-compliance
Lightning Source LLC
Chambersburg PA
CBHW051132120626
46547CB00012B/771